The Philosophy of Autism

The Philosophy of Autism

Edited by Jami L. Anderson & Simon Cushing

ROWMAN & LITTLEFIELD PUBLISHERS, INC.
Lanham • Boulder • New York • Toronto • Plymouth, UK

Published by Rowman & Littlefield Publishers, Inc.
A wholly owned subsidiary of The Rowman & Littlefield Publishing Group, Inc.
4501 Forbes Boulevard, Suite 200, Lanham, Maryland 20706
www.rowman.com

10 Thornbury Road, Plymouth PL6 7PP, United Kingdom

British Library Cataloguing in Publication Information Available

Library of Congress Cataloging-in-Publication Data

Anderson, Jami L.
The philosophy of autism / Jami L. Anderson & Simon Cushing.
p. cm.
Includes bibliographical references and index.
ISBN 978-1-4422-1707-2 (cloth : alk. paper) -- ISBN 978-1-4422-1709-6 (electronic)
1. Autism--Philosophy. I. Cushing, Simon, 1968- II. Title.
RC553.A88A53 2012
616.85'882--dc23

2012036099

The paper used in this publication meets the minimum requirements of American National Standard for Information Sciences Permanence of Paper for Printed Library Materials, ANSI/NISO Z39.48-1992.

Printed in the United States of America

Contents

Acknowledgments

We both want to thank Marissa Parks, Associate Editor at Rowman & Little-field; she was immediately excited about this project and has been fantastically supportive through the whole process.

The initial idea for writing this book was not mine, but once the idea was in my head, I was able to do my part because of the encouragement and assistance I have received from people I would like to thank. I took my first philosophy course, a freshman seminar, when I was barely seventeen years old and had no idea what I was doing with my life, from Jeffrie G. Murphy. He is a brilliant teacher, truly gifted at showing how important and relevant philosophy is. Although always supportive of my philosophical efforts, he recently suggested that I write a philosophical reflection on my experiences of parenting an autistic son; his kind and encouraging words inspired me to write my chapter. Mike Brownell, Jennifer Sopka, Carol Fast, and Katie Kramer have each been terrific sources of information about autism, but more importantly, each was tremendously helpful to us and was (or, with Mike, continues to be) a fabulous teacher and friend for our son. Emily Van Brocklin, our Mary Poppins, has made the last six years possible and our son's life wonderful. There simply is no way we could have gotten through them without her. Zea (a.k.a. Zena, Zeke, Zach) Miller's gifted assistance and (almost) constant good cheer made working on this book sheer joy. Let's work together on another book! And, of course, I want to thank my boys, all three of them.

(JA)

My life would have been very different if it had not been for Anthony Grayling, who was not only my first philosophy teacher, but the person who suggested to me that I should try the Graduate School Thing. I only applied to one graduate school (the one he suggested) where I met my future co-editor and life partner on the first day. So he's got a lot to answer for. On matters pertaining to the subject matter of this book, I would like to thank Elizabeth Anderson for some great advice, and join Jami in thanking Emily Van Brocklin, who has been perhaps the most important figure in our son's life since he was a baby. If this book were dedicated to anyone, it would be to her. Finally, the book almost certainly would not have happened if not for Zea Miller, by-now graduate student at Purdue, who put in many hours of invaluable editing work and really should be listed as co-editor if we weren't such glory-hunting credit-hogs.

(SC)

Introduction

Jami L. Anderson and Simon Cushing

From when our son was about twenty-four months old, until he was twenty-six months old he was enrolled in a nearby Montessori preschool. One day his teacher and her assistant called Jami in for a meeting. Since all parent–teacher meetings for our older son were always happy events, we did not think this would be anything otherwise, since, if anything, our younger son hit milestones earlier than when our older son did. Our younger son had known his alphabet and could count to one hundred by the time he was twelve months old and by eighteen months old was "coding" his answers to questions. What could be the problem? The teacher did not say anything directly but suggested that he be taken "to a specialist." Given that other kids in the class had been known to hit, bite, cry, or have day-long temper tantrums, whereas our son was a jolly chap quite thrilled with life, happy to be with others and content with whatever came his way, this suggestion seemed inexplicable. Jami asked, "Is he…*slow*?" "Oh, no! But he's not talking—though of course he is just twenty-six months old. But…he is very, very…" At this point, the conversation just…sort of…petered off. We were sitting precariously on tiny chairs, each about eight inches tall, circled around a tiny table. It would have been hilarious except that the subtext of the conversation was so terrifyingly bizarre. Obviously realizing that Jami was not "getting" the point, the teacher plunged onward. "We just feel—don't we?—that he needs to see a specialist. We think that would be best." At that they shuffled their papers and that was the end of the meeting. At no point was the term "autism" spoken nor was Jami told what sort of "specialist" to consult. So far, autism had not yet entered our world.

Our son was diagnosed unofficially by Simon's father and stepmother while we were visiting England. Simon and his father were watching our son play in the surf on a beach, and Simon's father asked, "What are you going to

do about him?" Puzzled, Simon asked what he meant. "Well, it's obvious
he's autistic," he replied. As one might imagine, this cast somewhat of a pall
over the vacation. When we returned to the States, our primary-care physician regarded the diagnosis as absurd but begrudgingly agreed to refer us to a
neurologist. During a very brief meeting, the neurologist diagnosed our son
as "PDD-NOS" (Pervasive Developmental Delays-Not Otherwise Specified),
then cheerfully bid us good day. In the fog that followed, Simon contacted a
couple of distinguished philosophers, whom he had asked for minor favors,
to let them know that his immediate plans had changed, and mentioned the
reason. Both responded that they understood, because they, too, had children
"on the spectrum." Since these philosophers were the very first fellow academics we had "outed" our son to, it seemed an amazing coincidence that
they, too, had children on the spectrum.

Neither of those distinguished philosophers had written on the subject of
autism, despite the fact that at least one of them had obviously done copious
research and was, as a result, able to be an enormous help to us in finding
services for our son, including recommending perhaps the most eminent
expert on autism working in our state.

When we were able to get an appointment with him, one of the first things
he asked us was what each of us did for a living, and his reaction on hearing
that we were both philosophers was "Well, no wonder!"

He is not unique in this attitude. In an article in the online edition of the
New York Times, Andy Martin wrote:

> I don't want to maintain that all philosophers are autistic in this sense. Perhaps
> not even that "You don't have to be autistic, but it helps." And yet there are
> certainly episodes and sentences associated with philosophers quite distinct
> from Wittgenstein and Russell that might lead us to think in that way…One
> implication of what a psychologist might say about autism goes something like
> this: you, a philosopher, are mindblind and liable to take up philosophy pre-
> cisely because you don't "get" what other people are saying to you. You, like
> Wittgenstein, have a habit of hearing and seeing propositions, but feeling that
> they say nothing (as if they were rendered in Chinese). In other words, philos-
> ophy would be a tendency to interpret what people say as a puzzle of some
> kind, a machine that may or may not work. I think this helps to explain
> Wittgenstein's otherwise slightly mysterious advice, to the effect that if you
> want to be a good philosopher, you should become a car mechanic. [1]

Despite this anecdotal evidence of a link between an interest in philosophy
and autism, it appears that the amount of philosophical writing directly about
autism is scanty indeed. This strikes us both as odd. Surely the philosopher's
first impulse when confronted with any major life issue should be to subject
it to analysis. In retrospect, it was and is perfectly understandable: work
should be a refuge from the general shittiness of real life. Admittedly, we

both found it very hard for a couple of years to read anything that might expose us to a gloomy prognosis about the life prospects for autistic people, and by implication, our son. Why ruin the enjoyment of our undoubtedly odd, but undoubtedly happy and lovable, son's childhood with depressing foreshadowing?

Yet the postdiagnosis years are a colossal mindfuck and while friends and family intend to be supportive, what we both wanted—what we *needed*—was to make intellectual sense of autism. Because nothing being said to us made sense: the diagnosis did not make sense; the sub-categories of autism did not make sense; the therapy regimes proposed were inconsistent with one another and seemed, given the realities of life, ridiculous if not brutal. Moreover, embracing the diagnosis "autism" required accepting as pathological the very features of our son that we found most endearing and did not want to change. (Like his "odd play," to give but one example.)

We have mixed attitudes towards academic philosophy and are (probably unfairly) dismissive to a great deal of what is labeled "continental" philosophy precisely because we both find it to be almost completely unreadable. And if individuals who have been trained in philosophy (who can wade through the multi-claused sentences of Hume and Mill and emerge thinking that they are propounding obvious common sense) find continental philosophy unreadable, what hope for the uninitiated? Simon had an undergraduate professor whose lectures were clear, and whose philosophical position he found utterly convincing and important. But then he turned to his written work and found it barely penetrable (and managed then only because of his lectures). Simon actually asked him why his writing and speaking styles were so different, and he responded by saying something on the lines of "it's expected in the field." And this by a contributor to *Radical Philosophy*! He has since been a winner of some award for "most tortured sentence" (or some equivalent) given out by an organization that crusades for clarity.

So we side with analytic philosophy because of its (professed[2]) commitment to clarity and argumentative rigor. But analytic philosophy has too often ceded important areas of discussion to the dark side. Why is it that if you are interested in gender you are almost forced to read Judith Butler, another deserved winner of the tortured sentence award?[3] And why do certain very narrow, and to the general public, minor issues dominate philosophical discussion, while issues of immediate concern to people's real lives go relatively unaddressed?[4]

The subject of autism is rich with philosophical possibilities. First, exactly what *is* autism? What does the concept cover? Analytical philosophy has obsessed with conceptual analysis to the point that it is somewhat passé these days, but surely now is the time to analyze the concept "autistic" as it is just exploding into use by the general public. This is a crucial time in the evolution of meaning of the term. Until recently the term has been almost exclusively the preserve of psychiatrists, but with the vast increases in diagnoses and the corresponding spike in attention by the media, the scope of the concept (or concepts) attached to the term has become broader and the term has acquired various connotations that will affect those labeled by it in serious ways throughout their lives. As parents of a child diagnosed on the autistic spectrum, we, and all others in the same situation, want to know: what does that *mean*?

The issue of what exactly autism is is inextricably bound up with the epistemological question of how to tell that a person is autistic. When a diagnosis is made, what are the signs that justify that diagnosis? And why is it that they *are* the signs that justify a diagnosis of autism?

Complicating matters is the fact that in the medical community "terminology centering on autism is something of a minefield."[5] The current edition of the American Psychiatric Association's official *Diagnostic and Statistical Manual of Mental Disorders* (the *DSM-IV-TR*) specifies three distinct autism-related conditions as members of a group of pervasive developmental disorders. These are "autistic disorder," "Asperger disorder," and "PDD-NOS."[6] Thus, according to the *DSM-IV*, there are three distinct "subtypes" of autism, each distinct from the other, with differing diagnostic criteria. Furthermore, each of these three is termed a "disorder" rather than the more neutral "syndrome" or simply condition. However, studies performed in the years since the publication of the first edition of *DSM-IV* in 1994 have led some researchers to think of autism instead on the model of a spectrum of conditions, each bleeding into the next. In particular (and of particular relevance here), studies have shown that family members of individuals diagnosed autistic typically display a few of the symptoms of autism, but well below the threshold required for a diagnosis:

> An aunt, for example, may have had speech and language therapy as a child, and was slow to learn to read; a brother or sister may have had difficulty in making friends at school and have chosen a career with minimal contact with other people; the father may be an avid collector of something, with unusual factual knowledge relating to his hobby.[7]

(Or his parents may simply be philosophy professors...) The name for this phenomenon of mild signs of autism among relatives of an autistic individual is "broader autism phenotype" (BAP). Thus, it seems likely that instead of autism being on the analogy of Down syndrome, where there is a detectable genetic marker that separates all Down syndrome individuals from those who are not (even if, of course, there is a wide spectrum of abilities among individuals who have this condition), individuals diagnosed as autistic look likely to be simply individuals who have clustered in one person symptoms that separately, or in milder forms, are present in a huge number of individuals never diagnosed. That is not to say that the various categories are necessarily vacuous—the existence of dusk does not mean that there is no day or night, and the term "spectrum" does not imply that there are no colors—but it certainly throws into question the rigidity of the categories in the current *DSM*.

So, how to tell whether or not someone fits in "autistic" or "PDD-NOS"? Answering that question depends on what, at bottom, we think any of the categories of disorder or syndrome actually *are*. In Simon Cushing's chapter, "Autism: The Very Idea," Cushing subjects "autism" to conceptual analysis to see if we can say with confidence what it is that individuals labeled autistic have in common. If each of the subtypes of autism is defined simply as constituted by a set of symptoms, then the criteria for its observation are straightforward, although, of course, some of those symptoms themselves might be hard to observe definitively. Compare with telling whether or not someone is *bleeding*: while it might be hard to tell if someone is bleeding internally, we know what it takes to find out, and when we have the right access and instruments we can settle the issue. But matters are not so simple for the autism subtypes. For one thing, how do we settle which symptoms to group together under one heading? One key difference between "autism disorder" and "Asperger's disorder" is that the former exhibits language delays (sometimes extreme), whereas the latter does not. But is that a sign of genuinely distinct conditions or is that an artifact of the distinct groups of subjects that Leo Kanner (the American psychiatrist whose 1943 study[8] is credited with defining autism) and Hans Asperger (the Austrian physician who published a study[9] in 1944 that was not translated into English until 1991) worked with? And in general, although there are certainly types of behavior that are taken to be indicative of autism, none by itself is taken by diagnosticians to be either necessary or sufficient for a definitive diagnosis for any of the autism subtypes. What is the diagnostician to do? This is not merely an academic issue, as many parents can attest. Our primary care practitioner was practically scornful of the suggestion that our son was autistic, in part because he is not remotely touch averse (although clothing tags annoy him) and has comparatively good eye contact. But the neurologist our physician referred us to took the fact that our son would not point to objects by himself but instead would grab a parent's hand and use *that* to point with as a sure sign. Are we in a situation, then, that each practitioner has his or her own "pet" signs that are the "real keys" to the diagnosis? That would be chaotic (and indeed, is). That would also suggest that the term "autistic" might meet the fate of the outdated term "neurotic," which turned out to be a pseudo-scientific term for an inexact clumping together of unrelated phenomena.

What anyone of a scientific bent hopes for is that the question of whether or not a particular individual is autistic will follow the lead of the question of whether or not a particular liquid is water. Back when the name was initially coined, and water was distinguished from other liquids, a far wider range of substances would have counted as such than would today. Now we say we have a sure-fire way of telling whether or not something is water: if it is H_2O. The assumption among specialists seems to be that we will reach that point with autism: there will be a root essence to autism whose presence or absence settles a diagnosis. If that is to be the case, however, we have to settle the *level of application* of the concept. Does the term apply to people who exhibit particular behaviors? Or is it possible to exhibit "autistic" behaviors without actually being autistic, because autism is instead a particular feature of the mind (as, for example, in Baron-Cohen's "impaired theory of mind module" theory, discussed below) which usually but not necessarily has behavioral effects? Or is autism located instead in the brain, perhaps in damage to key areas, which in turn would typically have an effect on modules of the mind? Or perhaps autism is located in genetics or biology, so that some people with damage to the brain caused by accidents and exhibiting autistic symptoms would not actually be autistic. This is not simply a dry academic issue, because there genuinely are individuals (for example, Kim Peek, the savant who was the inspiration for *Rain Man*) who display "autistic" symptoms, but whose status as "actually" autistic is questioned. Conversely, supposing one had an "autistic brain" but showed none of (or not a sufficient number of) the symptoms, would one not be autistic? The assumption is that the genotypes and phenotypes will line up neatly, but if they do not, what happens to the concept "autistic?" (There is an analogy in the philosophy of sex and gender: androgen insensitive individuals tend to self-identify as female and have outward female traits, but have XY chromosomes—should we go with chromosomes or self-identity in assigning sex category?) Finally, the implications for these complications for diagnosis and categorization, with the attendant social and medical implications are discussed. The typical assumption of the medical profession is that autism cannot be "cured." That assumes that autism is *not* simply the symptoms. However, at the same time, the tests used to diagnose ASDs (Autism Spectrum Disorders) work simply from the symptoms (for example, Baron-Cohen's Sally/Anne test described below—which ASD children of a certain age almost all fail, but which practically no ASD adult fails). This implies an inherent confusion over the status of the concept. Cushing's conclusion is that attempts to make sense of some *true* or *accurate* summary of what it is to be autistic (such as one would find in the *DSM*) are almost certainly misguided and will vanish into history along with "neurotic." But as with racial terms, which are similarly shifting and perverse, the term has already passed into the public sphere and will have a lasting and dangerous influence beyond its short scientific shelf life.

Almost certainly the most influential theory of what is essentially distinct about autism is the one[10] that has been developed over the past couple of decades by the British psychologist Simon Baron-Cohen.

Baron-Cohen's work would seem to give lie to the earlier suggestion that philosophy has had little connection with the subject of autism, because articles of his have appeared in anthologies with,[11] and been cited extensively by, influential work in the philosophy of mind. This is in part because Baron-Cohen has himself been influenced by a particular school in philosophy of mind, specifically the *Theory-Theory* camp, which takes the view that neurotypical humans are able to interpret the behavior of others because their brain furniture includes a "theory of mind module" (ToMM).[12]

> ToMM is a system for inferring the full range of mental states from behavior—that is, for employing a "theory of mind."…The first thing that is…needed is a way of representing the set of *epistemic mental states* (which include pretending, thinking, knowing, believing, imagining, dreaming, guessing, and deceiving). The second is a way of tying together all these mental-state concepts (the volitional, the perceptual, and the epistemic) into a coherent understanding of how mental states and actions are related. ToMM does just these things. It has the dual function of representing the set of epistemic mental states and turning all this mentalistic knowledge into a useful theory.[13]

We say "neurotypical" because of course Baron-Cohen has made the prediction that on the basis of what he thinks to be true about the brain, "in autism virtually all aspects of ToMM should be impaired."[14] Indeed, impairment of ToMM is, on this view, what is distinctive about autism, what *makes* an individual autistic. In the terminology that Baron-Cohen employs, while neurotypical individuals are capable of "mindreading" because of ToMM, autistic people are "mindblind."

Central to Baron-Cohen's argument for this conclusion are tests that purport to demonstrate an impaired theory of mind in autistic children. Although many variants of the test have been used, the canonical version was described in a 1985 paper by Baron-Cohen, Leslie and Frith:[15]

> There were two doll protagonists, Sally and Anne.…Sally first placed a marble into her basket. Then she left the scene, and the marble was transferred by Anne and hidden in her box. Then, when Sally returned, the experimenter asked the critical Belief Question: "Where will Sally look for her marble?" If the children point to the previous location of the marble, then they pass the Belief Question by appreciating the doll's now false belief. If however, they point to the marble's current location, then they fail the question by not taking into account the doll's belief.[16]

Not only do autistic children fare worse on "Sally/Anne" style false belief tests than neurotypical children, but also worse than children of a similar age who have Down syndrome; so the three authors concluded that "the failure shown by the autistic children...constitutes a specific deficit...that is largely independent of general intellectual level and has the potential to explain both lack of pretend play and social impairment by virtue of a circumscribed cognitive failure."[17]

There are several assertions basic to Baron-Cohen's research that no contributor to this anthology questions, such as that autism almost certainly has a genetic basis and that early psychoanalytic claims, most notoriously associated with the work of Bruno Bettelheim, that autism was the result of "refrigerator mothers" were fundamentally misguided. Baron-Cohen has also worked to destigmatize autism. However, other distinctive positions of his are exposed to critical analysis in various chapters in this anthology. In his piece, "I Think, Therefore I Am. I Am Verbal, Therefore I Live," Nick Pentzell questions both the Theory-Theory and the conclusion drawn from the false belief tests that children with autism lack ToMM. Pentzell self-identifies as a person on the autism spectrum who only became fully verbal at age thirteen, and thus is in a position to remember and outline how language development affected the subsequent organization of his thinking, and how fluency of communication increased his awareness of other people's thoughts and feelings. Pentzell suggests that the supposedly poor performance of autistic children in Sally/Anne style tests is better explained by sensory overload, limited verbal fluency, and a resulting inexperience with interpersonal relationships than by "damage" to a particular module of the mind. If Pentzell is right, this suggests that Baron-Cohen et al. have failed to identify the true essence of autism, and perhaps, furthermore, that a more essential element of autism might be sensory processing difficulties.

Anna Stubblefield takes up this idea. (Stubblefield's central goal in her piece "Knowing Other Minds: Ethics and Autism" is to challenge conclusions reached by Deborah Barnbaum in her book *The Ethics of Autism*, and we will come to that argument below, but a part of her article merits mention here because in doing so Stubblefield also questions Baron-Cohen's analysis of autism as an absence of a theory of mind which Barnbaum's work explicitly presupposes.) Stubblefield argues that it is more accurate to define autism in terms of sensory and movement challenges, which is in keeping with the evidence that people labeled with autism do demonstrate empathy and the capacity for moral agency. On a related note, Stubblefield argues further that people labeled with autism experience alienation because neurotypicals fail to empathize with those labeled autistic, pointing to the appalling abuse that non-neurotypical individuals routinely endure.

Two other writers take aim specifically at Baron-Cohen's more recent work, albeit to different ends. In works published in 2005 and 2006,[18] Baron-Cohen suggested that the route into mindreading was through "the empathizing system," and that, in effect, if you are defective in empathy, you are defective in mindreading. The empathizing system is to be contrasted with the systemizing mechanism: the former is more developed in females, and the latter, which autistic people rely on by default, more developed in males. Hence Baron-Cohen's view is now the "extreme male brain" view of autism.

Michelle Maiese believes that Baron-Cohen has gone astray in conjecturing that empathy is related to the Theory-Theory of mind. In her view, empathy is not so strictly cognitive a process. To understand empathy fully we need to be aware of the essentially embodied, emotive, enactive interaction processes involved in social cognition. Maiese develops the idea of *affective framing*, whereby our bodily feelings and cares influence our patterns of cognitive focus and attention. Affective framing is, at bottom, nonconceptual and nondeliberative: an individual's interpretations of the world are shaped to a large extent by her desires, goals, fears, and values and grounded in her habitual patterns of bodily response. This view suggests that the mentalistic understanding of social interaction that Baron-Cohen defends is too narrow. Subjects engaged in conversation, for example, do not observe and then infer, but instead enter into what Maiese characterizes as "a shared dance" with their conversation partner or partners. Empathy involves modulation of one's mental and emotional state by coming into bodily contact with other persons' mental states, so that one literally feels with them. Understanding other people's minds and behavior thus relies necessarily on the embodied interaction process itself. Maiese argues that autistic individuals are cut off from empathy so understood because autism involves impaired affective framing, and as such, autistic subjects' bodily feelings do not play their usual role in focusing attention or attuning them to other people's mental states. A correlated effect is that autistic subjects do not exhibit the same sort of bodily modulation that ordinarily takes place during face-to-face interpersonal interactions. Maiese concludes by investigating the implications of her account of empathy on the moral powers of autistic individuals.

In her chapter, Ruth Sample challenges the "extreme male brain" view of autism. In particular, she identifies what she takes to be Baron-Cohen's central argument for his claim, which she calls "The Common Cause Argument," and charges that it both rests on dubious premises and is, in fact, invalid. The argument can be broken down as follows:

1. Fetal testosterone is causally relevant to male-typical behavior.
2. Fetal testosterone is causally relevant to ASD.
3. Both male-typical behavior and ASD are more common in males.
4. Male-typical behavior is a milder version of ASD: they are part of the same phenotypic expression. Therefore,
5. ASD is the Extreme Male Brain.

Sample argues not only that Baron-Cohen has failed to provide evidence for the key claims of the premises, but that the conclusion would not follow even if, for example, fetal testosterone *were* causally relevant to autism. Sample concludes that even though the prevalence of autism is significantly sexually dimorphic, it would be a mistake to see it as a phenotypical expression of the male brain, just as it would be a mistake to see disorders found more often in girls (such as Rett syndrome, which is almost exclusively female, and used to be regarded as a form of autism) as the Extreme Female Brain. "Sexing the brain" adds nothing to our understanding of autism. Neither does it add to our understanding of what causes, or how to remediate, autism. In addition, promoting this equivalence has serious social implications that should not be ignored. The equation of autism with the male brain advances another agenda endorsed by Baron-Cohen: what Erik Turkheimer calls "belligerent defenses of stereotypical masculinity in evolutionary psychology."[19] Baron-Cohen uses The Extreme Male Brain theory to argue that the low representation of women in the natural sciences, mathematics, computer science, and engineering is a product of biological differences in the brains of men and women. This has clear political implications, despite Baron-Cohen's professed neutrality.

As should be evident in the forgoing, it is practically impossible to separate discussion of what, if anything, constitutes the "essence" of autism from discussion of related normative issues. Perhaps the most vital and contested issue surrounding autism is whether (or not) it should be labeled a "disorder" at all. On the one hand, the origin of the label in medicine and psychology, along with the fact that the children studied by Kanner and Asperger were brought to them by worried parents who wanted to know what was wrong with their children, suggests that, *of course* it is a disorder. And, while Baron-Cohen has worked to take away the stigma from the label (and indeed advocates the use of the term "autism spectrum *condition*" rather than the more common *disorder*[20]), it is still true that the suggested causes, "weak central coherence," "executive dysfunction," and his own "mindblindness" all carry negative connotations.

In her chapter, "A Dash of Autism," Jami L. Anderson describes her "post-diagnosis" experiences as the parent of an autistic child, those years in which she tried, but failed, to make sense of the overwhelming and often nonsensical information she received about autism. Anderson argues that immediately after being given an autism diagnosis, parents are pressured into making what amounts to a life-long commitment to a therapy program that (they are told) will not only dramatically change their child, but their family's financial situation and even their entire mode of existence. Moreover, despite information overload in the form of books, pamphlets and videos about autism, many treatment programs for autism rely on empty jargon and make completely unrealistic promises, so parents are left feeling overwhelmed and panicked. Even well respected therapy programs encourage parents to spend liberally buying special education equipment, clothing, bedding, and play equipment that may be purposeless. Indeed, autism therapists, who help construct what Anderson refers to as the Culture of Autism, advise parents to commit to a minimum of thirty-five to forty-five hours of intensive therapy with their child every week. The implications are clear: for a parent who works full time, their autistic child becomes a second full-time job. While treatments and therapies are big business right now, they are pushing parents to the brink of desperation, so it is not too surprising that there is a desperate cry for a more *permanent* solution—which is why researchers seek to cure autism.

But there are two ways to conceptualize cure. A Therapeutic Cure model (TC) conceives of a cure as a beneficial treatment for the patient that eliminates or ameliorates the harms of the disease or condition. But the notion of a therapeutic cure for autism is highly implausible, given the complexities of autism. Indeed, at this point, the vast majority of researchers have come to the conclusion that the idea of a *therapeutic* cure for autism is simply a nonstarter. Therefore the bulk of research seeking a cure for autism focuses instead on a second approach, which Anderson refers to as the Negative Eugenics Cure model (NEC).With this model, the intention is to eliminate the disease or condition without regard for the health or well-being of the organism carrying the disease or condition. So, with regard to autism, researchers are focusing on identifying genetic markers for autism that can be detected *in utero*, or in embryos, so that autistic fetuses can be eliminated and autism eradicated by preventing the existence of autistic individuals. Anderson reviews both models and argues that both fail to provide convincing arguments that the "solution" either offers is desirable. Both rest on the assumption that autism renders a life not worth living which, all things considered, is false. Instead of pushing to cure autism, an idea pervasive in this Culture of Autism, Anderson contends that autistics are individuals with lives worth living. Moreover, rather than expend millions on research to search for the means to eliminate autism, we should instead expend our resources to ensure individuals have better access to any therapeutic resources they may need. If the phenomenology of autism were better understood and appreciated, the panicked demand for a cure for autism might abate and perhaps autism could be seen as having value in and of its own right.

Indeed, many people who self-identify as autistic are challenging the conception of autism as a disorder, preferring to argue for a position called *neurodiversity*. One thing that stands in their way is that, although it is true that many autistic individuals exhibit certain "splinter skills" like extraordinary memory or mathematical ability, the kinds of behavior that are liable to lead to a diagnosis in a child are things like hand flapping, repeatedly ordering objects (e.g., toys) in rows, and profoundly restricted routines, which it is *prima facie* hard to construe as anything but disabling. Indeed, the view expressed in the *DSM IV-TR* is that many of these behaviors lack adaptive function or purpose, interfere with learning, and constitute the nonsocial behavioral dysfunctions of those disorders making up the Autism Spectrum. As the *DSM IV-TR* continues to be the reference source of choice for professionals working with individuals with psychiatric difficulties, its characterization of the Autism Spectrum holds significant sway.

However, in their chapter "Embodying Autistic Cognition: Towards Reconceiving Certain 'Autism-Related' Behavioral Atypicalities as Functional," Michael Doan and Andrew Fenton argue that, while "interventions in the lives of some of those diagnosed with ASDs are sometimes justified and desirable," many of the so called "aberrant behaviors" or "restricted interests" can be seen to have a useful function, and as such should be viewed as desirable and, in themselves, nondisordered. Fenton and Doan make this argument against the backdrop of Extended Mind and Enactive Mind Theories, which theorize that mind (or cognition) is embodied and environmentally embedded. They offer a fine-grained taxonomy of what have been called "Restrictive Repetitive Behaviors and Interests" (RRBIs), distinguishing between RRBIs with and without function, and, in the former category, among *adaptive, maladaptive,* and *neutral* behavior, and argue that of functional RRBIs, only those that are maladaptive (the kind that positively hinder active cognitive engagement with physical and social environs) are uncontestable bases for interventions. In contrast, adaptive and neutral RRBIs can be the means by which individuals on the spectrum are *able* to engage, and intervention can be positively harmful. To support their case, Fenton and Doan include the testimony of two individuals on the spectrum describing how certain RRBIs enable them to make order where otherwise there is debilitating sensory chaos. Fenton and Doan seek to carve out a "middle way" between the pathologizing medical view of autism as a disorder and RRBIs as functionless symptoms of impairment and a relativistic view whereby *no* RRBI should ever be questioned or seen as a sign that intervention could be helpful. We should have a more nuanced view that is directed both by the testimony of autistic individuals themselves and a sophisticated conception of cognition that should facilitate greater acceptance of the sensory needs of those on the spectrum and the related behavioral atypicalities that can mediate and support their physical and social environments, or otherwise have value for them.

One of the supposed defining features of autism is an impairment in empathy. At the same time, there is a tradition in ethics that sees an ability to empathize as essential to moral agency. A combination of these two theses would portray the autistic individual as something less than a moral agent, which, in itself, would put them on very unsure footing, as there is a further tradition in ethics that makes moral personhood, and in effect, moral worth, contingent on moral agency. Several of the chapters in this anthology analyze one or more of the foregoing theses.

In her book *The Ethics of Autism*, Deborah Barnbaum defends versions of these claims. Barnbaum agrees with Baron-Cohen's contention that autistic people lack a theory of mind. Yet, Barnbaum goes further: she asserts that one cannot experience either empathy or genuine human relationships without a theory of mind, and that therefore the moral agency of autistic individuals is compromised. Anna Stubblefield challenges Barnbaum's claims at every step of the way: autism is *not* absence of a theory of mind (it should be thought of in terms of sensory and movement challenges), and autistic people do *not* lack empathy (if anything, neurotypical people fail to empathize with people on the spectrum) and therefore are capable of moral agency. Perhaps more damning, Stubblefield charges that Barnbaum inaccurately summarizes the words of autistic people to demonstrate their lack of empathy and moral agency, and that when the context of the quotes she summarizes and the full quotations are restored, a different picture of what it is to be labeled autistic emerges. Ultimately, Stubblefield asserts, Barnbaum's arguments amount to "blaming the victim." The alienation that people on the spectrum experience has much more to do with the ostracism and abuse directed at them by the very individuals who are supposedly full moral agents and fully able to experience empathy than any supposed deficiencies of mental capacity on the part of autistic people.

The question of the extent to which autistic individuals can be said to be autonomous agents is taken up further in David DeVidi's chapter, "Advocacy, Autonomy, and Autism." DeVidi, who has worked as an advocate for people who meet the criteria for a diagnosis of "classic" autism (in particular, sometimes extreme language delays), starts by considering a challenge to the point of his advocacy: while it is common for people who advocate for people with disabilities to argue that we as a society should structure things so that they have *full citizenship, self-determination,* and *meaningful, reciprocal relationships* with others in the community, there are reasons to wonder whether this rhetoric can be intended in good faith for people diagnosed as autistic. Diagnostic criteria for autism include such things as a "lack of social reciprocity or emotional reciprocity" and a "failure to develop peer relationships appropriate to developmental level."

DeVidi argues that, once we understand what autonomy is, and the requirements that even neurotypical individuals need met to achieve it, we will see that individuals with classic autism are capable of realizing it. DeVidi uses as a basic definition of autonomy the following, owing to John Christmas: "Put most simply, to be autonomous is to be one's own person, to be directed by considerations, desires, conditions, and characteristics that are not simply imposed upon one, but are part of what can somehow be considered one's authentic self."

DeVidi focuses on three limitations typically faced by autistic people, and in particular, those who require *facilitated communication*, that might be seen to impair expression of this authentic self. These limitations are *inflexibility, poor impulse control*, and *communication difficulties*. This last would appear to make it difficult to know that authentic self, especially when it is occasionally unclear exactly how much an assistant is contributing to the communication that he or she is facilitating.

For each instance of these limitations that might call into question the capacity for autonomy of autistic individuals, DeVidi points to equivalent limitations faced by neurotypicals that are not seen to compromise their autonomy because of the existence of strategies for coping with them that are so familiar and commonplace as to go unremarked upon. DeVidi asserts that no person, on the spectrum or not, gets by without what he calls "externalizing" strategies, and that once we face that fact, and are aware of the strategies that can work for even those on the spectrum who might be considered comparatively "low-functioning," it is possible to defend their status as autonomous, and thereby capable of full citizenship. This is not to downplay serious concerns that we might have for such individuals: DeVidi cautions that those who act as advocates must not lose the distinction between "helping someone to think something through" and "doing someone's thinking for him." But so long as the right safeguards are in place, he concludes that "advocating for self-determination for people with autism need be no mere rhetorical ploy, but can be done with a clear conscience." All people require support to achieve autonomy: the supports autistic people require are "statistically unusual," but justice requires that we "push for the creation of the right sorts of supports to make [their] autonomy more than potential."

REFERENCES

American Psychiatric Association. 2000. Diagnostic and Statistical Manual of Mental Disorders. 4th Edition, Text Revised. Washington, DC: American Psychiatric Association.
Baron-Cohen, S. 1995. *Mindblindness: An Essay on Autism and Theory of Mind*. Cambridge, MA: Bradford Books/MIT Press.
Baron-Cohen, S. 2005. The Empathizing System: A Revision of the 1994 Model of the Mindreading System. In *Origins of the Social Mind*, eds. Ellis and Bjorklunk. New York: Guildford Press.
Baron-Cohen, S. 2006. Two New Theories of Autism: Hyper-Systemising and Assortative Mating. *Archives of Disease in Childhood* 91:2–5.
Baron-Cohen, S. 2008. *Autism and Asperger Syndrome*. Oxford, UK: Oxford University Press.
Baron-Cohen, S., Alan M. Leslie, Uta Frith. 1985. Does the Autistic Child Have a "Theory of Mind?" *Cognition* 21(1):37–46.
Boucher, J. 2009. *The Autistic Spectrum: Characteristics, Causes and Practical Issues*. London: Sage.
Martin, Andy. 2010. The Stone: Beyond Understanding. *New York Times Online*, November 10.
Turkheimer, E. 2010. The It Strikes Back. *PsycCRITIQUES* 55(24): No Pagination.

NOTES

1. *New York Times Online*, 2010.

2. As Ed McCann has observed, if you compare the writing of the Hegelian, F. H. Bradley, and G. E. Moore, the supposed founder of analytic philosophy, it is the former who displays the clarity and precision of argument.

3. Sally Haslanger has made an admirably clear and incisive analytical contribution to the philosophy of gender, but she admits that she gets raised eyebrows when she tells fellow philosophers what she writes about.

4. To give one example: no philosophy of religion textbook fails to include extensive discussion of the ontological argument, which few even ardent believers find convincing and for effectively none of whom is a reason for belief, yet the same textbooks invariably do fail to analyze either the topic of prayer or the topic of heaven, surely two of the most basic subjects of interest to real worshippers.

5. Boucher 2009, 36.

6. APA 2000.

7. Boucher 2009, 24.

8. Kanner L. 1943. Autistic Disturbances of Affective Contact. *Nervous Child* 2:217–50.

9. Asperger, H. 1991. Autistic Psychopathy in Childhood. In *Autism and Asperger Syndrome*, trans. U. Frith, 37–92. Cambridge: Cambridge University Press.

10. If indeed it is a single theory. It could be argued that Baron-Cohen's recent work is distinct enough from his original suggestions to be a different account altogether.

11. A couple of key early examples are *Folk Psychology*, ed. Davies and Stone (Oxford: Blackwell, 1995) and *Theories of Theories of Mind*, ed. Carruthers and Smith (Cambridge: CUP, 1996).

12. Baron-Cohen takes the term from the work of Alan Leslie, specifically "ToMM, ToBy, and Agency: Core architecture and domain specificity," in *Mapping the Mind: Domain Specificity in Cognition and Culture*, ed. L. Hirschfeld and S. Gelman (Cambridge: CUP, 1994).

13. Baron-Cohen 1995, 51.

14. Baron-Cohen 1995, 69.

15. Baron-Cohen et al. 1985.

16. Ibid.,41.

17. Ibid., 44.

18. Baron-Cohen 2005; Baron-Cohen 2006.

19. Turkheimer 2010.

20. "I prefer the acronym ASC, since individuals in the high-functioning subgroup are certainly different—they think differently and perceive differently—but is arguable whether these differences should be seen as a disorder… The term 'condition' simultaneously acknowledges the disabling aspects of autism and Asperger syndrome, and the fact that the differences in functioning do not lead to global disability, and may in some individuals even result in talent" (Baron-Cohen 2008, 14).

Chapter One

Autism: The Very Idea

Simon Cushing

There are many pressing questions that one might ask about autism. These include:

How will I know if my child is autistic?
What will be the prognosis if she is?
Is autism treatable?
Is autism curable?
Should autism be eradicated?
Why wasn't autism discovered before the 1940s?
Why have the rates of diagnosis risen so sharply over the past couple of decades?

Before those questions can be addressed, the more fundamental question must be answered: what *is* autism? Answering this question is tricky. For one thing, there is more than one way to take the question. It could be asking what *kind* of thing autism is (the *genus*, you might say): a complex of behaviors? a psychological condition? a kind of neurology? a genetic condition? Alternatively, it could be asking what makes it its own special instance of that kind (the *differentia*): *which* behaviors? *what* psychological condition/neurology/genetics? Call these *categorical* issues. On the other hand, it could be asking whether or not autism is a real knowledge-independent entity in the world for which we have just recently coined a term (on the model of something like Down syndrome) or if the concept is a human artifact that either does not track any real entity (like "neurotic" or other now-abandoned theoretical notions) or tracks behavior that is a product of human culture of a specific time and place (like "hipster"). This is a *metaphysical* question. As Locke might put it: once we establish the *nominal* essence of autism (the content of our concept of autism), we want to know if there is a *real* essence out there in the world. We want to know if autism is like "water," where it emerged that there really was a distinct kind of molecular substance to the stuff we just used to pick out by its wetness, clarity and ability safely to slake thirst.

THE CRITERIA FOR DIAGNOSIS

Before we can address either categorical or metaphysical questions, we need to have a first pass of a description to work with, and it seems appropriate to begin by returning to the source: the seminal paper "Autistic Disturbances of Affective Contact"[1] in which Leo Kanner first posited the existence of a syndrome that we now know as autism.[2] Commenting on Kanner's article more than forty years after its publication, (now Sir) Michael Rutter wrote:

> There are few scientific papers that have stood the test of time as well as Leo Kanner's first description of the syndrome that came to bear his name. The fact that he was the first person to recognize that this constellation of behaviors constituted a condition that was different from the general run of problems grouped under "mental retardation" or "schizophrenia" was quite enough for the paper to receive an honored place in the history of psychiatry. It was indeed a reflection of Kanner's remarkable clinical acumen that he was able to see so clearly that which had escaped the notice of his many distinguished contemporaries and predecessors... [F]urther research demonstrated that he had been correct in his identification of the key features that held the syndrome together. As Leon Eisenberg commented in his preface to the 1973 collection of Kanner's papers on autism, "The genius of the discovery was to detect the cardinal traits...in the midst of phenomenology as diverse as muteness in one child and verbal precocity in another."[3]

Kanner's achievement, then, was picking out a "constellation of behaviors" that were the "cardinal traits" or "key features" that "held the syndrome together" that has since come to be called autism. So what were these key features? Kanner writes that "even a quick review" of the eleven case studies of children that had been brought to him "makes the emergence of a number of essential common characteristics appear inevitable," characteristics that together "form a unique 'syndrome,' not heretofore reported."[4] Those characteristics (the vast majority of which are today considered either indicators of autism or seen to be commonly related phenomena) included: late speaking; a use of language that was rote and focused mainly on the use of nouns to identify objects, colors, or numbers; excellent rote memory; "delayed echolalia" (delayed because the "parrot-like repetitions" could be stored for later); personal pronouns "repeated just as heard, with no change to suit the altered situation;" common failure to attend to people calling on them; fussiness about food; adverse reaction to loud noises and moving objects; lack of spontaneity; treatment of people like objects; possession of "good cognitive potentialities" and "strikingly intelligent physiognomies;" clumsiness in gait allied with skill in finer muscle coordination.[5]

What kind of an answer is this to the question we began with? Suppose we say that *this* is autism: the exhibition of the set of characteristics in Kanner's list. Call this analysis the Bundle of Behaviors (BoB) Model. It is the simplest answer to the question "what is autism?" It is the answer: "what Kanner observed." In some ways it is the most optimistic, because it implies that the condition can be discarded in the way that any behaviors can be ended, however difficult that might be, and that successful behavioral therapy would not simply be a way to *mask* autism, but be a cure. Children could be autistic, and then later, not.[6]

Is it a satisfactory answer? Well, not really, for a number of reasons.

First, it seems more likely that the *essence* of autism lies deeper than the surface. Consider an analogous behavioral analysis of what "homosexuality" is.[7] To keep it simple, let's focus on what seems to be the key piece of behavior for homosexuality: same-sex sex acts. This is unsatisfactory as an analysis of what it is to be homosexual, because it seems neither necessary (the concept of a homosexual virgin makes perfect sense) nor sufficient (sex workers who perform same-sex sex acts could perfectly well be heterosexual). The behavior in each case seems to be an *effect* (or "symptom" in the medicalized language that used to apply to homosexuality and still does to autism) of the condition rather than itself *constituting* the condition.

Second, there is the problem of vagueness of boundaries. While some examples of behavior are clear-cut (e.g., misuse of pronouns), others are vague and meeting them would seem to be a matter of opinion and context. Just about every child is fussy about food to a certain extent—what counts as the degree necessary to meet the criterion here? The suspicion is that it is not the *degree* that matters but the *cause*. But referring to a (presumably nonbehavioral) cause means abandoning a simple behavioral model.

Third, we need to know if *every single* item on Kanner's list is necessary for a diagnosis of autism. Should lacking even one of those characteristics be sufficient to establish that one is not autistic? We are accustomed to think that this would be too strict a requirement, that "milder" versions of certain syndromes can lack one or two of the symptoms of the "full-blown" syndrome. But the simple BoB model is just a conjunction of all the "cardinal traits." There is no reason to believe that each trait cannot occur in people who do not have the condition. We cannot know whether or not there is a *separate* condition that lacks just one of the traits (a particular issue if we believe that Asperger syndrome is distinct). A diagnosis of autism would be like a conviction for breaking and entering in this respect: you can only be guilty of breaking and entering if you meet *every* requirement (breaking or entering/a building/without the owner's or tenant's permission/with intent to commit a felony). Meeting any but the full quota is not a mild version, it is no version at all (which is a relief to those of us who have forgotten our keys, or to firefighters intent on rescuing possible inhabitants of a burning building).

Perhaps the standards might be loosened somewhat. Suppose that I claim to have discovered "William Shatner Syndrome," the compulsive need to behave like that much impersonated actor, and give as constituent elements an exhaustive list of his behavioral characteristics. This would be analogous to the BoB model of autism, in that there is no theorizing about 'a deeper cause:' the syndrome just is the set of behaviors. Suppose further that a patient comes in who is suspected of having the syndrome. Would he have to exhibit every single item on my exhaustive list? Perhaps, instead, we could make a decision on what was the *essence* of "Shatnerosity" and insist that the behaviors that were part of this core cluster were essential, while the others were just "comorbid symptoms," likely indicators of the possibility that one had the syndrome, but not individually necessary. Of course, deciding on where to draw the line between the essential and the accidental characteristics would be a fraught issue. We have seen something like that in the debate over whether or not language delays are essential (ruling out Asperger syndrome as a kind of autism) or not. But who is the "William Shatner" of autism? Would it be the eleven children in Kanner's original study? Surely, though, we want to leave open the possibility that one or more of those was *not* autistic, or at least, even if all were, that they were not so *simply by definition*. However, on the simple BoB model, it would be an analytic truth that they were autistic, because autism would be defined as "behaving like those children."

Clearly this is not the assumption that clinicians have operated on, because it is just not the case that Kanner's list has been seen as sacrosanct. The most authoritative current list of characteristics that merit a diagnosis are to be found in the fourth edition of the American Psychiatric Association's *Diagnostic and Statistical Manual of Mental Disorders*. This manual is the resource to which a vast number of clinicians turn in deciding whether or not a patient is autistic. It was originally brought into existence to standardize diagnoses that had up to that point varied wildly among clinicians.[8] The entry on "Autistic Disorder" in *DSM-IV* presents an alternative strategy from both the simple method of requiring *every single* characteristic and making a distinction between a set core and an outer ring of nonessentials. The approach might be called the Cluster of Behaviors (CoB) model. Here are the diagnostic criteria:

A. A total of six (or more) items from (1), (2), and (3), with at least two from (1), and one each from (2) and (3):

1. qualitative impairment in social interaction, as manifested by at least two of the following:

    a. marked impairment in the use of multiple nonverbal behaviors such as eye-to-eye gaze, facial expression, body postures, and gestures to regulate social interaction

    b. failure to develop peer relationships appropriate to developmental level

    c. a lack of spontaneous seeking to share enjoyment, interests, or achievements with other people (e.g., by a lack of showing, bringing, or pointing out objects of interest)

    d. lack of social or emotional reciprocity

2. qualitative impairments in communication as manifested by at least one of the following:

    a. delay in, or total lack of, the development of spoken language (not accompanied by an attempt to compensate through alternative modes of communication such as gesture or mime)

    b. in individuals with adequate speech, marked impairment in the ability to initiate or sustain a conversation with others

    c. stereotyped and repetitive use of language or idiosyncratic language

    d. lack of varied, spontaneous make-believe play or social imitative play appropriate to developmental level

3. restricted repetitive and stereotyped patterns of behavior, interests, and activities, as manifested by at least one of the following:

    a. encompassing preoccupation with one or more stereotyped and restricted patterns of interest that is abnormal either in intensity or focus

    b. apparently inflexible adherence to specific, nonfunctional routines or rituals

    c. stereotyped and repetitive motor mannerisms (e.g., hand or finger flapping or twisting, or complex whole body movements)

    d. persistent preoccupation with parts of objects

B. Delays or abnormal functioning in at least one of the following areas, with onset prior to age three years:

1. social interaction,
2. language as used in social communication, or
3. symbolic or imaginative play.

The CoB approach is to identify key *types* and demand that each be instantiated by one or more *tokens*. No single individual characteristic is essential, but each type must be represented.

However, what this list gains in flexibility, it loses in specificity. Now it seems that a wide variety of differing individuals could all meet the same diagnosis. One person might meet the diagnosis by being A1ab2a3aB1, while another by being A1cd2b3bB2, and so on. Why should we assume that there is some essentially similar syndrome that they share? (The assumption is that each person, while exhibiting different behaviors, is exhibiting the same set of types of behaviors. But if the behaviors are different enough to warrant separate descriptions, then even if they share being *one* type of behavior, each differs from the other in other respects, like being "play" or "communication.")

One could respond that each unique individual who scored above a threshold level on this points system shares a "family resemblance" (as all things called "games" do in Wittgenstein's famous example) to any other, and that this is enough. But that would undermine the status of the diagnosis as a precise scientific one. It begins to seem less likely that this checklist is picking out a condition that "carves nature at the joints," but rather that it is a rough-and-ready way of sorting people into groups for some predetermined social purpose. It seems to be treating an autism diagnosis on the model of entrance criteria into a prestigious university: to make the grade you have to be "well-rounded." Medically, however, it would appear to make more sense to avoid the "catch-all" diagnosis of autism altogether and focus instead on the various individual criteria.

To put it another way: one key problem with BoB was explaining the "string" that bound the bundle of various characteristics into a *syndrome*. Why *those* characteristics? Moving to CoB seemed to make the collection less arbitrary but, conversely, we now need to know why no individual item on Kanner's list is necessary (and some have been dropped altogether). What motivated the shift? (This is especially pressing given that some of the things that Kanner described but that are left out of the new list—sensitivity to various kinds of sensory stimulation for example—should be recognizable to a huge number of parents of autistic children. Why have those criteria been excised?) It wasn't motivated by an attempt to describe the eleven original children more accurately, because only Kanner himself attempted any follow-up.

What is more, the original problem with BoB recurs at a new level: what is it that binds the three *types* together into a syndrome? Why those, and only those *types*?

A FORAY INTO METAPHYSICS

It might seem academic to wonder about the justification for the difference between the diagnostic lists provided by Kanner and the *DSM-IV*—Kanner, after all, was only the first person to talk about the syndrome and could be expected to have made some mistakes that could be corrected by advances made since. Why shouldn't we simply say "we know more about autism now?"

Such a response, however, is not available to a theory that is committed to either a Bundle or a Cluster theory. Recall William Shatner Syndrome: what is the "more" that we could know? Such an account cannot appeal to anything outside of the Bundle or Cluster to justify altering the components. We shall shortly address theories that suggest that the characteristics on the list are *effects* or *symptoms* of autism, rather than constitutive elements of it, but for now the puzzle remains. What is more, the issue of providing a justification for a changed list of characteristics is very pressing because the fifth edition of the *DSM*—the first major revision in seventeen years—is soon to be released, and while there is some dispute about what effect the changes in the definition of what is now called "*Autism Spectrum* Disorder"[9] will have it seems clear that the changes will (and perhaps are intended to) restrict the numbers of people who meet the diagnosis, as the following quotes illustrate:

> "We have to make sure not everybody who is a little odd gets a diagnosis of autism or Asperger disorder," said Dr. David J. Kupfer, a professor of psychiatry at the University of Pittsburgh and chairman of the task force making the revisions, which are still subject to change. "It involves a use of treatment resources. It becomes a cost issue."[10]

> "The changes would narrow the diagnosis so much that it could effectively end the autism surge," said Dr. Fred R. Volkmar, director of the Child Study Center at the Yale School of Medicine and the author of the new analysis of the proposal. "We would nip it in the bud."[11]

Suppose we interpret such statements as suggesting that the changes between *DSM IV* and *V* were partly motivated by financial considerations. How should one respond to that as a justification for changes to the standards for diagnosis? Different responses track different metaphysical views, depending on whether or not it is thought that the essence of autism is to be found solely in the intrinsic properties of those labeled as autistic or to depend also on social facts extrinsic to them.

On one view, this is either irresponsible or only justified by a belief that the earlier standard of diagnosis cast too broad a net. A *realist* would take the view that the number of people who *really are* autistic is unaffected by words in a book. For the realist, autism should be viewed on the model of conditions like Down syndrome: a biological phenomenon that humans have had throughout the centuries but which has been identified and named only comparatively recently.[12] But a realist would never be happy with the implication that cost *alone* should be a motivation for setting the standards of diagnosis: the goal of a diagnosis would be to capture as closely as possible all and only those people who genuinely have autism.

On the other hand, one could draw a contrasting lesson from this controversy. To the extent that "autism" has reality, it is realized in the individuals who are picked out by diagnosticians as autistic. And exactly who is picked out as autistic depends greatly on the definition given in the *DSM*. So rather than the diagnosis being driven by the attempt to capture an independently existing reality, the explanatory arrow could be reversed: the existence of the phenomenon depends on the diagnosis, where the content of the diagnosis could be driven by ideology or economics more than medical science. This is the view that autism is a "socially constructed" phenomenon.

There are two main ways autism could be socially constructed. It could be like *race*: that is, although there are biological (although not necessarily genetic) bases for things like skin pigmentation, eye and/or nose shape, hair texture and other characteristics that have been taken as race *traits*, there is nothing in nature that marks those traits as distinctively racial. Not only is the collection of traits arbitrary (Why not ear size, belly button type or "tongue rollability?") but there is no "glue" that groups (for example) all the supposedly "black" traits together, so that they either all occur together in particular individuals or not at all. For this reason, biologists have asserted that racial *categories* have no biological reality. "Race" is a socially constructed phenomenon that arbitrarily groups traits together that have no underlying common cause, genetic or otherwise. If autism were like that, then it would lose status as a medically useful category.[13] That would not mean, however, that the conditions that make it up, such as language delays, social difficulties, problems of proprioception, problems with sensory integration *et al.*, would not each be conditions worth studying and treating, just that they are not all linked by being *autism* traits.

(A more extreme social constructivist view of autism would imply that the condition itself is a human creation, that the label has provided a source of identity for people who might otherwise be just awkward.[14] On this view "autism" would turn out to be like "female hysteria"—something whose diagnosis was just self-reinforcing. On this view even the so-called symptoms are not biological realities but culturally produced chimeras. I think this latter view can be dismissed.)

To summarize: the two major metaphysical views about autism are *realism*, the view that what Kanner first identified *is* a genuine cross-cultural (and possibly even cross-species) psychological/biological phenomenon whose true essence will soon be captured (in the way that the essence of AIDS turned out to be the HIV virus, or the essence of Down syndrome turned out to be an extra chromosome), and *social constructivism*, the view that "autism" is a concept that groups together independently existing, and independently treatable conditions—and no biological basis for *that* will be found, any more than we will find the "fabulousness" gene or the chromosomes responsible for the combination of liking country music at the same time as being Catholic. (Or for acting like William Shatner.) I think it safe to say that the predominant view is realism. One aim of this chapter is to argue that the vagueness surrounding the concept of autism undermines attempts to isolate something intrinsic shared uniquely by those labeled autistic, and that, therefore, the possibility that there *is* no real essence corresponding to the concept of autism, and that it is a social construct, should be more seriously entertained.

However, this conclusion concerning the metaphysical question is premature, as so far we have only considered the behavioral answers to the categorical question.

Recall that both the Bundle and Cluster theories faced the challenge of explaining why it was that we should group the various behaviors (whether tokens or types) under a single heading, and relatedly, how we could ever justify adding or subtracting behaviors from the group. What was it that tied the bundle together?

Obviously if there were a *common cause* of the behaviors then this would answer both challenges. All behaviors that were effects of the same cause should be counted as evidence for the presence of the same condition, and any that were not could be dropped from the criteria for a diagnosis. And the kind of thing that could underlie and explain behaviors in this way would be a *psychological* condition.

PSYCHOLOGICAL ACCOUNTS

Recall the analogy with homosexuality with which I called into question strictly behavioral analyses: a better account of what it is to be homosexual posits a *psychological phenomenon* that would underlie and explain the behaviors taken to be evidence of homosexuality. How about *same-sex sexual attraction*?[15] Locating the essence of homosexuality at the psychological level allows for the phenomenon of being "closeted" and of discovering oneself to be gay without actually having had sex. A psychological phenomenon can cause certain behaviors, but can be counteracted by other psychological states, so that it can be present without obvious behavioral results. Autistic adults can learn to "act normal."

It is important to distinguish between *being in a particular psychological state* and *having a certain psychological tendency*. If we defined homosexuality just as *actually experiencing* same-sex sexual attraction, then, again, homosexuality would be a "gappy" condition: for example, even one prone to excessive arousal would still not be homosexual while in a dreamless sleep. So a more sophisticated, but perhaps somewhat tendentious account (how could you falsify it?) would define being homosexual as "being such that, if one *were* to experience sexual attraction, it would be to someone (whom one perceives as) of the same sex."

What are the implications of a model that locates the essence for a condition at the level of psychological states?

The first is one already mentioned, that one could have the condition and it might not be evident to observers. For example, if one was not yet of a stage in one's development that one experienced *any* sexual attraction, then there would be no evidence that one was homosexual. (Of course, this is what makes the "sophisticated" psychological account suspicious—we cannot tell whether or not the condition is *absent* or "dormant"). And, of course, many children do not display symptoms of autism until at least eighteen months of age.

Second, such an analysis would be *agnostic on the genesis* of the psychological condition. For homosexuality it allows equally that one could be born a homosexual, one could be conditioned into homosexuality, or one might even choose it. Viewing autism in this light leaves open the possibility of "acquired autism," where the relevant psychological states could result from any number of causes (the mother having rubella while pregnant, for example). And, in fact, a distinction is now made between "idiopathic" autism, whose causes are unknown, and what is called "secondary" autism where the causes are said to be understood. That this distinction is made implies that autism itself is not located at the level of causes, even if these were genetic. However, I think our intuitions would rebel at calling somebody autistic who was neurotypical until his thirties but on being the victim of head trauma suddenly displayed Kanner's symptoms.

Third, a psychological model allows for the possibility of a "cure:" whatever one's genetics or history, it is in theory possible for one to cease to have any particular psychological state.[16]

Contrast this with the behavioral account: one is always in the position to choose to perform whatever behavior characterized the condition, but one cannot choose to have an attraction or choose to be "mindblind."[17]

Suppose we agree that autism is essentially a psychological condition (the genus part of categorization). The question then turns to the *differentia: what* psychological condition? It has to be one that can explain the behaviors that we are now taking to be *symptoms* of autism (rather than *components* of autism). There are two clear ways a proposed condition could fail to be a satisfactory explanation. First, it cannot simply be "whatever it is that causes those symptoms" because this begs the question in favor of a single condition and a single cause, while at the same time committing the *virtus dormitiva* sin of pretending to provide an answer without actually saying anything "contentful." Second, it must not simply be that a contentful psychological state is chosen that, on the face of it, cannot explain all of the disparate behaviors that make up the diagnosis of autism, but recalcitrant ones get dropped or artificially redescribed to suggest a unity that was not there before.

Did Kanner see a unity underlying his original traits? In a paper written some twenty-eight years after his seminal paper, he appears to suggest as much: "The outstanding pathognomonic characteristics were viewed as (a) the children's inability from the beginning of life to relate themselves to people and situations in the ordinary way, and (b) an anxiously obsessive desire for the preservation of sameness."[18]

I think there is a little bit of revisionism in his description: as noted in the previous section, in the original paper he describes *behaviors*, and they include a broad range, not easily clustered under only two headings (although he does stray from this in one instance, as I discuss below). But besides this, it is not clear how helpful these groupings are. An "inability…to relate…in the ordinary way" is at best a vague and woolly classification that could fit an enormous range of behaviors. It points to a need to research the cause of the inability without giving any clues as to where that might be found. And "anxiously obsessive desire" is, if anything, a step backwards from the simple description of the behaviors, loaded as the adjectives are with either rather dated or unjustifiably specific psychological notions.

The one glaring instance where the original study departs from a cautiously objective cataloguing of behaviors and indulges in psychological theorizing comes when Kanner attributes to the children "an all-powerful need for being left undisturbed." That the children have this "need" is then used to explain a range of behaviors:

> Everything that is brought to the children from the outside, everything that changes his external or even internal, environment, represents a dreaded intrusion.
>
> *Food* is the earliest intrusion that is brought to the child from the outside…Our patients…anxious to keep the outside world away, indicated this by the refusal of food…
>
> Another intrusion comes from *loud noises and moving objects*, which are therefore reacted to with horror…Yet it is not the noise or motion itself that is dreaded. The disturbance comes from the noise or motion that intrudes itself, or threatens to intrude itself, upon the child's aloneness.[19]

Is Kanner offering up the various kinds of behavior as evidence for the general psychological "need" or is he instead interpreting the behavior in light of a presupposed theory? While the former would be more defensible methodologically, it is of dubious explanatory worth. Furthermore, in the examples above he attempts to give an explanation for sensory issues for which the more likely explanation is biological. It looks like an overreach by a psychologist. In fact, I think we have cause now to question Kanner's descriptions of the traits as prejudiced by a preconceived speculation on an underlying mechanism, a speculation for which he could not have had adequate support.

What are some more recent suggestions for psychological essences or bases of autism? The three major candidates are: impaired theory of mind (the most influential version of which is Simon Baron-Cohen's "mindblindness" theory), weak central coherence, and executive dysfunction. As it turns out, the criticisms of each of these turn on its inability to account for certain symptoms taken to be essential indicators of autism.

In his 1995 book *Mindblindness*, Simon Baron-Cohen contended first, that neurotypical people understand others by having a "theory of mind" and second, that this faculty is impaired in autistic individuals. This view has been criticized from many different perspectives: from the charge that his evidence for this claim (the "Sally/Anne" false belief test) is inconclusive at best (hardly any autistic adult fails the test, while many nonautistic yet intellectually impaired and most deaf children are similarly delayed in their capacity to pass it[20]) to the criticism that the notion that *anybody* has a "theory of mind" is based on a misconception of how the mind works. But perhaps most seriously for an account of autism, the theory fails to account for what are deemed essential elements of it. Many autistic children are obviously so at an age before *any* child is deemed to have a "theory of mind," and the theory has nothing to say about repetitive behaviors, narrow interests and physical issues like being touch averse or hyper-sensitive to sensory inputs.[21]

Baron-Cohen now acknowledges that this theory alone is inadequate, but believes that it can be part of a complete theory, the "empathizing-systemizing" theory. As he ties this account closely with what he calls the "extreme male brain" theory, I will postpone discussion until the section on brain-based accounts of the essence of autism. Let us turn now to the second psychological theory.

Uta Frith suggested the following "hypothesis about the nature of the intellectual dysfunction in Autism":

> In the normal cognitive system there is a built-in propensity to form coherence over as wide a range of stimuli as possible, and to generalize over as wide a range of contexts as possible. It is this drive that results in grand systems of thought, and ultimately in the world's great religions. It is this capacity for

coherence that is diminished in autistic children. As a result, their information-processing systems, like their very beings, are characterized by detachment.[22]

A number of experiments led Frith to this conclusion, in particular ones that showed a superior ability to pick out specific details (faces hidden in pictures, for example) which she interpreted as showing that autistic children were not concentrating on the whole, trying to find meaning in it, but instead viewing each part individually.

Frith has modified this "weak central coherence" (WCC) theory substantially over the years, and there is some suggestion that it could link up with theories about the autistic brain that show "short range overconnectivity" but "long range underconnectivity"—that is, that more neurons than in neurotypical brains link local areas in the brain but fewer link distant areas.[23]

WCC appears to show promise in explaining a range of phenomena indicative of autism:[24] Besides enhanced perception of visual detail, there is also hypersensitivity to change (because any detail is noticed) face recognition difficulty (because only the parts of the face are perceived, not the whole face), and a well-known tendency to play with the parts of toys (e.g., the wheels of a toy car) rather than the whole toys. That said, however, the explanation is at best "loose" (are we seriously to believe that the autistic child does not *know* that the whole thing is a car?) and furthermore, several of these conditions are well known, and indeed severe, in people not labeled as autistic.[25] Moreover, however much you modify WCC, it seems that it could, at best, explain a subset of the characteristics first noticed by Kanner, and none of the motor issues so characteristic of autistic children.[26]

"Executive function" is the ability to control activities, both mental and physical. Defects in this function could impair *inhibitory* control (the ability to stop doing what one is doing), *flexibility* (ability to change activities or switch attention to new projects) and the ability to *initiate* new activities. The major features of autism that executive dysfunction is said to explain are the repetitive behaviors, reliance on routine, "obsessive" interests and (purported) lack of creativity,[27] as well as the inability to plan a schedule for oneself. However, it does not seem equipped to explain any sensory issues or the things the other theories purport to explain, viz., social difficulties or enhanced perception of detail, so it is at best incomplete. Also, repetitive behaviors, reliance on routine, etc., are features of other distinct psychological conditions, like Obsessive Compulsive Disorder or Tourette's syndrome, so even if executive dysfunction explained these things it would not be a unique indicator of autism. Finally, as with the other theories, there are many criticisms of the inferences drawn from the various tests that supposedly support the theory.[28]

So we see that no single psychological mechanism yet proposed can capture all of the core features of autism. We must conclude that if there is a psychological essence to autism it consists of more than any single one of these. We are then faced with a familiar dilemma, only one layer down from before: is autism *simply* a bundle or cluster of psychological mechanisms, or should we look deeper for a common cause that unites all in the cluster? A related but distinct question concerns whether or not the presence of any of these mechanisms alone is sufficient to warrant a diagnosis for autism (even if we allow that autism *consists of* more than the mechanism alone), or if one can have a psychology that exhibits the mechanism and yet not be autistic.

Theories that posit particular psychological modules or mechanisms as explanations of behavior face a further challenge: explain what exactly the module or mechanism *consists in*. Where exactly are these psychological phenomena located? As each of them is a *deficiency*, what *exactly* is it that autistic people lack?

Such challenges inevitably lead us to biology, and, more specifically, neurobiology. Let us turn now to discussion of the "autistic brain."

BRAAAAAAAAINS!

When we talk about the autistic brain, what exactly do we mean? We could mean one of three things: the brain that *results* from autism, the type of brain states that *constitute* autism or the brain that *causes* autism. Which of these it is depends on what level autism is located at, an issue that we have yet to settle. We began with the idea that autism *was* a "constellation of behaviors." But the strange implications of BoB and CoB pointed towards a psychological account. Were there a single unified psychological account, we would still want to know what underpinned that psychological state. Assuming that psychological states *reduce* to states of the brain (that is, psychological states cannot exist except where there are brains in certain states), it is still an open question whether or not we should *identify* autism as a psychological state with a condition of the brain ("identifying" reductivism[29]) or say that, while brain states are all there is to the psychological states in question, one cannot just talk in the language of brain biology and capture the essence of those psychological states ("constitutive" reductivism[30]).

Finally, if it turned out that there was an "autistic gene," then, if we decided that *that* was the essence of autism, then the type of brain that uniquely resulted from that genetic nature would be an *effect* of autism, and not the cause *or* essence.

But, of course, we have not found a satisfactory unified psychological account, which suggests either that autism is not a unified phenomenon, but in fact a bundle of distinct, often comorbid, but actually independent conditions (and that the term "autism" does not carve nature at the joints any more than the term "Coca-Cola" captures a natural kind), or that, if autism is a single state, then it must be the common cause of these disparate psychological conditions. This suggests that (a) a particular kind of brain is what constitutes autism (just as a particular molecular structure constitutes "water") and (b) for autism to be a real, distinct phenomenon, this should be a single particular kind of brain, and not a set of conditions that can occur independently of each other.

What have studies shown? Sadly, there is as much disunity among brain researchers as we have seen among psychologists. This is not surprising though, because, as Jill Boucher writes:

> The implications of findings on brain function are easily identified because the research is always hypothesis-driven. That is to say, each study is designed to test a specific hypothesis concerning the neural activity that occurs when the person being tested is carrying out a specific task. [31]

In other words, the brain research does not drive the psychological theorizing but rather the reverse. To give a single example, consider the study "Decreased Connectivity and Cerebellar Activity in Autism during Motor Task Performance." [32] This study was referred to in an article entitled "New Insight into the Neurological Basis of Autism," which described the study as follows:

> Researchers used fMRI scans to examine the brain activity of 13 children with high functioning autism and 13 typically developing children while performing sequential finger tapping. The typically developing children had increased activity in the cerebellum, a region of the brain important for automating motor tasks, while children with autism had increased activity in the supplementary motor area (SMA), a region of the brain important for conscious movement. This suggests children with autism have to recruit and rely on more conscious, effortful motor planning because they are not able to rely on the cerebellum to automate tasks.
>
> Researchers also examined the functional connectivity of the brain regions involved in motor planning and execution in order to compare the activity between different brain regions involved in the same task. The children with autism showed substantially decreased connectivity between the different brain regions involved in motor planning and execution. These results add to increasing evidence that autism is related to abnormalities in structural and functional brain connectivity, which makes it difficult for distant regions of the brain to learn skills and coordinate activities. [33]

There are several points worth noting in this study. The first is that this is a study of only thirteen children. (Of course, while this number seems tiny, it is still two more than Kanner's original study.) Second, it is assumed that these thirteen children *all* are autistic, while none of the control group are. This is worth noting in particular because these children are all "high functioning" (HFA) and thus closer to "normal" children. But that assumes that we *know what autism is*, and can recognize it perfectly when we see it, something it has been a point of this chapter to challenge. (And if we could do that *perfectly*, then what exactly are we discovering with these brain studies? What if we discovered variance among the brains of similarly-behaving children? In fact, we always *do* discover variance, but it is glossed over.)

Then, of course, there is the assumption (inherent in the title of the article, if not the study itself) that conclusions about HFA children can be generalized to all autistic individuals.

Finally, in the study itself (and unremarked on in the article), we find this:

> Some of the children with HFA were taking psychoactive medications, and the potential impact of this cannot be discounted. Future investigations might benefit from exclusion of children taking medications, though this would have a detrimental impact on recruitment of numbers sufficient to examine group differences using BOLD fMRI.[34]

One would have thought that this would be a very serious strike against the study, reminiscent of the study that claimed to show an essential difference between the brains of gay men and those of straight men, but whose "gay brains" were all the brains of men who had died of AIDS.[35] Yet the authors of the study justify proceeding because of the difficulty of recruiting participants. Not ideal circumstances for good science.

Supposing we put these criticisms aside: what lessons should be drawn from a study of reaction times of finger-tapping? The lead author of the study, Dr. Stewart H. Mostofsky, a pediatric neurologist in the Department of Developmental Cognitive Neurology at the Kennedy Krieger Institute, had this to say:

> Tapping your fingers is a simple action, but it involves communication and coordination between several regions of the brain. These results suggest that in children with autism, fairly close regions of the brains involved in motor tasks have difficulty coordinating activity. If decreased connectivity is at the heart of autism, it makes sense social and communication skills are greatly impaired, as they involve even more complex coordination between more distant areas of the brain.[36]

The generalizing assumptions at work here are breathtaking, especially in light of the facts noted about the study above. Why, one might wonder, are such generalizing assumptions necessary? Why study reaction times instead of, you know, the *social and communication skills themselves*? The article author offers an explanation:

> While autism is characterized by impaired communication and social skills, these abilities are hard for scientists to measure and quantify. In contrast, the neurological processes behind motor skills are well understood, and motor tasks can be objectively observed and measured.[37]

One is reminded of F. Lee Bailey's favorite analogy of a person who had dropped money on a dark street, looking for it under a street light some distance away "because the light was better there."

Put aside all the criticisms I have so far raised and assume that this study really does demonstrate a brain difference between thirteen genuinely autistic children and thirteen "perfectly" neurotypical children—perhaps the most damning assumption built into Mostofsky's claim is that all individuals who have the motor skills issues will have communication and social issues as well. That is exactly the "unifying" assumption about autism that we want brain studies to be testing. And note that these are "high functioning" children whose communication difficulties might be less serious. Meanwhile, Kanner himself noted of the children in his study that "[s]everal of the children were somewhat clumsy in gait and gross motor performances, but *all were very skillful in terms of finer muscle coordination*,"[38] suggesting that generalizing across motor abilities in autistic children is inadvisable. A person who worked with many autistic adults once told me that she knew someone who was a regional tennis champion yet was unable to tie his own shoelaces. Perhaps this was evidence of some lack of connectivity, but if so, then it is clearly possible to excel at some tasks while connectivity is impaired, so to suggest that communication difficulties can automatically be explained in this way seems rash.

Earlier I noted that Baron-Cohen linked his recent empathizing-systemizing with what he calls the "extreme male brain" theory. Briefly, as you may imagine, he believes that brains are "sexed," that female brains are different from male brains.[39] One might think that he arrived at this view *from a study of brains*, but one would be wrong. The "brain" theory is actually a theory about ways of thinking. Essentially, Baron-Cohen claims that one can distinguish between empathizing (of which mindreading is the "cognitive" aspect, but it also has an affective component of "having an appropriate emotional reaction to another person's thoughts and feelings"[40]) and "systemizing" ("the drive to analyze or construct systems"). Males, he claims, are better at the latter than the former, and for females it is the reverse. Meanwhile, autistic people are *much* better systemizers than empathizers. Now, Baron-Cohen's theory is open to all sorts of criticisms, including several in this volume, but I will focus here on the following claim:

> Recently the extreme male brain theory has been extended to the level of neurology, with some interesting findings emerging. Thus, in some regions of

the brain that on average are smaller in males than in females, people with
autism have even bigger brain regions than typical males. [41]

That first sentence should give one pause: it is only recently that a theory
called the extreme male brain theory has been "extended" to the level of
neurology. But that aside, of course, we would want to be very certain that
we had correctly identified the full array of types of people who are autistic
and compared their brains with the full array of people who are "neurotypical" (recall the study of "gay" brains that were all from people who had died
of AIDS), and if, as has been suggested, female autistic individuals tend to go
underdiagnosed, then this might be problematic. [42] But this aside, Baron-
Cohen follows up the previous bold claim with this rather pathetic qualifier:
"not all studies support this pattern but some do." [43]

It would seem that Baron-Cohen's theory is an extreme example of
Boucher's assertion that the research is "hypothesis driven." Now, this is not
necessarily bad, especially if one espouses a Popperian hypothetico-deduc-
tive model of scientific progress. But Popper would, I think, want more effort
put towards *falsifying* the claim than in searching for *some* study that appears
consistent with it. The fact that only *some* studies "support" this pattern
might be enough to undermine the hypothesis already. Furthermore, what we
do *not* have here is anything like the evidence we would want to claim that
there is a uniquely identifiable autistic brain that explains and unifies the
disparate elements of autism, thereby justifying the label of autism as a
natural kind of phenomenon.

IN THE GENES

Given all of the problems we have noted, what is to be gained by going one
stage further and investigating the genetic basis for autism? We have failed
to come to a satisfactory account of what the evidence of autism is, or what
people to count as autistic so that we know whose genes to study.

However, there are reasons to believe that autism could be located at the
genetic level even with the problems outlined above. Consider the following:

> There is now considerable evidence from family and twin studies that, for a
> subgroup of autistic individuals, the etiology is mainly genetic. The risk of
> recurrence of autism in families (i.e., the frequency of autism in subsequently
> born siblings) is estimated at 6%-8%, or up to 200 times the risk in the general
> population. Three twin studies of geographically defined populations detected
> pairwise concordance rates of approximately 65% (the average over the three
> studies) and 0% in monozygotic and dyzogotic pairs, respectively, producing a
> heritability estimate of over 90%. Further, there is no convincing evidence that
> perinatal factors play an important role in the etiology of most cases of aut-
> ism. [44]

What recent studies seem to show is that autism is *genetic* (like Down syndrome) because of the high rate of concordance in monozygotic twins, *familial* (unlike Down), but that *environmental factors* also must play a part (because in 10 percent of cases one monozygotic twin has autism but the other doesn't at all, and in cases where both have it, the severity can vary widely).[45]

Kanner himself suggested a genetic basis in his original study,[46] but that theory was not investigated for some time because, as Folstein and Rutter noted in the introduction to a landmark 1977 study of twins, "[t]here is no recorded case of an autistic child having an overtly autistic parent and it is decidedly unusual for a family to contain more than one autistic child." That these appeared to be the facts at the time did not undermine a genetic basis because, they argued: "First, it is extremely rare for autistic persons to marry...and there is only a single published report of one having given birth to a child...Second, autism is a very uncommon disorder, occurring in only about 2-4 children out of every 10,000."[47] Both reasons now seem rather quaint. Of course the diagnosis of autism has skyrocketed, but what about the claim that autistic individuals do not marry or even reproduce? This is where the *broader autism phenotype* (BAP) comes in. According to one of the earliest studies to refer to this phenomenon it is "a behavioral phenotype that is qualitatively similar to but more broadly defined than that which defines autism occurs more commonly in relatives of autistic individuals than in the general population."[48] Or, as Baron-Cohen puts it, "mild echoes" of autism:

> This might take the form of being socially withdrawn or confused by social interaction, or mildly obsessive (in the sense of having strong narrow interests or a need for sameness) or having excellent attention to detail and remarkable memory. Although [the close relatives of autistic individuals] don't have autism or Asperger syndrome itself, they have a milder manifestation of the same characteristics.[49]

The existence of BAPs in families of autistic individuals is taken both to lend support to the idea that autism has a familial, genetic basis, and to explain how it is that the reproducing happens, if it is not to be done by severely autistic individuals. It would also explain the apparent high incidence of autism in the children of academics in such disciplines as philosophy and in such places as Silicon Valley: the kind of focus and interest that leads one to succeed in certain intellectual pursuits is itself evidence of a broader autism phenotype.

At the same time, however, this very notion of BAPs might be taken to undermine the idea that autism can have a status as a distinct, self-contained phenomenon. If the conditions that are taken to be evidence for the presence of autism can occur individually, without the others that are needed for a diagnosis of "full-blown" autism, then the bundle is broken, the cluster unclustered, and autism just becomes shorthand for a collection of not necessarily related phenomena, rare in the way that left-handed stamp-collecting Elvis-loving archeologists are rare, and equally devoid of a common explanation.

One clear rebuttal to this would be the following suggestion: autism *is* essentially a certain genetic condition that *tends* to produce defects in all the areas noted by the *DSM*, but whose effect can be blunted by other environmental factors or indeed, interaction with other genetic conditions. (This would also make sense of the spectrum model of autism.) Those who do not exhibit *all* the symptoms only do not because other factors have interfered with the influence of their autistic genes on their brain and psychology. On this account, autism is essentially a genetic condition. An "autistic brain" would be a likely (but not essential) effect of possession of the relevant gene(s). Autism would no more be curable than any genetic condition, only eliminable from the population by selective abortion on the basis of an *in utero* or PGD genetic test. One could actually be autistic, however, and "pass" as nonautistic (as, one would assume, huge numbers of individuals "passed" while only the extreme version was counted as autistic), if the influence of the genes were sufficiently blunted.

Conversely, there could be many individuals who exhibited Kanner's symptoms because of nongenetic influences on their brains who would *not* be autistic since their symptoms did not have the specific genetic cause.

Compare with water. We now say that water *is* H_2O, but knowing something is H_2O without knowing its specific environment won't tell us whether or not it is solid, liquid, gas, opaque, scattered or gathered in a sphere. Conversely, things that are not H_2O can have almost identical tendencies (totally identical, if we allow the possibility of a Putnamian twin earth[50]) without being water.

This would achieve the unity of essence for autism in the face of a great range of realizations of the condition, but at the cost of breaking the necessary connection between autism and the syndrome described by Kanner in the first place. It might turn out that "the autistic" include in their number many people who would not meet any behavioral diagnosis, and exclude many who would. At this point one might well question whether or not we really had discovered the genetic essence of autism or instead discovered that autism had to be located at a higher level (behavior/psychology/brain type) and had no real essence. Our position on this would not be a matter that science could settle. Science could (at best) tell us that this particular genetic makeup had this particular effect in these particular circumstances, but there are distinct issues that should affect our decision that are based on human interests.

Consider the issue of biological sex in humans. While throughout history sex determination has usually been made on the basis of genitals and secondary sexual characteristics, it is now generally accepted that to be female is to have XX chromosomes, while to be male is to have XY chromosomes. The trouble is, there are individuals with conditions that mean they are neither XX nor XY, such as Turner Syndrome, or XO, which is when the individual lacks a second X chromosome, and Klinefelter Syndrome, or XXY, where the individual has an extra X chromosome. What are we to say is the sex of such individuals? Furthermore, some individuals have a "mosaic" of sex chromosomes: they have XX in some cells, XY in others and possibly other types in other cells. And finally, there are cases of individuals who outwardly appear one sex but are chromosomally the other.

Consider the case of Maria Patino, twenty-four years old in 1985 and at the time Spain's top female hurdler (or so she thought), who had to take a chromosomal "sex test" in order to compete as a woman in World University Games in Kobe, Japan. Such tests were the norm for athletes at the time and she thought nothing of it until, just before she was to compete in her first race, she was informed that she had failed the sex test: in the eyes of the International Olympic Committee (IOC) she was not, in fact, a woman.[51] It emerged that Patino had Androgen Insensitivity Syndrome (AIS), so named because typically an XY fetus develops male genitalia as a result of exposure to androgen *in utero*, but AIS individuals do not respond to that androgen. As a result, they are usually designated female at birth, and grow up thinking of themselves in that way.

Imagine yourself in Patino's position—how would you react? The reaction that Patino in fact had, was to deny that the chromosomes should be the deciding factor concerning her sex. "I knew I was a woman in the eyes of medicine, God, and most of all, in my own eyes," she insisted.[52] It seems hard to argue with Patino's conclusion, and increasingly it is accepted that "transgender" individuals whose genitals "match up" with their chromosomes, but who identify with the other sex should be allowed to classify themselves how they want. One's sex, then, is not simply settled by one's chromosomes.[53]

Wouldn't the same be true of autism even if we did find an "autism gene?" Clearly one's status as autistic does not play as basic a role in one's identity as one's sex (at least for the majority of people), but it is a status that carries with it certain social and economic riders. So, just as imprisoned transgender individuals are campaigning to be moved to a prison that reflects their self-identity (or at least, removed from one that doesn't), so a self-identified autistic individual might demand rights to certain services that, increasingly, states are requiring be made available to autistic individuals, especially if that individual, while not having the requisite genetic makeup, had the behavioral or sensory challenges we have associated with autism.

All of this assumes that there *is* a simple, definite genetic basis to at least the majority of the conditions we have been associating with autism. However, a study of papers published between 1961 and 2003 on the genetics of autism (and that cites over 200 of them) reached the following conclusion:

> Although many genes and proteins have been implicated as causes of autism, too little is known about their functions or their role in brain development to generate a parsimonious hypothesis about the brain dysfunctions that underlie autism. Evidence from multiplex families with the broader autism phenotypes, together with twin studies, indicates that single-gene defects are rare even within families....Despite the profusion of investigations into the genetics of autism, few significant genetic linkages to autism have been identified. [54]

Scientists have been saying for years that the "gay gene" is about to be discovered, and we seem no nearer. And what it is to be gay is, if anything, simpler to state than what it is to be autistic.

CONCLUSION

We do not have a clear conception of what autism is. The closest "official" definition is the diagnosis in *DSM-IV* that is, as befits a diagnosis available to the general practitioner, in terms of observable behaviors. However, one of the several problems with a behavioral definition is that it makes the changes soon to come in *DSM-V* either arbitrary or solely politically/economically motivated. (This should come of no surprise to those familiar with the history of the APA's changing attitude towards homosexuality.) Attempts to locate the essence of autism at a deeper level than observable behavior have been varied but unsatisfactory. Various psychological "modules" either fail to explain all of the behaviors picked out as distinctive of autism, appear present in some people not labeled autistic, or are so vaguely defined that their essence seems simply to be "whatever it is that would underlie the behavior that needs explaining." If autism is to be a *collection* of such modules (or defects in various modules) then we either need to know the justification for grouping them together (the "bundle" problem again) or we need a common explanation at the level of neurology. However, suggested brain conditions are again either specific to only a subset of the symptoms of autism or not distinctive to autism alone. Finally, genetic bases are suggested by the familial grouping of autistic-like symptoms, but if the same genetics explain BAPs as explain "full-blown" autism, then again, the net is cast too wide.

In general, while most people would no doubt think that "science" is driving a deepening understanding of what autism is, I would argue that science is, if anything, demonstrating that there is no such thing as "autism" if we are to understand it on the model of something like Down syndrome. At best there are several conditions that can occur independently of each other, but seem to co-occur, that can vary significantly in severity, and that seem to cluster in families, but not necessarily always. I propose that we focus instead on specific deficiencies, like sensory processing disorders, communication difficulties or food sensitivities and stop trying to cluster them together as something called "autism." To do so is like dividing hair types into "black hair" and "Caucasian hair." As any hairdresser with a diverse clientele knows, there is huge variety in each, and some types of "black" hair are much closer to some types of "Caucasian" hair than to other types supposedly racially similar.

EPILOGUE: SO WHAT?

Recall the list of pressing questions I gave at the start. Let us look at how each of these is affected by what categorical or metaphysical position one takes on the issue.

How will I know if my child is autistic?

The "true test" will either be behavioral, psychological (which would essentially put the child into a position where her behavior would exhibit a supposed underlying deficit, as in the case of the "Sally-Anne" false belief tests for theory of mind), neurological (say, using "three dimensional brain scans," recently developed by researchers at the University of Pittsburgh Medical Center[55]) or chromosomal, depending on what level one places autism at (the "genus" issue). But either this will mean that "autism" is much more narrowly defined than presently, or being told that one's child is autistic will be remarkably uninformative. But that should be familiar to parents who have been through a diagnosis anyway.

What will be the prognosis if she is?

Again, BAPs significantly cloud the issue. I suspect that a great number of very successful, creative, funny, and/or athletic individuals would turn out to be classifiable within the Broader Autism Phenotype. Conversely, if a brain scan did show a significantly nonneurotypical brain, then I think it would be progress in neuroscience that would enable experts to explain exactly what difficulties the owner of that brain might be expected to have. And I don't think this would be usefully defined as an advance in our knowledge of *autism*, just an advance in our knowledge of *brains*.

Is autism treatable?

That depends. It seems evident that each aspect of autism can be treated, but by different specialists and in different ways. Special diets, both edible and sensory, various speech therapies, and simple loving interaction are all salutary. If autism is genetic, or consists in "disorganized" brain wiring, then these therapies couldn't really be said to be treating *autism*. But should we care that they are not if they are making life easier and open to more opportunities to the individual so labeled? And the downside to the label is that treatments that might be of benefit to a wide range of children are only provided *on the condition* that one is so labeled.[56] Parents have then to make a decision to strive to get their child a diagnosis in order to get treatment, knowing full well the stigma that comes attached to it. A separate issue is the turf wars that have emerged over treatment of autism that turn on just such disputes about what exactly autism is. Consider the issue of special gluten-/casein-/soy-free diets. On the one hand, there is the claim that switching to a special diet can "cure" a child of ASD. As we have seen, the idea that autism is curable is rejected by scientists who predict that it will be found to have a genetic basis. These same scientists tend to dismiss any claims made by people who purport to offer a cure. But it nonetheless appears clear that for a number of children diagnosed as autistic, a special diet can, like the "sensory" diet, have a calming effect, reduce wild mood swings and instances of acting out, and in general make life better for children and parents. In this respect, some of the apparent symptoms of autism are ameliorated. So this might be viewed as a clash between those who define autism as the behavioral symptoms Kanner listed, such that if some of the more disturbing ones disappear, allowing the child to be calmer and more social, then in a real sense the *autism* is being treated, and those who locate autism at a genetic level, so that a diet could never affect it. One can feel that one is siding with the quacks in attempting a diet regime that could actually help greatly. All of this could be avoided with a more measured and focused description that avoided talk of autism (and the entrenched camps and interest groups that have developed around that term) altogether.

Is autism curable?

The talk of a "cure" for autism seems to be geared towards finding a genetic test for it. This would not, of course, be a way to "cure" it in an individual, but rather as an attempt to prevent autistic people being born in the first place. A better "cure" might be to change society so that it is more accepting of and accessible to individuals with differences of the kind Kanner first noted. Perhaps a first step towards this would be to get rid of the label "autistic." Of course, this suggestion is just like the idea that we should get rid of racial labels, and ignores the fact that some people are relieved to be labeled, either because it "makes sense" of difficulties they have struggled with for a long time,[57] or because it gives them a group to identify with when much of society has regarded them as alien. But more narrow, precise, and syndrome-specific labels could do that too. And just as there is racism, there are already many negative stereotypes about autistic individuals, in particular that they lack empathy and are dangerously violent.

Should autism be eradicated?

If autism is identified with inability to communicate, self-harming and perseverative activities and all of the most extreme and debilitating indicators, then one can see how this might be appealing. But it matters greatly if this is to be achieved by making therapies available to those whose opportunities in life would widen greatly as a result, or by *eugenics*. If "autism" really is socially constructed, then I'm all in favor of its elimination. The people will still be the same, but they won't be encumbered with a catch-all term weighted down with decades of bad theorizing and "Rain Man" assumptions.

Why wasn't autism discovered before the 1940s?
Why have the rates of diagnosis risen so sharply over the past couple of decades?

It's interesting that social constructivism has an answer to this that would be the same as similar questions about rates of diagnosis of female hysteria or multiple personality disorder. Realists would say that the phenomena were always there (like the famous cases of "feral children," like Victor the Wild Boy of Aveyron in the 1780s) and it's only now that we have developed a concept that maps precisely onto the real essence of a biological condition, so that we can clearly see what was always there. But, as I hope I have shown, our concept is anything but clear, and indeed, progress can only come from abandoning it and starting from scratch. There will never be consensus in all the various brain and chromosome studies if they all compete to be the explanation of *autism*. But if instead they just attempt to explain some narrow feature of the human condition (that has often been lumped in with autism), then the competition dissolves and clarity emerges from discord. But how easy would it be to get grants or to raise funds or to get laws changed without the magic word "autism" to rally behind?

REFERENCES

Baron-Cohen, Simon. 1995. *Mindblindness: An Essay on Autism and Theory of Mind*. Cambridge, MA: The MIT Press.

Baron-Cohen, Simon. 2008. *Autism and Asperger Syndrome: The Facts*. Oxford: Oxford University Press.

Boucher, Jill. 2009. *The Autistic Spectrum: Characteristics, Causes and Practical Issues*. London: Sage.

Byne, William and Mitchell Lasco. 1999. The Origins of Sexual Orientation: Possible Biological Contributions. In *Same Sex*, ed. John Corvino. Lanham, MD: Rowman and Littlefield.

Carlson, Alison. 1991. When Is a Woman Not a Woman? *Women's Sports & Fitness* 13:24–29.

Donnellan, Anne M., ed. 1985. *Classic Readings in Autism*. New York: Teachers College Press.

Fausto-Sterling, Ann. 2000. *Sexing the Body*. New York: Basic.

Folstein, Susan, and Michael Rutter. 1977. Infantile Autism: A Genetic Study of 21 Twin Pairs. *Journal of Child Psychology and Psychiatry* 18:297–321.

Frith, Uta. 1989. *Autism: Explaining the Enigma*. Oxford: Blackwell.

Grinker, Roy Richard. 2007. *Unstrange Minds: Remapping the World of Autism*. Philadelphia: Basic Books.

Kanner, Leo. 1943. Autistic Disturbances of Affective Contact. Donnellan 1985, 11–50.

Kanner, Leo. 1971. Follow–up Study of Eleven Autistic Children Originally Reported in 1943. See: Donnellan 1985, 223–34.

Locke, John. 1690. *An Essay Concerning Human Understanding*.

Mostofsky, Stewart H., Stephanie K. Powell, Daniel J. Simmonds, Melissa C. Goldberg, Brian Caffo, James J. Pekar. 2009. Decreased Connectivity and Cerebellar Activity in Autism During Motor Task Performance. *Brain* 132(9):2413–25.

Muhle, Rebecca, Stephanie V. Trentacoste, Isabelle Rapin. 2004. The Genetics of Autism. *Pediatrics* 113(5).

Nazeer, Kamran. 2006. *Send in the Idiots: Stories from the Other Side of Autism*. New York: Bloomsbury.

Parfit, Derek. 1995. The Unimportance of Identity. In *Personal Identity*, eds. Raymond Martin and John Barresi. Oxford: Blackwell.

Piven, Joseph, Pat Palmer, Dinah Jacobi, Debra Childress, Stephan Arndt. 1997. Broader Autism Phenotype: Evidence from a Family History Study of Multiple–Incidence Autism Families. *American Journal of Psychiatry* 154:185–90.

Putnam, Hilary. 1973. Meaning and Reference. *Journal of Philosophy* 70(19):699–711.

Rutter, Michael. 1985. Commentary on Kanner's Autistic Disturbances of Affective Contact, in Donnellan 1985, 50–52.

Wing, L. and J. Gould. 1979. Severe Impairments of Social Interaction and Associated Abnormalities in Children: Epidemiology and Classification. *Journal of Autism and Childhood Schizophrenia* 9:11–29.

NOTES

1. Kanner 1943.

2. As is now well known, Hans Asperger was working along similar lines to Kanner in Austria at the time. I do not mean to say that in some sense Kanner "won the race," just that Kanner had a head start on influencing the concept in the English-speaking world, as Asperger's work was not translated from the German for many decades.

3. Rutter 1985, 50–51, emphasis added. Historian Chloe Silverman notes that the continuing relevance of Kanner's descriptions contrasts markedly with contemporary descriptions of other mental disorders that sound hopelessly archaic today (Grinker 2007, 44).

4. Kanner 1943, 41.

5. This list, and each quote, comes from Kanner 1943, 42–48.

6. Kamran Nazeer relates meeting as an adult the teacher who knew him as a child labeled as autistic. When Nazeer exhibited a sense of humor and an apparent ability to interpret her behavior, she said "you're not autistic." Nazeer 2006, 183.

7. Why homosexuality? Because it was a condition first identified by psychologists and labeled as a disorder, and over the nature of which there is continuing debate. Like autism, it was also blamed on "refrigerator mothers." Further parallels are noted in the discussion of brain studies below.

8. See Grinker 2007, 107–121.

9. The notion that autism is a spectrum was first proposed in Wing and Gould 1979 (where it is called a "continuum"). Wing was the person who translated Asperger's work into English and named the syndrome after him. See Boucher 2009, chapter 2, for a discussion of the merits

of the "subtypes" (*DSM–IV*) vs. "spectrum" views of autism. It seems that the spectrum view has won out, at least terminologically.

10. Amy Harmon, "A Specialists' Debate on Autism Has Many Worried Observers," *New York Times*, January 20, 2012.

11. Benedict Carey, "New Definition of Autism Will Exclude Many, Study Suggests," *New York Times*, January 19, 2012.

12. Many people who study autism assert a strong parallel with Down syndrome, predicting that autism will be found to have a genetic marker, and an *in utero* test will eventually be available. See discussion of genetics below.

13. It is sometimes claimed that keeping track of race data is medically useful, because of racially specific conditions like sickle-cell anemia. But in fact there is no disease that tracks racial categories, even if some diseases can be traced back to a common origin in a specific region.

14. Consider this diatribe from comedian Dennis Leary on p. 87 of his book *Why We Suck* (New York: Viking, 2008): "There is a huge boom in autism right now because inattentive mothers and competitive dads want an explanation for why their dumb-ass kids can't compete academically, so they throw money into the happy laps of shrinks...to get back diagnoses that help explain away the deficiencies of their junior morons. I don't give a shit what these crackerjack whack jobs tell you—yer kid is NOT autistic. He's just stupid. Or lazy. Or both." (He does go on to talk about "true" autism, so his overall view might be realism.)

15. There might still be behaviorists who want to define "attraction" in terms of empirically observable changes in behavior (blushing, perspiring, increased pulse, et al.), but there remains the possibility that a skilled actor could either hide attraction that was present or exhibit behavior consistent with an attraction he did not have, and that it is the attraction, not the resulting behavior, that is essential.

16. However, because of the first implication noted above, it would be very hard to know if a cure had actually been achieved or if the "therapy" was just masking or counteracting the effects of a still-present psychological phenomenon. Compare the different attitudes to so-called reparative therapy that purports, in flagrant disregard of the APA's ban on such claims, to "cure" homosexuality: one side claims it to be a genuine cure, the other that the "cured" are just in the closet, suppressing their real desires.

17. Contrast also with locating autism at a genetic level: one cannot change one's genes, so talk of a "cure" for autism would on a genetic account be at best science fiction. This is discussed below.

18. Kanner 1971, 229.

19. Kanner 1943, 44.

20. Baron-Cohen himself points out that "a range of clinical conditions show forms of mindblindness (such as patients with schizophrenia, or narcissistic and borderline personality disorders, and children with conduct disorder), so this may not be specific to autism and Asperger syndrome" (Baron-Cohen 2008, 61).

21. "Its shortcoming is that it cannot account for the non-social features" (Baron-Cohen 2008, 61).

22. Frith 1989, 100. Perhaps it is the autistic in me that sees the production of the "great religions of the world" as of dubious merit.

23. Baron-Cohen 2008, 56.

24. Boucher 2009, (102) uses WCC as an example of "one-too-many" explanation, where one theory explains many phenomena.

25. Well-known neurologist Oliver Sacks is so face-blind that he cannot tell if he is looking at his own reflection in a pane of glass or through it at somebody else (until, as he recounted humorously on a radio interview, that person moved). The painter (ironically, of faces) Chuck Close is also almost totally face-blind.

26. See Boucher 2009, 211; 213. My personal complaint is that this theory presents a caricature of the autistic individual as one who cannot see the forest for the trees. However, I have already noted how prevalent I have found autism to be among the children of philosophers, and I would hazard a guess that the "analytic tendency" is just this predilection to focus on the basic building blocks of things. The same would be true among theoretical scientists. Yet

there is no paucity of "grand systems" in philosophy or the natural sciences. I find it odd, indeed, that Frith sees the culmination of systematizing as the "great religions," which seems to me the least systematic modes of thinking. It is worth noting that Baron-Cohen's most recent theory posits instead that autistic individuals are superior "systemizers" [sic] where "systemizing is the drive to analyze or construct systems" (Baron-Cohen 2008, 63, emphasis added). Perhaps both theories could haggle over Wittgenstein (a common choice in the "diagnose the famous autistic person" game): Baron-Cohen could have the Wittgenstein of the *Tractatus*, while Frith could have the *Philosophical Investigations*. Kant has always leaped out to me as someone with autistic tendencies, insofar as there are such things, and nobody could accuse him of lacking systems.

27. I say "purported" because there seems to be ample evidence of creativity even among quite severely autistic individuals. Consider Derek Pavancini, the blind British pianist, who, while he has memorized "an enormous repertoire" of jazz songs, is also able to improvise on the spot (Baron-Cohen 2008, 104). There are more and more examples of autistic artists as well.

28. See discussion of the "windows task" and the Wisconsin Card Sorting Test, Boucher 2009, 171–74.

29. The terminology is Derek Parfit's, see Parfit 1995, 294.

30. Ibid., 295. Parfit gives the example of a statue which, while it is simply made of bronze, is not to be identified with the bronze, because you can melt the statue and still have the bronze but not the statue.

31. Boucher 2009, 139.

32. Mostofsky et al. 2009.

33. http://www.news-medical.net/news/2009/04/29/48951.aspx.

34. Mostofsky et al. 2009, 2421.

35. Byne and Lasco 1999, 116.

36. http://www.news-medical.net/news/2009/04/29/48951.aspx?page=2.

37. Ibid.

38. Kanner 1943, 47.

39. This has interesting parallels in the "science" of homosexuality. According to Byne and Lasco (1999), the vast majority of biological studies on homosexuality have presumed what they call the "intersex assumption," which is the claim that there are male and female brains plus the assumption that what it is to be gay is to have the "wrong sex brain." They point out several devastating problems for this view, most relevant of which for our current interests is the fact that not one of the (over one thousand) brain studies that have been done in the last century that have yielded published results has produced evidence to support the claim that there are distinct male and female archetypes of the human brain.

40. Baron-Cohen 2008, 62.

41. Baron-Cohen 2008, 74.

42. This point, along with several criticisms of the extreme male brain theory are made by Rachel Cohen-Rottenberg, who self-identifies as autistic, in http://www.journeyswithautism.com/2009/07/02/a-critique-of-the-extreme-male-brain-theory-of-autism/.

43. Baron-Cohen 2008, 74. One can only imagine the homosexuality-as-"central nervous pseudohermaphroditism" and autism-as-male-brain theorists arguing over whether or not they were looking at the brain of a lesbian, an autistic female, or a neurotypical male.

44. Piven et al. 1997, 185.

45. Boucher 2009, 118.

46. "We must, then, assume that these children have come into the world with innate inability to form the usual, biologically provided affective contact with other people, just as other children come into the world with innate physical or intellectual handicaps...here we seem to have pure-culture examples of inborn autistic disturbances of affective contact" (Kanner 1943, 50).

47. Folstein and Rutter 1977, 297.

48. Piven *et al.* 1997, 185. As evidence, the authors offer: "Wolff *et al*... interviewed the parents of autistic children and the parents of nonautistic mentally retarded comparison subjects

and found that the parents of the autistic children were more often judged to lack emotional responsiveness and empathy, show impaired rapport with the examiner, and have histories of oversensitivity to experience, special interest patterns, and oddities of social communication... Gillberg, in a study of the parents of 23 children with Asperger syndrome, reported social deficits in 11 of the 23 fathers that were similar to, but milder than, those seen in Asperger syndrome." Ibid., 186.

49. Baron-Cohen 2008, 93.

50. Putnam 1973.

51. Carlson 1991, 25. See also Fausto-Sterling 2000, chapter 1. Patino agreed to fake an injury at the Kobe games so that the reason for her dismissal did not get out and cause embarrassment, and she was encouraged to keep training. However, four months later, at the first meet of the Spanish indoor season the head of the Spanish federation told her she would have to fake another injury—this time supposedly career-ending—or risk exposure in the media. She refused, won her race, and, as promised, she was exposed in the media, lost her boyfriend and many friends, and all of her records were stripped from the books.

52. Carlson 1991, 27. The International Amateur Athletic Federation (IAAF) finally conceded the point, and in 1992 Patino was allowed to rejoin the Spanish Olympic Squad (and the IOC finally abandoned sex testing in 1999).

53. It might be that "biological sex" is actually a socially constructed notion, just as I have argued that race is, and thus open to change by transgender activists. What constitutes one's sex could be located at the level of outward physical appearance. In that case, sex-reassignment surgery really would achieve a change of one's sex. Alternatively, if sex is psychological, then the point of such surgery would just be to give someone the body that matches what their sex already is. Finally, if sex is at the chromosomal level then sex-reassignment surgery does not achieve a change of sex, but merely enables one to "pass" even while naked. These are important legal matters, of course—see the case of *Littleton v. Prange* (1999).

54. Muhle, Trentacoste, and Rapin 2004, e482.

55. Paul Steinberg, "Asperger's History of Overdiagnosis," *New York Times*, January 31, 2012.

56. "A 1992 United States Department of Education directive contributed to the overdiagnosis of Asperger syndrome. It called for enhanced services for children diagnosed as being on the autism spectrum...The diagnosis of Asperger syndrome went through the roof...The downside to this diagnosis lies in evidence that children with social disabilities, diagnosed now with an autism-spectrum disorder like Asperger, have lower self-esteem and poorer social development when inappropriately placed in school environments with truly autistic children. In addition, many of us clinicians have seen young adults denied job opportunities, for example in the Peace Corps, when inappropriately given a diagnosis of Asperger syndrome instead of a social disability." Paul Steinberg, "Asperger's History of Overdiagnosis," *New York Times*, January 31, 2012.

57. For example, Tim Page, former music critic for the *Washington Post*; see "Parallel Play," *The New Yorker*, August 20, 2007, 36–41.

Chapter Two

Embodying Autistic Cognition: Towards Reconceiving Certain "Autism-Related" Behavioral Atypicalities as Functional

Michael Doan and Andrew Fenton

Autistic Disorder, Asperger's Disorder and Pervasive Developmental Disorder-Not Otherwise Specified constitute the Autism Spectrum Disorders (ASDs).[1] Within psychiatry the ASDs are characterized by clinically significant atypical cognitive or behavioral profiles in three distinct areas: (i) social interaction, (ii) communication, and (iii) profoundly restricted activity and interests.[2] Interventions in the course of the ASDs in one or more of these three areas of cognitive or behavioral difference tend to target young children. Profoundly restricted activities and interests are targeted for various reasons, prominent among which is their role in (further) isolating the relevant children from their educators and peers. There are other reasons, of course, including the self-destructive nature of some of these behaviors (e.g., head banging, hair pulling, biting), and the fact that other behaviors are thought to interfere with cognitive development (e.g., fixation on objects or their parts). In this chapter, we are primarily concerned with those behaviors that are thought to interfere with the cognitive development of autistic persons.[3] These behaviors, such as fixation on objects or so-called aberrant self-stimulation (e.g., finger flipping, hand flapping, mouthing objects), are typically thought to interfere with the relevant autistic person's ability to learn.[4] Teaching the autistic person to suppress, replace, or eliminate these behaviors will, according to this view, facilitate the development of greater cognitive functionality than would otherwise be the case.

A dissenting perspective to this characterization of ASD-related "aberrant behavior" is emerging. This perspective is partially inspired by autistic activists—often self-identifying as "neurodiverse"[5]—as well as by a growing concern that previous behavioral research has been misled by a language of deficit and impairment that has effectively obscured positive ASD-related capacities and the cognitive potential of perhaps many of those diagnosed along the Autism Spectrum.[6] It is the contention of this dissenting perspective—which we will refer to as the Neurodiversity Perspective—that many of these so-called aberrant behaviors and restricted interests aid, rather than impede, autistic cognition and learning. On this view, teaching autistic children to suppress, replace, or eliminate atypical behaviors and abandon restricted interests could actually be hampering rather than helping their cognitive development (e.g., by raising anxiety levels that interfere with their ability to cognitively engage with the world).

In this chapter we critically examine the Neurodiversity Perspective and suggest a middle way between a conception of atypical behaviors as dysfunctions or impairments properly targeted for behavioral intervention, and one that sees them not only as inappropriately targeted for intervention, but also as beneficial to those individuals who express them. We will introduce two theories of embodied cognition as lenses through which these behaviors might be reimagined as functional and adaptive. The strength of these theories lies in providing a conceptual space within which researchers and autistic advocates can both interrogate previous behavioral research and explore more affirming ways of conceiving the behavior of those on the Spectrum. It is not our intent to deny that interventions in the lives of some of those diagnosed with ASDs are sometimes justified and desirable. Thus, we do not assume a one-size-fits-all approach to restricted interests or atypical behaviors diagnostic of ASDs.

Our first section will provide a brief orientation to the Autism Spectrum, particularly as it relates to stereotypies, restricted interests and rituals. Introducing the voices of some of those on the Spectrum will then motivate interest in the potential of Extended Mind and Enactive Cognition Theories for communicating and exploring a reconception of ASDs, which will be the focus of our next section. Our final section will suggest how these two theories both meet the concerns of those self-identifying as neurodiverse when encountering currently dominant scientific views on the nature and value of their atypical behaviors, while also helping to translate those concerns into novel avenues for research in the cognitive sciences.

AUTISM SPECTRUM DISORDERS

As mentioned in the introduction, the Autism Spectrum is typically characterized by a clinically significant deviance from the norm in capacities for reciprocal social behavior and communication, as well as "stereotyped behavior, interests, and activities."[7] Examples of behavioral atypicalities offered in the literature include difficulties with common social practices such as eye contact, sustaining interactive conversations beyond certain restricted interests over an extended period of time, adjusting to novel circumstances or breaks with routine, as well as engaging in repetitive behaviors that are commonly described as functionless or at least as obstructing the relevant individual from engaging with others and the world around them. As an individual matures they may exhibit significant difficulties initiating and maintaining social relationships, using language in nonliteral ways and achieving the capabilities necessary for independent living.[8] "Pervasive Developmental Disorder-Not Otherwise Specified" is used when diagnosing individuals whose autistic traits, though clinically significant, do not meet all of the requisite criteria used to diagnose Autistic Disorder or Asperger's Disorder. Asperger's Disorder can be distinguished from Autistic Disorder on the basis of a lack of, absence, or significant delay in early language development, or delay in early cognitive development typical of children at or below the age of three.[9]

CONCEPTUAL AND EMPIRICAL ISSUES SURROUNDING BEHAVIORAL ATYPICALITIES

In charting what we regard as a middle way between the Neurodiversity Perspective and an understanding of the ASDs in terms of dysfunction and impairment, we will adopt "Restricted, Repetitive Behaviors and Interests (RRBIs)"[10] as a description of the third diagnostic characteristic or feature of ASDs. This is to disambiguate "behavioral atypicalities," as this term can also be used to refer to atypicalities in social domains discussed under the first and second diagnostic character or feature of ASDs.[11] As mentioned above, RRBIs are thought to both isolate the child from her educators and peers and interfere with the child's active cognitive engagement[12] with her physical and social worlds. Complicating discussions of this third diagnostic characteristic or feature of ASDs is a great deal of heterogeneity in what qualifies as an RRBI. Given the diversity of behaviors historically bundled together under this umbrella term, it is not surprising that there has been extensive debate in both empirical and clinical circles over the relative merits of (sub) classificatory schemata, not to mention mixed—and often inconsistent—terminological usage among behavioral and cognitive psychologists, neuroscientists, educators, and other related professionals.[13] Nevertheless, for the purpose of determining their distinctive neuroanatomical localizations and biomechanical underpinnings—and from a clinical perspective, for identifying possible targets for behavioral and pharmacological intervention—it has been useful to differentiate this class of behaviors from apparently similar behavioral phenomena such as habits, mannerisms and gestures on the one hand, and more or less complex motor tics, paroxysmal dyskinesias and so forth, on the other.

If RRBIs form a distinct class of behaviors, then what are their central differentiating features or criteria of inclusion? On this matter expert opinion has been mixed and not uncommonly value laden. RRBIs have been variously described as involuntary, topographically invariant, rigid, repetitive, perseverative, consistent, ritualistic, rhythmic, and coordinated (i.e., patterned or even periodic, and therefore to some extent predictable in form and amplitude), as well as self-stimulatory and insensitive to changes in features of the environment, whether social or nonsocial. They have also been cast as having no apparent function, or as plainly purposeless, functionless, counterproductive, bizarre and inappropriate (i.e., both developmentally and socially); and in certain instances, as aberrant, pathological, dangerous, and destructive—although more sophisticated techniques of analysis and assessment, combined with greater attentiveness to the self-reports of those under study, have gradually eroded the tendency to leap to these sorts of conclusions.

Some researchers have suggested that RRBIs can be differentiated from other classes of behavior according to their (i) typical age of onset and developmental trajectory (i.e., the consistency and degree of fixity in their patterning over time); (ii) topographical location, frequency, and duration; (iii) association with specific antecedent sensations, urges and desires to perform; or (iv) (sometimes multiform) behavioral functions and characteristic maintaining contingencies. However, it has proven quite difficult to draw very sharp lines between, for example, RRBIs, habits, mannerisms and gestures, especially in cases where the behaviors in question are more complex, are susceptible to both endogenously and exogenously facilitated change over time, and are possibly communicative in nature (e.g., in cases of echolalia).

Murky and oft-debated terminological and classificatory issues aside, what *is* perfectly clear is the fact that RRBIs have been widely considered problematic, subjected to intense criticism and ultimately deemed worthy of clinical attention. Indeed, in practice the term "RRBI" carries diagnostic weight and has wide-ranging implications for the clinical treatment of those diagnosed with various developmental disorders, psychiatric disorders, and neurological conditions. Whatever RRBIs turn out to be, or what as of yet unforeseen functions they may turn out to serve, most agree that something has to be done about them, and quickly (i.e., while the brains of children are at their most plastic and malleable). This sense of urgency appears to be largely due to the immediate impact RRBIs tend to have on the parents, educators, and peers of children who exhibit them, not to mention both their empirically demonstrated and perceived effects on personal safety (i.e., in cases where they may become self-injurious), prospects for learning and cognitive development, adapting to physical and social environs, and becoming socially accepted, well-integrated and esteemed. [14]

While it has been challenging to classify RRBIs in general, it has also been quite difficult to characterize their specificity in autism. [15] This is true in spite of the fact that RRBIs occupy a rather large proportion of the behavioral repertoires of those diagnosed with ASDs, [16] especially around the time when children have reached an age appropriate for securing diagnosis. There is widespread consensus that RRBIs are not unique to individuals on the Spectrum (i.e., as opposed to those diagnosed with other developmental disorders, psychiatric disorders, and neurological conditions; not to mention, RRBIs have been reported in a number of studies of typically developing children[17]). It is also generally accepted that none of these behaviors are type-specific to autism. [18] Nevertheless, it has been shown that their frequency and severity correlate with "severity of illness, cognitive deficiency, impairment of adaptive functioning, and symbolic play." [19] Thus, their specificity among those diagnosed with ASDs appears to be quantitative in nature, not qualitative, and their rate of occurrence tends to be bound up with broader trends in the global development of the children who exhibit them.

RRBIs have been associated with the clinical profile of autism ever since Leo Kanner first described the disorder in the early 1940s. [20] Yet from an empirical standpoint, more than a half century later it was still clear that "work on the objective measurement of repetitive behavior in autism has not been done." [21] Today it remains apparent to neurobiologists that the "continuities and discontinuities in the normative and pathological expression of these behaviors have not been the subject of systematic study." [22] Ultimately, "little is known about the pathophysiology" of RRBI's in general, [23] or about their developmental trajectory in children at risk for being diagnosed with autism in particular. [24] As such, it is not at all clear how RRBI's can be reliably distinguished from other, apparently benign repetitive behaviors (e.g., strategies for acquiring and communicating information, as well as for building socially-"scaffolded"[25] abilities and more complex motoric skills) that may play significant roles in early infantile and childhood development. [26]

For some further conceptual clarity in this area of autism research, we can usefully distinguish motor mannerisms from restricted interests and insistence on sameness. [27] Motor mannerisms can include auto-stimulation (e.g., finger-flicking, hand-flapping, spinning, rocking), awkward movements (e.g., walking on tip-toes), and "complex whole-body movements." [28] Self-mutilation or damaging behavior (e.g., self-biting, head banging) falls under this category. Restricted interests can include an extended and unusually concentrated interest in, and attachment to, whole objects or their parts (e.g., gazing at lights, fixating on the wheels of toy vehicles), video clips, or domain-specific facts (e.g., train timetables, calendars, dinosaurs). An insistence on sameness can be observed in certain rituals (e.g., lining up toys in rows, sorting objects into specific colors), routines (e.g., insisting that a certain route is followed away from and back to home, or that a certain route is taken in particular stores), and a difficulty negotiating even minor changes in daily routines or the physical layout of home or work. Under the RRBI heading, Szatmari et al. draw a distinction between Repetitive Sensory and Motor Behaviors (RSMB) and Insistence on Sameness (IS).[29] This cuts across two of the three subcategories we have suggested, with IS behavior incorporating what we have included under insistence on sameness as well as restricted interests.

There are at least four possible ways of construing RRBIs conceptually. A basic or fundamental dichotomy will distinguish RRBIs with and without function.[30] We construe "function" here as including the production of positive stimuli (e.g., watching certain video clips), reducing the impact of noxious stimuli (e.g., covering one's ears to reduce sound perceived as too loud), and both expressing and regulating negative or positive affective and emotional states[31] (e.g., certain instances of rocking or hand flapping). Under RRBIs with function one can distinguish among adaptive behaviors (i.e., those which facilitate active cognitive engagement with physical and social environs), maladaptive behaviors (i.e., those which hinder such engagement) and neutral behaviors. Perhaps the clearest examples of maladaptive behaviors will involve self-injury (e.g., self-biting, head banging), but we also include behaviors that are maladaptive in certain contexts (e.g., tantrums in public spaces).[32] We allow that adaptive behavior can include covering one's ears to dampen noxious sounds or temporarily withdrawing from contexts in which one is overwhelmed by sensory stimuli. Our motivation for this allowance arises from the difficulties involved in nonarbitrarily excluding such behavior from that which is unproblematically regarded as adaptive. Think here of the difficulty of nonarbitrarily distinguishing typical and atypical individuals covering their ears in response to loud sounds or temporarily withdrawing from contexts of overwhelming sensory stimulation (e.g., a fairground or crowded party). Neutral behaviors might include auto-stimulatory behaviors that, while pleasant, merely relieve boredom. Depending on the behavior in question, each of these ways of functionally categorizing RRBIs can be found in the literature in this area of autism research.

Of particular importance for our focus here, arguably only those RRBIs that are maladaptive can be regarded as relatively *incontestable* legitimate targets for behavioral intervention.[33] That is to say, without (detailed) reference to the needs of the relevant individuals diagnosed on the Spectrum, it is *prima facie* reasonable to think it is in their best interests to intervene when their behavior is maladaptive, but the same is not true of nonmaladaptive behavior (i.e., adaptive or neutral behavior).[34] This is not to claim that a defense cannot be effectively made for intervening in other RRBIs, but this will require details that outline how such interventions are in the interests of those targeted. Pressures from self- or parent advocates gain greater weight when the behavior targeted for intervention is not maladaptive, even if it lacks a function. Arguably, in such circumstances the expressed wishes of those who are otherwise targets for intervention, or their advocates,[35] ought to figure in analyses of what is in their interests. This would be no less true if these individuals were neurologically typical (think here of age-matched children), and the current diagnosis of individuals on the Spectrum does not clearly warrant a differential treatment. Again, more details are needed that highlight how such interventions are in their interests.

It is important that we are not read as advocating that *only* maladaptive behavior warrants intervention. In very broad terms, good parenting involves shaping a child's behavior over time to instill a character, or set of behavioral dispositions, that equip the child for engaging with the physical and social world. This is an important form of "behavioral intervention," albeit of a less technical sort. A good parent is not limited to shaping a child's behavior only when it is maladaptive (e.g., consider training the child in table etiquette, or to sit quietly during religious services). Arguably, interventions in the lives of young people on the Spectrum need not be viewed in a different light, though parents may rightly seek help from those who understand the needs, environmental saliencies, and interests of their children (e.g., clinicians and educators who are trained to work with autistic children, and who are skillful in working with them, as well as autistic advocates). What should cause pause is targeting the RRBIs of an autistic individual in a fashion that is disproportional to atypical behavior among neurologically typical individuals simply because that individual is on the Spectrum.

In exploring how nonmaladaptive RRBIs might be reconceived in a more positive light, in the next section we turn to an examination of first-hand descriptions provided by two individuals on the Spectrum. These descriptions engage our previous discussion of RRBIs by challenging widespread claims that such behavioral atypicalities are functionless or purposeless.

VOICES FROM THE SPECTRUM

The importance of including the views of those on the Spectrum in this discussion is at least threefold: (i) as we have suggested, the objections of self- or parent advocates to the targeting of behavioral atypicalities gain greater weight when the behavior targeted for intervention is not maladaptive; (ii) all things being equal, acting in the interests of individuals should take account of their expressed preferences (when they are able to express them); (iii) should proxies choose, or advocates agitate, on behalf of others, attention should be given to careful reflection on what is in the interests of those in their care. These claims all share a common motive in respecting the interests of those whose behavior is targeted for intervention: (i) it is situated in the context of good parenting; (ii) it is grounded in the recognition that an appeal to best interests, even if indexed to accounts of flourishing, can ill afford to impose interventions that so depart from the expressed preferences of individuals that they cause suffering or disrespect their standing as persons; (iii) it reflects the danger of proxies or advocates acting in accord with their own interests, or greater social interests, rather than the interests of the individuals they represent. The situation is unsurprisingly acute when proxies or advocates have little or no experience with the embodiments of the individuals whose behavior is targeted for intervention. Autistics such as those quoted in what follows give voice to interests that may not be properly considered in contexts where decisions are routinely made by individuals who are neurologically typical. This is not to indict the motives of those making the decisions. It is, however, to encourage a healthy recognition of their epistemic fallibility.

Let us now turn our attention to some of the voices on the Spectrum. Amanda Baggs is an autistic activist and occasional video blogger who has received a great deal of attention for her 2007 web-video *In My Language*.[36] Although she is nonverbal, Baggs communicates through written word, a voice synthesizer and, according to her, repetitive behaviors. In her video, Baggs describes the repetitive behaviors she performs and records as follows:

> The previous part of this video was in my native language. Many people have assumed that when I talk about this being my language that means that each part of the video must have a particular symbolic message within it designed for the human mind to interpret. But my language is not about designing words or even visual symbols for people to interpret. It is about being in a constant conversation with every aspect of my environment. Reacting physically to all parts of my surroundings.[37]

Notice that Baggs's claims about her "native language" (i.e., her repetitive behavior) contrasts starkly with a standard view according to which such behavior is merely self-stimulatory. Such a view would place special emphasis on the rewards that Baggs receives from engaging in this sort of behavior (e.g., arousing sensory stimulation) while effectively ignoring the other possibilities that she presents here (more on these matters shortly). In characterizing her own repetitive behavior as communicative, interactive, and responsive, Baggs is implying that this behavior has cognitive value for her.

In the scene where Baggs is running her fingers through water, she writes:

> In this part of the video the water does not symbolize anything. I am just interacting with the water as the water interacts with me. Far from being purposeless, the way that I move is an ongoing response to what is around me. Ironically, the way that I move when responding to everything around me is described as "being in a world of my own" whereas if I interact with a much more limited set of responses and only react to a much more limited part of my surroundings people claim that I am "opening up to true interaction with the world."[38]

Here Baggs is clearly challenging the view that her repetitive behaviors are purposeless or merely self-stimulatory. Again it is noteworthy that from Baggs's perspective her behavior is not only purposeful but communicative and interactive. Perhaps more importantly, Baggs is calling upon her observers to understand her repetitive behavior as responsive to a remarkably broad range of stimuli in her surroundings. She contrasts this promiscuous responsiveness with what would typically be asked of her in contexts of intervention. In such contexts she understands her behavioral responsiveness as being artificially narrowed and constrained to suit the interests of others. According to Baggs, when her behavior is made to resemble that which is expressed by those who are neurologically typical her capacity to respond to the world is diminished considerably. Consider one final passage:

> The way I naturally think and respond to things looks and feels so different from standard concepts or even visualization that some people do not consider it thought at all but it is a way of thinking in its own right.[39]

Here Baggs suggests that her behavior has been misunderstood because of the differences that exist between the experiences and embodiments of those on and off the Spectrum. The reference points available to those who are neurologically typical are understandably informed by their peculiar styles of engaging the world cognitively, but perhaps these are poor (or at the very least, limited) grounds for understanding life on the Spectrum.

Dawn Prince-Hughes is an anthropologist and primatologist at Western Washington University. Diagnosed with Asperger's Syndrome when she was thirty-six years old, she has since recounted her years growing up on the Spectrum undiagnosed. She writes of her childhood:

> As I got older, around four or five, I started to have fascinations with objects: kitchen utensils, rocks, tools. I like to watch tools and gadgets work over and over. Mixers and wrenches were great. I delighted in watching my grandparents use these things and perform the same motions over and over. I remember feeling like these tools and devices had *meaning* and *perfection*.[40]

These statements shed light on Prince-Hughes's fascination with objects as well as the repetitive manipulations of objects by other people. As in the case of Baggs's descriptions of her own repetitive interactions with the objects in her immediate environs, these encounters are once again described as meaningful rather than purposeless or even self-stimulatory. Though this description precludes more of a substantive claim than that, it motivates resistance to a unidimensional characterization of RRBIs, while also redirecting attention to their potential cognitive value.

Again thinking back to her childhood, Prince-Hughes writes:

> My need for repetition extended to routes, places, and activities. When we went to the store, the cleaner, or the park, I would insist on going the same way every single time. I would silently acknowledge landmarks as the route unwound, whether they were the buildings and hills or the flowers and trees. I had memorized everything. To me, each flower, tree, building, and hill was a person, a being with its own personality and sense of agency. If I did not see it, it missed me and felt abandoned. I would panic if we did not drive or walk by it, because it would think I didn't exist anymore and would be worried. In turn, I felt like I would disappear if I were not hemmed in by the familiar and unchanging.[41]

The childhood personification of objects and organisms is unsurprising. If these are veridical memories, they contrast with descriptions of autistics as deficient in imagination. More importantly for present purposes, Prince-Hughes speaks here of interacting communicatively with her surroundings. This is strikingly similar to some of the claims made by Baggs above. Regarding these environmental objects and features as possessing agency, Prince-Hughes understands herself to be maintaining a relationship with them through her insistence on taking the same routes, visiting the same places and engaging in the same activities. Though we can doubt the ascription of sentience to these objects and features, the perceived purpose served by her insistence on sameness is striking.

The statement at the end of this passage is also worth noting. Prince-Hughes alludes, in other parts of her autobiography, to occasionally being lost in an overabundance of sensory stimulation. We suspect that her reference to "disappearing" refers to these experiences. The importance of being "hemmed in by the familiar and unchanging"[42] hints at something distinctively cognitive. In particular, it hints at the function these regularly encountered environmental objects or features may have served in Prince-Hughes general active cognitive engagement with her surroundings. Prince-Hughes seems to be claiming that her bodily relationship with these objects and features provided her with stability within which she maintained a sense of integrity and, presumably, from which she was poised to act. Interestingly, she writes later:

Most autistic people need order and ritual and will find ways to make order where they feel chaos. So much stimulation streams in, rushing into one's body without ever being processed: the filters that other people have simply aren't there. Swimming through the din of the fractured and the unexpected, one feels as if one were drowning in an ocean without predictability, without markers without a shore…Autistic people will instinctively reach for order and symmetry: they arrange spoons on the table, they line up matchsticks, or they rock back and forth, cutting a deluge of stimulation into smaller bits with the repetition of their bodies' movements.[43]

What Prince-Hughes seems to be describing towards the end of this passage are cognitive "scaffolds." In this case, her ordering of environmental objects or bodily movements into symmetrical, repetitive sequences appears to facilitate a slowing down or "filtering" of perceptual experience, thus allowing her to better perceive the world around her. Prince-Hughes's claims need not be true of most individuals on the Spectrum to motivate a reconception of the kind of insistence on sameness she is describing.

These passages highlight the interests of two individuals on the Spectrum in actively engaging with their respective physical and social worlds in ways that are thoroughly embodied and interactive. It is through Baggs's repetitive behavior that she interacts communicatively with her environment, and in her youth it was through her insistence on sameness that Prince-Hughes maintained a relationship with her surroundings that furnished her with a sense of stability, integrity, and control. It is the thoroughly embodied character of the engagements captured in passages such as these that motivates our examination of two embodied theories of mind that are currently enjoying a significant amount of attention in philosophy and cognitive science. These relatively recently articulated theories seek to place cognition firmly in the body, thereby contrasting with theories that view mental states either as something other than physical (a position currently most often encountered in religious traditions concerned with survival after death) or as nothing other than brain states. As lenses through which to view the behavior of those on the Spectrum, these theories promise to offer autism advocates conceptual resources for challenging *carte blanche* approaches to RRBIs as pathological, while also unearthing imaginative possibilities for researchers keen to investigate the alleged functionality of RRBIs.

COGNITION, EXTENDED AND ENACTIVE

Over at least the last two decades[44] cognitive science, philosophy of mind, and the philosophy of cognitive science have seen the emergence of two broad approaches to human cognition—the Extended Mind Hypothesis and Enactive Cognition—which are committed to radically embodying the mind.[45] "Embodying the mind" in the sense relevant to these approaches involves moving away from craniocentric or neurocentric views that cast the mind as bounded by the head or brain.[46] That is, both approaches see cognitive capacities, and the mental states that often accompany them, as emergent from mechanisms and processes extending beyond the head or central nervous system. Thus, these approaches require a view of the mind as situated at the intersection of brain, body, and world.[47] Though this broad conception of an embodied mind is shared by both approaches, they have arrived at this conclusion in importantly different ways. Some of the elements that distinguish them will be pertinent to how they might shed light on repetitive sensory and motor behaviors, as well as an insistence on sameness.[48] It is to a brief characterization of these distinguishing elements that we now turn.

Extended Mind

The Extended Mind Hypothesis is a broadly functionalist approach to mind.[49] According to functionalism, mental states such as beliefs, desires and preferences are functionally differentiated. Minimally, a mental state is the thing it is by virtue of its functional relationships (i.e., what it does) within a greater intentional system[50] (i.e., a system comprised of intentional states or their relations).[51] For example, my belief that there is a tree outside my window is the thing it is because of its functional relationship with relevant perceptual processes, other mental states I possess (including other beliefs about trees, windows and the outdoors), and my behaviour in the world. It is important to note that the physical substrate of cognition is not restricted by this functional characterization of mental states.[52] This last observation permits the development of a view of the mind as unbounded by the central nervous system and organic body. What is important to such a theory is that functional relations hold between states implicated in instances of information processing and facilitating an individual's active engagement with her physical and social environments over time and across contexts. An example of extended cognition often appealed to in the literature involves mathematical calculations using pen and paper.[53] Imagine yourself engaged in long division, where the calculation is greater than what could be done "in your head" alone. As you write out each stage in the calculation process on paper, you are moving toward calculating the final answer. The whole process, once completed, qualifies as your mathematical reasoning, even though you could not have done this "in your head" alone and key steps in the calculation were accomplished by physically manipulating numbers on paper. Notice that the whole process is extended, including brain, body, and a part of the world. Another example involves the use of mnemonic devices to aid restaurant workers in servicing clients in restaurants or bars. Consider bartenders who use differently shaped or positioned glasses for particular (types of) drinks, cues from ingredients already in glasses, or the clients themselves to efficiently mix drinks while interacting with clients and colleagues. These external cues off-load what might otherwise have to engage their working memory in ways that slow them down or even increase errors in service.[54] In examples such as these, the relevant link between the agent and her world is such that the "scaffolds" on which she depends are transparent (i.e., they do not require her attention as she uses them), reliable, and play a constitutive role in bringing about acts of cognition.[55]

Enactive Cognition

Enactive approaches to human cognition regard the body behaving in the world as importantly implicated in cognitive processes.[56] What often distinguishes enactive from extended approaches is the former's reliance on action in explicating the processes constitutive of cognition. Enactive theorists using perception as their example implicate an individual acting against and towards objects in her physical environment in such a way that, over time, her understanding of those objects in various contexts (as encountered from various angles or circumstances) facilitates perceptual experience.[57] Examples include perceptual experiences of such simple objects as tomatoes, apples, or coins as solid bodies, fully shaped and substantive, even though the occurrent perceptual information received through the eyes and visual neural pathways does not fully convey such content. That is, our visual experience of these objects transcends what is visually presented to us in moments where we experience them as three dimensional, temporally extended, full of flesh (for tomatoes or apples) or spherical (for coins). The understanding that facilitates such a rich perceptual experience emerges over time and across action contexts where we have encountered and engaged in physical or sensory contact with the relevant objects while situating ourselves differently in space. Without such differently situated encounters our perceptual experience of objects would be markedly diminished.[58]

Since extended and enactive approaches allow that body and world can be partly constitutive of certain cognitive processes, how it is that we engage with the world bodily can play an integral role in perceiving and thinking. With this suggestion in mind we can begin to anticipate how theories of embodied cognition open up possibilities for reimagining the RRBIs exhibited by those on the Spectrum.

Embodying Autistic Cognition

It is worth returning briefly to the writings of Baggs and Prince-Hughes in order to chart connections between the lived experiences of some of those on the Spectrum and the two theories of embodied cognition explored above.

Baggs's descriptions of her repetitive behaviors fit nicely with an Enactive approach to cognition. Baggs understands her repetitive bodily movements, as well as her touching, smelling, and tasting of objects, as forms of promiscuous responsiveness to, and communication with, her surroundings. Perhaps better described as activities, they can be seen as enriching Baggs's interactions with environmental objects, fleshing out the content of her perceptual experience, and contributing to the constitution of her thoughts. From Baggs's perspective, a reduction of these intricate ways of responding bodily to the world in order to bring them in line with standards of "normality" (understood here as that which is more typical) effectively diminishes her active cognitive engagement rather than enhancing it.

Prince-Hughes's insistence on sameness, through which she is able to introduce order into her routines and activities, fits nicely with an Extended approach to cognition. Selective attention in the midst of rich and sometimes overwhelming sensory stimulation can be difficult to achieve for autistics such as Prince-Hughes. She describes this sort of stimulation as coming in waves, leaving her feeling as though she is drowning in a threatening, chaotic influx. Her insistence on sameness (e.g., ordering and sequencing objects) and engagement in repetitive behaviors (e.g., rocking) can be seen as reducing assaultive sensory stimulation and settling the world around her in ways that facilitate cognition. Viewed in this light, routines and repetitive activities play a constitutive role in subsequent cognitive engagements.

As lenses, Extended Mind and Enactive Cognition Theories offer fresh opportunities for understanding and investigating the alleged functionality of the RRBIs exhibited by those on the Spectrum. They provide autistics such as Baggs and Prince-Hughes with theoretical tools that are useful for situating how they experience and understand the world. Because of their increasing relevance to research communities in the cognitive sciences, these theories offer rich, increasingly robust and coherent frameworks through which the perspectives of autistics can be communicated and taken up. For researchers, these theories recommend the reimagining of atypical embodiments and routines, because they suggest how different ways of engaging the world bodily might shape or constitute those processes that give rise to complex mental lives. When understood in this manner, these theories can help bridge existing divides over the nature of RRBIs and their value to autistics by ameliorating the poverty of explanatory options currently on the table. It is to the poverty of these options that we finally turn.

THE POVERTY OF EXPLANATORY OPTIONS ON THE TABLE

A number of different theoretical perspectives have emerged over the past forty or so years in an effort to account for the occurrence of RRBIs in both human and nonhuman animals, several of which are geared specifically to explaining their occurrence in autistic individuals.[59] For example, it has been proposed that RRBIs might in some cases function as reward-inducing, provide sensory stimulation, ameliorate impoverished or over-stimulating environments, or reduce stress that arises from abnormalities in sensory processing and social cognition. Or perhaps RRBIs simply stem from abnormalities in inhibitory and control processes, as well as idiosyncratic styles of environmental exploration and delayed or atypical forms of learning.

The most influential theoretical perspective currently stems from the work of the behaviorist Ivor Lovaas, who described RRBIs as learned or operant behaviors that are maintained over time by the kind of reinforcement they provide (e.g., repetitive flapping of hands in front of the eyes might provide visual stimulation, prompting a child to continue flapping their hands[60]). Part of the enduring appeal of this approach is that it is often informed by, or else translates directly into, techniques of behavior modification. These techniques are frequently recommended to parents of autistic children as part of early intensive intervention programs designed to steer their children onto a more typical trajectory of learning and development. However, other research among behaviorists suggests that many RRBIs are not *self*-stimulatory in the specific sense intended by Lovaas, and that the same behavioral form can be multiply functionally determined (i.e., it may serve more than a single function in different contexts). These diverse sources of evidence indicate that certain RRBIs are maintained by social contingencies,[61] as well as other external or environmental factors[62] that may be both positively and negatively reinforcing for the individual in question.[63]

Shifting our attention away from work among behaviorists, another influential psychological perspective hypothesizes that RRBIs serve to reduce chronically high levels of arousal, stress, and anxiety.[64] This perspective gels nicely with the commonly held view that more socially acceptable repetitive behaviors (e.g., nail-biting, watching television), sometimes associated with relieving stress or anxiety, can be functional and adaptive. Building on this general line of thought, cognitive psychologists and like-minded philosophers have suggested that RRBIs might function as coping strategies useful for regulating anxiety that arises from trying to navigate a social world ill-suited to the unique social-cognitive styles of autistic individuals (i.e., their alleged "mind-blindness"[65]). Notice that this approach also fits with the embodied approaches to cognition outlined above. By contributing to the regulation of arousal, stress and anxiety, some RRBIs might serve to facilitate or enable further active engagements with the environment, or allow individuals to return to such engagements after a brief period of withdrawal.

The arousal-regulation approach contrasts with another hypothesis, also from cognitive psychology, which suggests that RRBIs arise directly as a result of specific executive dysfunctions. Executive functions are implicated in various forms of cognitive and motoric inhibition, working memory, and related processes that play various roles in the execution of goal-oriented behaviors. The basic idea behind this alternative perspective is that autistic individuals may have difficulties inhibiting certain behaviors, regulating or controlling them once they have been initiated, or experience additional difficulties planning and generating alternative behavioral projects.[66] As such, they might literally get "locked into" a repetitive behavioral sequence, such as spinning in place, from which it can be difficult and perhaps even distressing to disengage.

Other psychological perspectives have attempted to explain RRBIs as resulting from a tendency among autistic individuals to focus attention on apparently "inessential" or "irrelevant" environmental details, and a related weakness in the drive for "central coherence" (i.e., more gestalt-like or abstract forms of meaning) that is characteristic of information processing among typically developing individuals.[67] Some psychologists have also attempted to combine the sensory processing or weak central coherence approaches with the executive function[68] and arousal-regulation approaches.[69] Other such combinations are, of course, still possible. Some researchers have called for a yet more thoroughgoing pluralism, emphasizing that certain varieties of explanation are particularly well-suited to specific RRBIs, while others may have limited applicability.[70]

Unraveling the Options

Dysfunction plays a key role in all but the first of the explanatory options outlined here. What precisely is "dysfunctional" about RRBIs as they are exhibited in individuals with autism? We set aside self-injurious behaviors as we have allowed for this class of behavior to qualify as maladaptive. As mentioned above, one of the major complaints that has been issued by parents and educators of children with autism is that RRBIs such as hand-flapping, gazing at lights, noise-making or fixating on certain objects interfere with learning both *indirectly* and *directly*. It is claimed that RRBIs interfere with learning *indirectly* because their frequent occurrence and recalcitrance tends to be disruptive and socially stigmatizing for both the children who exhibit them and their parents, complicating social interactions and potentially reducing opportunities for learning (e.g., in public schools). Since RRBIs are "often perceived as age-inappropriate in form, focus, context, duration, or intensity,"[71] parents and educators may well be ill-equipped to respond to these behaviors in a developmentally appropriate manner, and they may in addition feel paralyzed by shock, confusion or discomfort. More relevantly for our purposes, it is also claimed that RRBIs interfere with learning *directly* by preventing learning from occurring at all. This is primarily because such behaviors are distracting and appear to completely absorb the child's attention, preventing her from staying on task both in the moment and over the days, weeks, and months it can take to undergo pivotal experiences and inculcate more complex habits of learning. This much has seemed just obvious.

It is, however, tremendously difficult to generalize in this area of autism research. The first-hand accounts surveyed above problematize a monolithic explanation of autism-related behavioral atypicalities, particularly when these behaviors are regarded as playing no positive cognitive role. Perhaps the most we can say at present is that *certain varieties of RRBIs* (and remember that there are many) occurring at a relatively *high rate of frequency* may directly interfere with *certain kinds of learning*, *some of the time*, at least in the cases of *some children*—namely, those who exhibit particularly abnormal or delayed patterns of development.

We are concerned that empirical attention has been directed at only *certain kinds of learning*: namely, the sort that might take place in a preschool or classroom filled with typically developing children, based on a curriculum tailored to their styles of sensory, affective and cognitive engagement, information processing and so forth. Perhaps of more concern are studies of autistic children that appear to focus on classical conditioning as the litmus test of their learning capacity. For example, a study conducted by Koegel and Covert found that so-called lower functioning autistic children who exhibit relatively high-frequency stereotypies fail to learn simple discrimination tasks while they are engaged in these behaviors, and that the (punishment-based) suppression of these behaviors leads to increases in task performance.[72] A parallel inverse relationship has been reported between stereotypies and spontaneous "appropriate" play with toys; although, once again, the frequency in occurrence of stereotypies among the subjects under study was very high, and only two "lower functioning" children were included.[73]

Moreover, it is worth noting that researchers have been interested almost exclusively in the learning of *very young children* who are diagnosed with autism, so there is remarkably little data linking early childhood predictors of learning success with adult outcomes, whether or not the children in question have been involved in early intensive behavioral intervention programs. In a recent review of the current level of understanding (and alleged *mis*understanding) of learning in autism, Michelle Dawson and colleagues at the Université de Montréal contend that "[d]escriptive and empirical accounts of autistics learning in unusual and successful ways have sporadically appeared and remained unexplained throughout the history of autism research."[74] While it has been convenient for psychologists to presume that what is "unusual" about autistic learning is straightforwardly pathological in nature, this presumption has also made it quite difficult to account for the noteworthy successes that have been documented over the past sixty or so years, especially those that were recorded before the emphasis on early intensive behavioral intervention programs.[75] Importantly, these successes include cases of children who reportedly engaged in high levels of RRBIs.

As lenses, the two theories of embodied cognition outlined above enrich the possibilities for understanding RRBIs and their role in autistic cognition. Learning occurs in autistics despite high frequencies of RRBIs, and even if these individuals remain restricted in what they learn, it need not be the RRBIs that are responsible for these restrictions. The passages from Baggs and Prince-Hughes suggest that it is *through* or *in virtue of* their RRBIs, not in spite of them, that they are able to actively engage with and make sense of their surroundings. Moreover, as Dawson and colleagues write,

> Learning in autism is characterized both by spontaneous—sometimes exceptional—mastering of complex material and an apparent resistance to learning in conventional ways. Learning that appears to be implicit seems to be important in autism, but autistics' implicit learning may not map directly onto non-autistics' implicit learning or be governed by the same constraints.[76]

The "spontaneity" to which Dawson and colleagues refer need not detain us. The suggestion that autistic learning may not follow the same constraints of neurologically typical learning or resemble the principles that underlie it does require a reimagining of cognition that both accommodates and highlights the significance of different styles of inhabiting and engaging the world bodily. The perspectives of people such as Baggs and Prince-Hughes provide further motivation for undertaking this reimagining because they are at least partly representative of the interests of those individuals whose atypical behavior is targeted for intervention. What we have been suggesting is that these authors' perspectives on their experiences and ways of understanding the world should not be dismissed out of hand as merely anecdotal or as incompatible with the theoretical frameworks currently available for guiding research in psychology and the cognitive sciences. Indeed, Extended Mind and Enactive Cognition Theories offer coherent and attractive theoretical spaces within which to begin reimagining the possible functions of RRBIs, particularly with respect to how they might enable learning and cognition.

CONCLUSION

Certain autistic advocates and their caregivers have argued against targeting behavioral atypicalities in interventions geared towards reducing the dysfunctions associated with ASDs. For those of us not on the Spectrum, it is important not to dismiss their arguments out of hand. There are options already on the table that may offer explanations for some RRBIs. High levels of arousal, stress, and anxiety are recurring themes in the autobiographies of individuals on the Spectrum. Behaviorally mediated mechanisms for arousal and stress regulation, as well as strategies for coping with anxiety, might account for a subset of behavioral atypicalities while also explaining some of the value attached to these behaviors by those who exhibit them. Though treating arousal, stress, and anxiety might alleviate the frequency of such behaviors, it might not eliminate them. What is more important for our purposes, in other cases behavioral atypicalities might derive their value from helping to order the environment and "filter" an assaultive influx of sensory stimulation, thereby enabling engagements with the world that are more comfortable and productive for the autistic individual, perhaps even facilitating learning and cognitive development. We are suggesting that a broader range of frameworks through which to understand RRBIs can provide more affirming means of understanding their value to those on the Spectrum, while also presenting alternative avenues of inquiry for both experimental and clinical researchers. None of what we have advocated is intended to detract from the difficulties of those on the Spectrum whose symptoms are best understood and addressed through a lens of dysfunction or impairment. It would be a mistake, however, to approach the lived experience and challenges of those diagnosed as autistic without a variety of theoretical perspectives that can accommodate the diversity existing on the Spectrum. In stressing the value of Extended Mind and Enactive Cognition Theories, we hope to have added to this variety.

REFERENCES

Ahearn, W. H., Clark, K. M., Gardener, N. C., Chung, B. I., and Dube, W. V. 2003. Persistence of Stereotypic Behavior: Examining the Effects of External Reinforcers. *Journal of Applied Behavior Analysis* 36:439–48.

American Psychiatric Association. 2000. *Diagnostic and Statistical Manual of Mental Disorders. 4th Edition, Text Revised.* Washington, DC: American Psychiatric Association.

Bach-y-Rita, P. and Kercel, S.W. 2003. Sensory Substitution and the Human-Machine Interface. *Trends in Cognitive Sciences* 7(12):541–46.

Bagatell, N. 2010. From Cure to Community: Transforming Notions of Autism. *Ethos, Special Issue: Rethinking Autism, Rethinking Anthropology* 38(1):33–55.

Baggs, A. 2007. *In My Language.* http://www.youtube.com/watch?v=JnylM1hI2jc (accessed December 11, 2011).

Baron-Cohen, S. 1989. Do Autistic Children Have Obsessions and Compulsions? *British Journal of Clinical Psychology* 28:193–200.

Beach, K. 1993. Becoming a Bartender: The Role of External Memory Cues in a Work-directed Educational Activity. *Applied Cognitive Psychology* 7:191–204.

Biklen, D. 2005. *Autism and the Myth of the Person Alone.* New York: NYU Press.

Bodfish, J. W., Symons, F. J., Parker, D. E., and Lewis, M. H. 2000. Varieties of Repetitive Behavior in Autism: Comparisons to Mental Retardation. *Journal of Autism and Developmental Disorders* 30:237–43.

Carruthers, P. 1996. Autism as Mind-Blindness: An Elaboration and Partial Defence, in P. Carruthers and P. K. Smith (eds.), *Theories of Theories of Mind.* Cambridge: Cambridge University Press: 257–73.

Castellanos, F. X., Ritchie, G. F., Marsh, W. L., *et al.* 1996. DSM-IV Stereotypical Movement Disorder: Persistence of Stereotypies of Infancy in Intellectually Normal Adolescents and Adults. *Journal of Clinical Psychiatry* 57:116–22.

Charlop, M. H. 1983. The Effects of Echolalia on Acquisition and Generalization of Receptive Labeling in Autistic Children. *Journal of Applied Behavior Analysis* 16(1):111–26.

Chen, Y. H., Rodgers, J., and McConachie, H. 2009. Restricted and Repetitive Behaviours, Sensory Processing and Cognitive Style in Children with Autism Spectrum Disorders. *Journal of Autism and Developmental Disorders* 39:635–42.

Clancey, W. J. 2009. Scientific Antecedents of Situated Cognition, in P. Robbins and M. Aydede (eds.), *The Cambridge Handbook of Situated Cognition*. New York: Cambridge University Press. 11–34.

Clark, A. 2005. Intrinsic Content, Active Memory and the Extended Mind. *Analysis* 65:1–11.

———. 2003. *Natural-Born Cyborgs: Minds, Technologies, and the Future of Human Intelligence*. New York: Oxford University Press.

Clark, A. and Chalmers, D. 1998. The Extended Mind. *Analysis* 58(1):7–19.

Cunningham, A. B. and Schreibman, L. 2008. Stereotypy in Autism: The Importance of Function. *Research in Autism Spectrum Disorders* 2:469–79.

Dawson, M., Mottron, L., and Gernsbacher, M. A. 2008. Learning in Autism, in J. H. Byrne (series ed.) and H. Roediger (vol. ed.). *Learning and Memory: A Comprehensive Reference: Cognitive Psychology*. New York: Elsevier: 759–72.

Dawson, M., Soulieres, I., Gernsbacher, M. A., and Mottron, L. 2007. The Level and Nature of Autistic Intelligence. *Psychological Science* 18(8):657–62.

Drickamer, L. C., Vessey, S. H. and Jakob, E. M. 2002. *Animal Behavior: Mechanisms, Ecology, Evolution*. Fifth Edition. New York: McGraw Hill.

Durand, V. M. and Carr, E. G. 1987. Social Influences on 'Self-Stimulatory' Behavior: Analysis and Treatment Application. *Journal of Applied Behavior Analysis* 20:119–32.

Fenton, A., and Alpert, S. 2008. Extending Our View on Using BCIs for Locked-in Syndrome. *Neuroethics* 1:119–32.

Foster, L. G. 1998. Nervous Habits and Stereotyped Behaviors in Preschool Children. *Journal of the American Academy of Child and Adolescent Psychiatry* 37:711–17.

Frith, U. 1989. *Autism: Explaining the Enigma*. Oxford: Blackwell.

Frith, U. and Happé, F. 1994. Autism: Beyond 'Theory of Mind.' *Cognition* 50:115–32.

Gallagher, S. 2005. *How the Body Shapes the Mind*. New York: Oxford University Press.

———. 2009. Philosophical Antecedents of Situated Cognition, in P. Robbins and M. Aydede (eds.), *The Cambridge Handbook of Situated Cognition*. New York: Cambridge University Press: 35–51.

Gould, J. L. and C. G. Gould. 1994/99. *The Animal Mind*. New York: Scientific American Library.

Harman, G. 1998/2004. Intentionality, in W. Bechtel and G. Graham (eds.), *A Companion to Cognitive Science*. Malden, MA: Blackwell: 602–10.

Harris, K. M., Mahone, E. M., and Singer, H. S. 2008. Nonautistic Motor Stereotypies: Clinical Features and Longitudinal Follow-Up. *Pediatric Neurology* 38:267–72.

Hutt, C. and Hutt, S. J. 1965. Effects of Environmental Complexity on Stereotyped Behaviours in Children. *Animal Behaviour* 13:1–4.

———. 1970. Stereotypies and Their Relation to Arousal: A Study of Autistic Children, in C. Hutt and S. J. Hutt (eds.), *Behaviour Studies in* Psychiatry, 175–204. Oxford: Pergamon Press.

Hutt, C., Hutt, S. J., Lee, D., and Ounsted, C. 1964. Arousal and Childhood Autism. *Nature* 204:908–9.

Jones, R. S. P, Walsh, P. G., and Sturmey, P. 1995. *Stereotyped Movement Disorders*. Chichester: John Wiley and Sons.

Joosten, A. V. and Bundy, A. C. 2010. Sensory Processing and Stereotypical and Repetitive Behaviour in Children with Autism and Intellectual Disability. *Australian Occupational Therapy Journal* (published online March 2010).

Kanner, L. 1943. Autistic Disturbances of Affective Contact. *Nervous Child* 2:217–50.

Kennedy, C. H., Meyer, K. A., Knowles, T., and Shukla, S. 2000. Analyzing the Multiple Functions of Stereotypical Behavior for Students with Autism: Implications for Assessment and Treatment. *Journal of Applied Behavior Analysis* 33(4):559–71.

Kinsbourne, M. 1980. Do Repetitive Movement Patterns in Children and Animals Serve a Dearousing Function? *Developmental and Behavioral Pediatrics* 1:39–42.

Kiverstein, J. and Clark, A. 2009. Introduction: Mind Embodied, Embedded, and Enacted: One Church or Many? *Topoi* 28:1–7.

Klin, A., Jones, W., Schultz, R., and Volkmar, F. 2003. The Enactive Mind, or from Actions to Cognition: Lessons from Autism. *Philosophical Transactions of the Royal Society B* 358:345–60.

Koegel, R. L. and Covert, A. 1972. The Relationship of Self-Stimulation to Learning in Autistic Children. *Journal of Applied Behavior Analysis* 5:381–87.

Koegel, R. L., Firestone, P. B., Kramme, K. W., and Dunlap, G. 1974. Increasing Spontaneous Play by Suppressing Self-Stimulation in Autistic Children. *Journal of Applied Behavior Analysis* 7:521–28.

Koegel, L. K., Koegel, R. L., and Smith, A. 1997. Variables Related to Differences in Standardized Test Outcomes for Children with Autism. *Journal of Autism and Developmental Disorders* 27:233–43.

Levin, J. 2008. Functionalism, in E. N. Zalta (ed.), *The Stanford Encyclopedia of Philosophy, Fall 2008 Edition*. http://plato.stanford.edu/archives/fall2008/entries/functionalism/.

Levy, N. 2007. Rethinking Neuroethics in the Light of the Extended Mind Thesis. *The American Journal of Bioethics* 7(9):3–11.

Lewis, M. H. and Bodfish, J. W. 1998. Repetitive Behavior Disorders in Autism. *Mental Retardation and Developmental Disabilities Research Reviews* 4:80–9.

Lewis, M. and Kim, S.-J. 2009. The Pathophysiology of Restricted Repetitive Behavior. *Journal of Neurodevelopmental Disorders* 1(2):114–32.

Llewellyn, A. and Hogan, K. 2000. The Use and Abuse of Models of Disability. *Disability and Society* 15(1):157–65.

Lopez, B. R., Lincoln, A. J., Ozonoff, S., and Lai, Z. 2005. Examining the Relationship Between Executive Functions and Restricted, Repetitive Symptoms of Autistic Disorder. *Journal of Autism and Developmental Disorders* 35(4):445–60.

Lord, C. and Bishop, S. L. 2010. Autism Spectrum Disorders: Diagnosis, Prevalence, and Services for Children and Families. *Social Policy Report* 24(2):1–27.

Lord, C. and Spence, S. 2006. Autism Spectrum Disorders: Phenotype and Diagnosis, in S.O. Moldin and J. L. R. Rubenstein (eds.), *Understanding Autism: From Basic Neuroscience to Treatment*. Boca Raton: CRC Press. 1–24.

Lovaas, O. I., Koegel, R. L., and Schreibman L. 1979. Stimulus Overselectivity in Autism: A Review of Research. *Psychological Bulletin* 86:1236–54.

Lovaas, O. I., Litrownik, A., and Mann, R. 1971. Response Latencies to Auditory Stimuli in Autistic Children Engaged in Self-Stimulatory Behavior. *Behaviour Research and Therapy* 9:39–49.

Lovaas, O. I., Newsom, C., and Hickman, C. 1987. Self-Stimulatory Behavior and Perceptual Development. *Journal of Applied Behavior Analysis* 20:45–68.

Lovaas, O. I., Schreibman, L., Koegel, R., and Rehm, R. 1971. Selective Responding by Autistic Children to Multiple Sensory Input. *Journal of Abnormal Psychology* 77:211–22.

Mason, S. A., McGee, G. G., Farmer-Dougan, V., and Risley, T. R. 1989. A Practical Strategy for Ongoing Reinforcer Assessment. *Journal of Applied Behavior Analysis* 22:171–77.

Menary, R. 2009. Intentionality, Cognitive Integrative and the Continuity Thesis. *Topoi* 28:31–43.

Murdoch, H. 2003. Stereotyped Behaviors: How Should We Think About Them? *British Journal of Special Education* 24:71–5.

Noë, A. 2008. Précis of *Action In Perception*. *Philosophy and Phenomenological Research* 76(3):660–65.

Prince-Hughes, D. (ed.). 2002. *Aquamarine Blue 5: Personal Stories of College Students with Autism*. Athens, OH: Swallow Press/Ohio University Press.

———. 2004. *Songs of the Gorilla Nation: My Journey Through Autism.* New York: Harmony Books.

Rapp, J. T. and Vollmer, T. R. 2005. Stereotypy I: A Review of Behavioral Assessment and Treatment. *Research in Developmental Disabilities* 26:527–47.

Repp, A. C., Karsh, K. G., Deitz, D. E. D., and Singh, N. N. 1992. A Study of the Homeostatic Level of Stereotypy and Other Motor Movements of Persons with Mental Handicaps. *Journal of Intellectual Disability Research* 36:61–75.

Ridley, R. M. 1994. The Psychology of Perseverative and Stereotyped Behaviour. *Progress in Neurobiology* 44:221–31.

Robbins, P. and Aydede, M. A. 2009. Short Primer on Situated Cognition, in P. Robbins and M. Aydede (eds.), *The Cambridge Handbook of Situated Cognition.* New York: Cambridge University Press, 3–10.

Rosenzweig, M. R., Breedlove, S. M., and Watson, N. V. 2005. *Biological Psychology: An Introduction to Behavioral and Cognitive Neuroscience, 4th Edition.* Sunderland: Sinauer Associates, Inc.

Singer, H. S. 2009. Motor Stereotypies. *Seminars in Pediatric Neurology* 16(2):77–81.

South, M., Ozonoff, S., and McMahon, W. M. 2007. The Relationship Between Executive Functioning, Central Coherence, and Repetitive Behaviors in the High-Functioning Autism Spectrum. *Autism* 11(5):437–51.

Standing Senate Committee on Social Affairs, Science and Technology. 2007. Pay Now or Pay Later: Autism Families in Crisis. http://www.parl.gc.ca/39/1/parlbus/commbus/senate/come/soci-e/rep-e/repfinmar07-e.htm (accessed January 27, 2011).

Symons, F. J., Sperry, L. A., Dropik, P. L., and Bodfish, J. W. 2005. The Early Development of Stereotypy and Self-Injury: A Review of Research Methods. *Journal of Intellectual Disability Research* 49(2):144–58.

Szatmari, P., Georgiades, S., Bryson, S., Zwaigenbaum, L., Roberts, W., Mahoney, W., Goldberg, J., and Tuff, L. 2006. Investigating the Structure of the Restricted, Repetitive Behaviours and Interests Domain of Autism. *Journal of Child Psychology and Psychiatry* 47:582–90.

Thelen, E. 1981. Rhythmical Behaviour in Infancy: An Ethological Perspective. *Developmental Psychology* 17(3):237–57.

Troster, H. 1994. Prevalence and Functions of Stereotypes Behaviors in Non-Handicapped Children in Residential Care. *Journal of Abnormal Child Psychology* 22:79–97.

Turner, M. 1997. Towards an Executive Dysfunction Account of Repetitive Behaviour in Autism, in J. Russell (ed.), *Autism as an Executive Disorder.* New York: Oxford University Press. 57–100.

Turner, M. 1999. Annotation: Repetitive Behavior in Autism: A Review of Psychological Research. *Journal of Child Psychology and Psychiatry* 40:839–49.

Tyler, M., Danilov, Y., and Bach-y-Rita, P. 2003. Closing an Open-Loop Control System: Vestibular Substitution Through the Tongue. *Journal of Integrative Neuroscience* 2(2):159–64.

Wilson, R.A. and Clark, A. 2009. How to Situate Cognition: Letting Nature Take Its Course, in P. Robbins and M. Aydede (eds.), *The Cambridge Handbook of Situated Cognition.* New York: Cambridge University Press, 55–77.

Zentall, S. S. and Zentall, T. R. 1983. Optimal Stimulation: A Model of Disordered Activity and Performance in Normal and Deviant Children. *Psychological Bulletin* 94:446–71.

NOTES

1. The *DSM* is currently undergoing revision, and proposed changes include adopting "Autism Spectrum Disorder" as a unitary diagnostic category that scopes over what is now distinguished under the categories of Autistic Disorder, Asperger's Disorder, Pervasive Developmental Disorder-NOS and Child Disintegrative Disorder (see http://www.dsm5.org/ProposedRevisions/Pages/proposedrevision.aspx?rid=94#). Child Disintegrative Disorder resembles Autistic Disorder but differs in onset and course. After at least two years, and perhaps as much

as ten years, of development within the standard norm, a child loses many social and communicative skills and engages in repetitive or restricted behaviors (APA 2000). Unlike many individuals diagnosed with Autistic Disorder, the characteristics or features diagnostic of Child Disintegrative Disorder remain "relatively constant throughout life" (APA 2000, 78).

2. APA 2000.

3. From time to time, we use "autistic person" or "autistic individual" instead of "person with autism" or "individual with autism" (i.e., we do not adhere to person-first language). This reflects the insight of autistic activists that person-first language encourages the incorrect view that autism is accidental rather than constitutive of the identity of the relevant people on the Spectrum. We do not suppose that all of those on the Spectrum would agree with this choice (see Biklen 2005; Standing Senate Committee 2007), and so we stray from a rigid adherence to this convention.

4. Lovaas et al. 1971; Lovaas et al. 1971; Koegel and Covert 1972; Lovaas et al. 1979. By "learning" we mean the understanding still prevalent in psychology: a change in the behavior of an individual due to their experience (Drickamer et al. 2002; Rosenzweig et al. 2005). The emphasis on behavior, though a reflection of the influence of behaviorism in this area of psychology, also reflects the need to accommodate learning how (e.g., learning how to ride a bicycle) and learning that (e.g., learning that the sun is our local star). Types of learning, with implications for changes in the relevant individual's intentional system (i.e., their mental states in relation to each other), include associative conditioning, operant conditioning, latent learning, observational learning, imitation, and so on (Drickamer *et al.* 2002).

5. Bagatell 2010. As we understand it here, the Neurodiversity Movement seeks a reconceiving of individuals diagnosed with neurological or neurodevelopmental disorders as fully human agents deserving of greater respect and tolerance than is currently experienced inside "the clinic." This reconceiving can have at least two possible expressions: (i) one that charts a middle way between a view that pathologizes those traits or features characteristic of ASDs, and a social constructivism that would see the category of autism as an artifact of a health-care system with an overly narrow construal of "normality"; or (ii) another that recommends an outright rejection of thinking of ASDs in terms of disorder. (ii) is much more radical than (i), though both require a reconceiving of ASDs so that many on the Spectrum are best regarded as *different* rather than *dysfunctional* or *deficient*.

6. Dawson et al. 2007.

7. APA 2000, 69.

8. APA 2000.

9. APA 2000.

10. Szatmari et al. 2006, 582.

11. A further complication is our occasional use of "stereotypical behaviors" or "stereotypies" instead of "RRBI." This reflects the appearance of these alternative terms in the scientific literature used in the relevant part of our discussion, and their exclusion of "insistence on sameness," which is subsumed under "RRBI."

12. Active cognition, as we use it here, occurs when the relevant individual plays an important role in the acquisition of knowledge (i.e., she learns by manipulating and experimenting with her environment), and decides, though perhaps not always consciously, what information, among the knowledge already possessed, will be used in future behavior (Gould and Gould 1994/99, 8; 114).

13. Turner 1999.

14. Jones et al. 1995.

15. Bodfish et al. 2000, 237.

16. Rapp and Vollmer 2005.

17. See, e.g., Troster 1994; Castellanos et al. 1996; Foster 1998; Harris et al. 2008.

18. Lewis and Bodfish 1998.

19. Singer 2009, 80.

20. Kanner 1943.

21. Lewis and Bodfish 1998, 81.

22. Lewis and Kim 2009, 115.

23. Lewis and Kim 2009, 126.

24. Symons et al. 2005.

25. "Scaffold" here merely denotes something that facilitates or enables something else.

26. E.g., Thelen 1981; for a relevant study of echolalia among autistic children, see Charlop 1983.

27. Szatmari et al. 2006.

28. APA 2000, 84.

29. Szatmari et al. 2006.

30. Problems with this basic dichotomy arise because the question of whether a particular RRBI "has a function" is likely to be sensitive to the developmental context in which it occurs—i.e., what at one stage in development is functionless might acquire a function as other developmental scaffolds settle into place (see Murdoch 2003).

31. We do not mean to suggest that certain affective or emotional states are, across contexts and individuals, essentially "negative" or "positive." These modifiers must be contextualized to remain sensible.

32. We grant these distinctions and examples while recognizing that, even with considerations of self-harm, what qualifies as maladaptive may be contextual. Certain examples of self-mutilation (e.g., nail biting, skin picking) are common enough to warrant occasional disapproval but usually not a diagnosis. This may reflect the importance of social norms at work in judging behaviors to be unacceptably harmful. As autistics can act in ways that are at odds with social norms, this may have undue influence on how their self-harming behaviors are perceived by others.

33. See the preceding footnote.

34. There is an epistemic problem lurking here: How exactly are we to distinguish between nonmaladaptive and maladaptive behaviors across variations in developmental trajectory (i.e., variations beyond what is common or typical)? It remains possible that what, at one point in development, is not adaptive (or perhaps even maladaptive) will later become adaptive.

35. There is a further question of who qualifies as an "advocate," particularly as this is an emotionally and politically charged decision space where the "real" interests of those directly affected are contested. This is a significant problem and one that may not be resolvable in a principled fashion (i.e., there may be no principle or rule that can definitively identify "the right" advocate). It is unclear whether this is a special problem for our view or one that attaches to any view that seeks to introduce proxies for those who are vulnerable and voiceless in decision spaces that are equally emotionally and politically charged.

36. Baggs's video *In My Language* can be viewed online at: http://www.youtube.com/watch?v=JnylM1hI2jc.

37. Baggs 2007.

38. Baggs 2007.

39. Baggs 2007.

40. Prince-Hughes 2002, 108.

41. Prince-Hughes 2004, 19–20.

42. Prince-Hughes 2004, 20.

43. Prince-Hughes 2004, 25.

44. The history of this emergent field of research can be given a much longer lineage of course. See Clancey 2009; Gallagher 2009.

45. For the purposes of simplicity we are using "cognition" and "mind" as synonyms.

46. Kiverstein and Clark 2009; Robbins and Aydede 2009.

47. Kiverstein and Clark 2009; Robbins and Aydede 2009.

48. Though we use Enactive Cognition Theory to focus on behavioral atypicalities expressed by individuals on the Spectrum, Klin et al. have examined some of the social difficulties faced by autistics using an Enactive model (Klin *et al.* 2003, 357). A similar approach to Klin *et al.* can be found in chapter 9 of Gallagher 2005.

49. Fenton and Alpert 2008; Levy 2007.

50. We use "intentionality" in Brentano's sense of the word: A belief is an intentional state because its representational content is about something (Harman 1998/2004, 602).

51. Levin 2008.

52. Levin 2008.

53. Clark and Chalmers 1998; Wilson and Clark 2009.

54. Beach 1993.

55. Clark and Chalmers 1998.For more examples of using environmental features or technological aids as aids for efficient cognition and action see Clark 2003.

56. Gallagher 2005; Kiverstein and Clark 2009.

57. Noë 2008.

58. For an application in the social domain see Klin *et al.* 2003.

59. For an overview of relevant psychological research, see Turner 1999; for an overview of psychological, genetic and neuropathological research, see Lewis and Kim 2009.

60. Lovaas *et al.* 1987.

61. Durand and Carr 1987.

62. Ahearn *et al.* 2003.

63. See also Kennedy *et al.* 2000; Cunningham and Schreibman 2008.

64. Hutt *et al.* 1964; Hutt and Hutt 1965, 1970; Kinsbourne 1980; Repp et al. 1992; Zentall and Zentall 1983.

65. See Baron-Cohen 1989; Carruthers 1996.

66. Ridley 1994; Turner 1997; Lopez *et al.* 2005.

67. Frith 1989; Frith and Happé 1994; Chen *et al.* 2009.

68. South *et al.* 2007.

69. Joosten and Bundy 2010.

70. Turner 1999, 844.

71. Cunningham and Schreibman 2008, 3.

72. Koegel and Covert 1972.

73. Koegel *et al.* 1974.

74. Dawson *et al.* 2008, 762.

75. Dawson *et al.* 2008, 762.

76. Dawson *et al.* 2008, 768.

Chapter Three

Autism and the Extreme Male Brain

Ruth Sample

Extraordinary claims require extraordinary evidence. —Carl Sagan

What is autism, and what is "The Extreme Male Brain"? Autism, Simon Baron-Cohen claims, is not only more common in males, but so are "autistic traits," and these traits are, like autism itself, biologically based and generated (at least in part) by fetal hormones. Autism is accordingly the far end of a spectrum of cognitive and affective difference, and this difference is the "essential difference" between men and women.[1] However, this claim is no ordinary causal claim about the relationship between biology and behavior. The hypothesis of the Extreme Male Brain (EMB) moves from a specific understanding of a particular clinical diagnosis to claims of a deeper knowledge of men and women in general. There are interesting and deep philosophical questions here about whether such knowledge is even possible. Here I wish to discuss whether EMB is defensible, as well as the implications of hypothesizing essential differences in mental traits along the lines of gender.

My aim is to investigate the relationship between recent claims made in psychology and neuroscience about autism spectrum disorders (ASD) and the broader claim that there is an "essential difference" between male and female minds.[2] Should we look at autism as an extreme version of the male brain? What, if any, arguments have been produced for this equivalence? More importantly, what would we gain by seeing autism as a gendered disorder?

Over the last decade, many other authors have tried to revive the idea that there are not only basic overall anatomical differences between men and women, but that our brains in particular are different too.[3] These brain differences, they argue, translate into behavioral, cognitive, and affective differences in ways that are consistent with received ideas about boys and girls, men and women. Furthermore, they claim that because of the differences in our brains, we can explain the differences in the way that men and women are positioned in society: in our schools, our employment patterns, in our hobbies and interests, and in our personal relationships. Baron-Cohen predicates his EMB theory on the idea of a Male Brain. He argues that we should see autism and certain male-typical traits as part of a broader phenotype generated by sex differences in the brain.[4] Some researchers have called this equation of autistic traits and maleness "intriguing."[5] Steven Pinker has enthusiastically endorsed it and, in an unfortunate cover blurb for the paperback edition, wrote that "*The Essential Difference* is essential reading." Others have accepted EMB and expanded his model to include an Extreme Female Brain as a pathological condition.[6] However, the argument equating EMB and autism has not yet been carefully scrutinized.

I shall try to show that although it seems *prima facie* plausible that EMB is true, it is not. The most important basis of this equivalence is an argument that I call the Common Cause Argument. It is an argument that Baron-Cohen never explicitly makes, but I aim to show that is implicit in what he does argue. I think it is the strongest, most plausible argument in favor of the equivalence between autism and EMB. It is structurally valid. It does not, however, succeed. One of the premises *is* true, but that premise is not relevant to establishing the thesis. However, none of the remaining premises that are relevant to the conclusion has been clearly established. Without a sound argument equating autism with the male brain, we should avoid doing so. Even though the prevalence of autism is significantly sexually dimorphic, it would be a mistake to see it as a stronger "dose" of The Male Brain, just as it would be a mistake to see disorders found more often in girls (such as Rett syndrome) as the Extreme Female Brain.

The primary reason for rejecting EMB is that it is not a well-supported hypothesis. Should it turn out the specific claims invoked in favor of EMB are confirmed, the confirmation of those claims would not confirm EMB. "Sexing the brain" adds nothing to our understanding of autism. It adds nothing to our understanding of what causes autism. It adds nothing to our understanding of how to remediate autism. EMB has the potential to divert research funding from other research programs that could enhance our understanding of autism and provide insight into remediation, if not a cure, for autistic symptoms.

In addition, promoting this equivalence has serious social implications that we should not ignore. Baron-Cohen has stated explicitly that science should be distinct from social policy,[7] and has said that some of his critics (such as neuroscientist Cordelia Fine) are merely advancing a feminist political agenda.[8] Instead, even if unintentional, the equation of autism with the male brain advances another agenda: what Erik Turkheimer calls "belligerent defenses of stereotypical masculinity in evolutionary psychology."[9] Baron-

Cohen uses EMB to argue that the low representation of women in the natural sciences, mathematics, computer science, and engineering is a product of biological differences in the brains of men and women. This has clear political implications, despite Baron-Cohen's professed neutrality. More recently, he has argued that the male brain is "truth-seeking" in a way that the female brain is not.[10] While his goal may be to valorize certain forms of autism and increase tolerance for poor empathizing, the sexist implications are clear: we should not expect women to succeed at the same rate as do men in the higher-paying, higher-prestige disciplines of math, science, and engineering.

WHAT IS AUTISM?

Important scientific research, including that of Baron-Cohen, in the last two decades has helped us to understand autism—and in particular, to understand the nature of autism as a biologically based neurodevelopmental condition. We now know more about what autism *is not* than ever before. We know that it is not psychogenically produced by "refrigerator mothers," to use twentieth century psychologist Bruno Bettelheim's cringe-making phrase. We know that vaccines do not cause autism. We know that autism has a significant genetic component, with hundreds of genes and epigenetic factors involved. We know that monozygotic twins have a higher rate of concordance in the diagnosis than the concordance of dizygotic twins, but the difference between MZ and DZ twin rates of concordance is much lower than previously thought. A 2011 Stanford University study shows that MZ twins have a concordance rate of .77 and .31 for ASD.[11] ASD is thus moderately heritable, whereas in the past autism was regarded as one of the most highly heritable of psychiatric conditions. Researchers suspect numerous spontaneous, noninherited mutations of having a cumulative causal effect.[12] In rare cases, maternal exposure to certain drugs during crucial periods of fetal development contributes to autism, although toxins account for a tiny minority of cases.[13] We also know more about how to remediate some of the symptoms of autism with behavioral interventions, particularly with various forms of applied behavioral analysis (ABA).[14]

There are several major contenders for conceptualizing autism.

1. "Weak Executive Functioning" theory implicates impairments in the ability to regulate cognitive and affective function.[15] Executive functioning allows us to regulate our emotions, respond to new information and adjust our behavior accordingly, and shift attention when necessary. Broad deficits in executive functioning could explain why

so many people with a diagnosis of ASD do poorly on the Sally-Anne test even when they do not have subnormal IQ.

2. "Weak Central Coherence" theory emphasizes the tendency among those with ASD to focus on particular parts of a situation or visual field rather than grasping the entity as a whole. Thus children with ASD often focus on parts of a face but have impairments in the ability to recognize the face as a whole, and they outperform typical children on certain detail-oriented tasks and the Embedded Figures test. [16]

3. "Mindblindness" emphasizes the deficits in people with autism in the area of recognizing and responding to the emotions of others. [17] Related to this is hypothesis of a hypo-functioning amygdala as the root cause of abnormal social interactions in those with ASD. [18]

4. Most recently, "Intense World Theory" hypothesizes that atypical development of the brainstem leads to multiple deficits in the ability to process sensory information in a modulated way. In essence, this theory attempts to explain *virtually all* the symptoms of autism (including many of those not listed in the last three versions of the *DSM* but widely recognized by researchers and clinicians) as sequellae of the autistic brain's extreme overreaction to stimuli. In contrast to the Mindblindness/Hypo-functioning Amygdala theory, this account postulates a *hyper*-functioning amygdala. [19] It also attempts to account, relying as it does on a theory of atypical brain stem development, for the difficulties with fine and gross motor skill observed in people with ASD, as well as atypical sensitivities to sound, light, taste, touch, and pain.

Still, we cannot yet claim to know what autism is, let alone claim to understand what causes it. The current science of autism is still very much dynamic. Despite the present consensus that autism is not psychogenic but is biologically based and is a disorder of the brain, ASD is always diagnosed symptomatically, usually using the criteria of the *Diagnostic and Statistical Manual of Mental Disorders* (*DSM*) of the American Psychiatric Association. These criteria have evolved over time, and may continue to evolve. Like almost all of the other disorders of the *DSM*, there is no physiological test for autism. No blood test, genetic test, or brain-imaging can diagnose autism, although genetic tests often differentiate between diseases with autistic symptoms (such as Fragile X) and autism. Measurable biological phenomena (such as seizures) and behaviors such as hand-flapping and self-stimulating behavior ("stimming") are associated with autism, but none of these associated phenomena are officially diagnostic. The prevalence of autism appears to be rising, and although some of the rise in prevalence can be explained by factors such as better identification, diagnostic substitution and parental age, a surprisingly large amount of it (by one estimate, perhaps 40 percent of the increase) remains unaccounted for.[20]

Although researchers and clinicians regard autism as a biologically based disorder, autism is not identified with its underlying biology. In particular, disorders that used to be considered forms of autism (such as the degenerative disorder Rett syndrome) have been reclassified as separate disorders principally because their specific biological basis and etiology has been identified. In the case of Rett syndrome, a specific *de novo* mutation of the MECP2 gene on the X chromosome causes virtually all cases of the disease. Consequently, although it appeared in the *DSM-III* as a type of autism, the fourth incarnation of the *DSM* (*DSM-IV*) removes it and Rett syndrome will not be associated with autism in the *DSM-V*.[21] Other disorders with known chromosomal or genetic causes such as Down syndrome, Fragile X, and tuberous sclerosis may involve some "autistic features" (especially in the case of boys with Fragile X), but are not classified under the general term "autism." In other words, it appears that when autism has a clearly identified genetically based culprit, clinicians and researchers no longer classify it as a form of autism.

Given all of this, it is difficult to make the case that we know what autism is. And yet Baron-Cohen argues that we do know what it is, and that it is a version of the Male Brain. It seems a dangerous error to use the emerging scientific research about autism, when autism is poorly understood, to understand sex differences in cognition and behavior more generally. Conversely, it seems dangerous to view autism through the lens of sex differences. To do so risks distorting both our understanding of autism and our understanding of sex differences.

THE SEXUALLY DIMORPHIC MIND

Philosophers have long attributed sexual dimorphisms in cognitive, emotional, and moral traits to humans, and from the ancient philosophers all the way to the early modern period of philosophy, those dimorphisms were derogatory toward women. Aristotle claimed that all females are a natural deformity, ultimately due to their lack of sufficient heat, and their reasoning faculty is defective in that it "lacks authority." Kant was famous for denying that women had a sense of justice, and worried that they were congenitally incapable of impartiality. Hegel thought that women were incapable of philosophical thinking.[22] These early theories of sexual dimorphism of the mind did not necessarily point to the *brain* as the source of the difference.

A few male philosophers such as John Locke[23] and John Stuart Mill[24] downplayed natural differences between the sexes, as did women such as Mary Wollstonecraft and Harriet Taylor Mill, but philosophers and "natural philosophers" (the precursors of experimental scientists) continued to defend the existence of sexually dimorphic mental traits well into the twentieth century.

The modern project makes use of research on hormones, brain structure, and various forms of brain imaging—especially functional magnetic resonance imaging (fMRI) in ways not previously possible. Most recently, the human genome itself has been targeted as the source of sex difference, although the idea of "two separate genomes" has been subject to significant criticism.[25] Additionally, some (but not all) contemporary versions of the theory insist that men's and women's brains and minds are fundamentally different, but one is not better than the other. Baron-Cohen argues that neither the male brain nor the female brain is superior to the other, but that these brain differences make us more or less suited for certain occupations and activities, some of which are more socially, culturally, and economically valued than others:

> People with the female brain make the most wonderful counsellors, primary school teachers, nurses, carers, therapists, social workers, mediators, group facilitators or personnel staff. . .People with the male brain make the most wonderful scientists, engineers, mechanics, technicians, musicians, architects, electricians, plumbers, taxonomists, catalogists, bankers, toolmakers, programmers or even lawyers.[26]

There are three parts to the modern version of this project, of which Baron-Cohen's EMB thesis is one example. The first part is to show that there are real and significant sex differences in the cognitive, behavioral, and affective traits of men and women. One scientist or another has argued that the following traits are sexually dimorphic: mathematical and verbal proficiency, performance on tasks of spatial rotation, orienteering, aggression, psychopathy, mind reading and empathizing, interest in competitive sports and competition generally, rough-and-tumble play, interest in children and child care, interest in people, sex drive, sensory-seeking behavior, left-handedness, and interest in color.

The second part is to show that differences in some combination of brain structure, brain functioning, brain development, and brain chemistry can explain the alleged dimorphism, *and* that these brain differences are not themselves due to culture. This is an important qualification. Those who reject the Extreme Male Brain hypothesis can accept that there are sex differences in behavior, affect, and interests that are based in the brain, but may argue that those brain differences are themselves a function of culture. While environmental factors can influence the direction of the structure and chemistry, biology, the argument goes, is the ultimate source of the difference and can explain it.

The third part of the project is to show that there is evolutionary pressure in favor of this dimorphism that explains its existence. Evolutionary psychologists, like the sociobiologists of the 1970s and 1980s, focus on the role the natural selection might play in the development of such dimorphisms. Evolutionary arguments are usually of the form "it makes sense that…" and come after a genetically based difference between the sexes is postulated. A natural selection argument shows how a genetic difference arose. Evolutionary psychologists argue that genetic differences between the sexes have been adaptive for humans by creating a division of labor between the sexes related to their reproductive roles. This third evolutionary part is not essential to the main project of explaining the alleged sexual dimorphism in mental traits, because not every biological difference, whether it is an average difference between, say, adult height among different populations of people, or whether it is an average difference in body mass between men and women, will have served an adaptive function. Some differences are random and have no identifiable function. It could be the case that such a dimorphism, were it to be demonstrated, plays no causal role whatsoever in reproductive success, but is just an accident of nature. Nevertheless, the evolutionary component is important, because scientists often use it as supporting evidence for the first two. Baron-Cohen himself speculates that evolution has played a role in selecting for the dimorphism he ascribes to humans. For example, the weaker empathizing that Baron-Cohen says is characteristic of men might be useful because it "makes it easier for you to hit or hurt someone, or in less extreme ways, simply to push them aside in competition, or abandon them when they are no longer useful to you."[27] On the other hand, stronger empathizing might be beneficial to women because "a high-empathizing female, engaged in childcare, is better equipped to create a community of friends who could watch over her children when she is unable to keep an eye on them all of the time."[28]

The thesis of the EMB fits squarely into a larger group of theories in the history of science. An interesting asymmetry in his theory is the focus on the Male Brain and its "Extreme" version, and not the Female Brain and its "Extreme" version. Why does Baron-Cohen focus on the Extreme Male Brain, and not the Extreme Female Brain? This asymmetry occurs because Baron-Cohen claims that ASD should be understood as an extreme amplification of typically male mental traits, with accompanying deficits in typically female traits. However, there is no developmental disorder identified with the amplification of any "typically female" traits—e.g., being very good at identifying and responding to emotions. Bernard Crespi and Christopher Badcock have defended the idea of schizophrenia as "The Extreme Female Brain" in a recent lengthy paper with commentary in *Brain and Behavioral Sciences*.[29] Badcock has turned the idea into a full-length monograph.[30] In *The Essential Difference*, Baron-Cohen seems to dismiss the idea of an extreme female brain.[31] However, more recently he seems to have changed his mind and has "postulated" an Extreme Female Brain; as of this writing he has not yet discussed it or defended it at any length.[32]

THE MALE BRAIN AND THE EXTREME MALE BRAIN

Which do we understand first? The Extreme Male Brain or the Male Brain? In places, Baron-Cohen seems to understand typical (i.e., nonautistic) human populations through the lens of autism. Thus it is useful to look at his conceptualization of autism first. He understands ASD as first and foremost, a failure of mind reading: a kind of "mindblindness" in which people have deficits in the ability to accurately ascribe and interpret the beliefs, emotions, and actions of others. These deficits lead to diminished ability to interact with others in normal (i.e., socially expected) ways. Initially, the focus was on the inability of children with autism to pass the famous Sally-Anne test, which he and many others regard as a test of the subjects' ability to accurately identify beliefs in others.[33] Later, the affective response to the mental states of others became the focus: people with autism do not merely have difficulties in understanding other minds, but they also do not have typical responses to the emotions they do identify. They are often less distressed or activated by others who are in distress, even when they *understand that* the other person is in distress.[34] He calls this combination of mindblindness and atypical responsiveness "hypo-empathizing."[35] Empathizing is "the drive to identify another person's emotions and thoughts and to respond to these with an appropriate emotion."[36] This drive, he argues, is underdeveloped in people with ASD.

But autism involves other features as a well as impairments of social interaction. The three main or "core" features presently identified with autistic disorders, according to the *DSM-IV*, are (1) impairments in social interaction, (2) impairments in communication, and (3) restricted interests and stereotyped or repetitive behavior. (The WHO has a slightly different set of criteria, but the *DSM-IV* is more widely used in North America.) However, the diagnostic criteria in the *DSM-IV* are highly disjunctive.[37] There is no simple set of necessary and sufficient conditions for receiving an autism diagnosis. The result is that many people with an autism diagnosis look very different from one another.

"Mindblindness" is Baron-Cohen's way of conceptualizing the impaired ability of people with ASD to understand and respond to what other people are doing and thinking: ASD people have an impaired or absent (or, some might argue, simply *delayed*) "theory of mind." Mindblindness with atypical (dampened) responsiveness to others' mental states conceptualizes the first diagnostic criterion: impaired social interaction. But what about the other two criteria? The second criterion, having to do with communication, is quite variable and not always pronounced in people with ASD. People with Asperger's do not have a delay in the acquisition of functional language, although sometimes they demonstrate atypical inflection and prosody. Yet those with Asperger's are part of the group of those with ASD, and Baron-Cohen includes them in his theorizing about the Extreme Male Brain. Indeed, they seem to be his *paradigmatic* cases of The Extreme Male Brain. Other people with ASD may have no functional language, and still others can communicate only through a keyboard or via pointing. However, the third criterion includes the restricted interests, and in many cases, the restricted interests of those with ASD involve so-called "static" (as opposed to dynamic) systems: systems of letters or numbers, train tables, actual trains. People—human beings—are Baron-Cohen's paradigmatic example of dynamic systems, because people are constantly changing in response to their inputs, and people cannot be described as functions with unique outputs for a given input. Electrical switches and mathematical formulas are his examples of static, lawful systems.[38] Baron-Cohen says that "systemizing is a new concept," and he is indeed using the term in an unusual way. A system in his sense is "something that takes inputs and deliver outputs [sic]."[39] In particular, systems with "predictive value" are particularly attractive to systemizers: systemizers prefer lawful systems with less variability in the possible outputs given inputs. The minds of people are not, he says, systems in this sense. People do not behave in a law-like, predictable manner; consequently, "[t]his is why systemizing the social world is of little predictive value."[40]

This last diagnostic criterion is the basis of Baron-Cohen's claim that ASD involves hypersystemizing, whereas the first criterion is the basis of his claim that ASD involves deficits in empathizing: the hypoempathizer also tends, he argues, to be a hypersystemizer, focusing on predictable, lawful systems. So Baron-Cohen's hypothesis of the Extreme Male Brain is a modification of his earlier hypothesis that ASD is essentially mindblindness: ASD is mindblindness *plus* inappropriate responsiveness *plus* "system-awareness:" hypoempathizing with hypersystemizing.

Baron-Cohen has argued that we should think of autism spectrum disorders as an extreme form of the kind of brain that men tend to have: a brain that "systemizes" well—or at least a lot—(hence the S-type) but does not "empathize" well—or at least a lot (hence the E-type). People with S-type "male" brains are not attracted to the world of people, but they are interested in machines, mathematics, and scientific, law-like systems. People with E-type or "female" brains are interested in people; they are prone to think about the minds of other people, and they tend to respond more appropriately to them. They find it rewarding to engage with other people. In general, he argues, women tend toward more E and less S, and men tend towards more S and less E, although most people have a more or less "balanced" brain, somewhere in the middle of the bell curve. Furthermore, Baron-Cohen postulates that those who hypersystemize tend to also be hypoempathizers: in other words, S and E are inversely correlated.[41] The combination of these two features in people with autism is not, he argues, a coincidence, but they are causally linked. Those who have this combination in an extreme enough form may be diagnosed with ASD.

However, Baron-Cohen also argues that his account of the nature of ASD does not just explain atypical or disordered brains, but also explains the distribution of E and S brains among the general population. And this in turn explains why we see gender divisions in social structures: on average, men are better at certain things than are women, and on average, women are better at certain things than are men. Baron-Cohen is emphatic that not all women are pure E and not all men are pure S, and that one's sex cannot serve as a certain predictor of one's brain type: some men have "the female brain" and some women have "the male brain." Rather, he argues that the *average differences* in the brains of men and women mean that women tend to be better empathizers and men tend to be better systemizers, although there is a normal distribution for both men and women of both of these traits. So some men are poor systemizers and strong empathizers, and some women are strong systemizers and poor empathizers. This, he argues, can explain the gendered division of labor in our culture, including the gendered division within family structures and the workplace. It can even explain our choice of toys and hobbies. He points out that he knows some women who are very good with computers and that he knows some men who are very nurturing and caring, and that we should not discriminate against women who want to engage in S-type activities or against men who want to engage in E-type activities. Being male does not automatically guarantee strong systemizing, and being female does not guarantee strong empathizing.[42] Nevertheless, there is a strong tendency of men to be good at what he calls systemizing and poorer than women at empathizing, and a strong tendency of women to empathize well but not systemize so well, and these differences in patterns of thought, emotion, and interest can be explained by biology. Furthermore, he argues that because of this, we should not be surprised when women are not represented proportionately to their numbers in systemizing professions, such as mathematics, computing, engineering, accounting, and the sciences. In fact, he argues that "we should not expect the sex ratio in occupations such as math or physics to ever be 50-50 if we leave the workplace to simply reflect the numbers of applicants who are drawn to such fields."[43]

Baron-Cohen appears to use the case of autism as *evidence* for the Male Brain/Female Brain dichotomy, because autism, in all of its various forms, is much more common among males. There is broad consensus that the ratio of boys to girls with autism is 4:1, and the ratio of boys to girls with Asperger's syndrome is 10:1. People with Asperger's, by definition, have normal IQs and do not have significant delays in language acquisition. This alone has led some to conclude that male brains are different from female brains because of their proneness to certain pathologies; but Baron-Cohen wants to argue that "non-pathological" (i.e., typical) humans without an ASD diagnosis show the same pattern of gendered traits. Hence the Extreme Male Brain theory appears to be the evidence for the Male Brain Theory.

AN ESSENTIAL DIFFERENCE?

The title of Baron-Cohen's popular book on this topic is *The Essential Difference.* However, what does he mean when he says that this difference between men and women is essential? Baron-Cohen does not explain what he means by "essential" in his book, despite the title. He does not use the word very much beyond the first page. So what could he mean? Baron-Cohen's book is about men and women as kinds of people and the characteristics of those kinds of people. Philosophers often talk about essences with respect to kinds. In this sense, an essence is the set of necessary and sufficient conditions that makes something an example of a kind of thing. For example, one might argue à la Kripke that the essence of gold is its atomic number 79, and the essence of water is its chemical structure H_2O.[44] Being malleable and yellow are not part of the essence of gold; something could have these features and not be gold. Something that is wet, clear, and potable is not necessarily water; it requires the structure H_2O. However, Baron-Cohen never argues that there is an essence, in the sense of necessary and sufficient conditions, of the male brain and he never argues that there is an essence of the female brain. He instead argues that "female brains are predominantly hard-wired for empathy. The male brain is predominantly hard-wired for understanding and building systems."[45] Elsewhere he amplifies this claim: he is talking about average differences between men and women. These are not essential differences.

What about individual essences? "Uniessentialist" views make claims about the unity and identity of individuals, rather than kinds.[46] Maybe having an S-type brain makes a person who he is or who she is, so that person would not be the same person if he or she did not have an S-type brain. Perhaps a person who had an S-type brain would cease to be the same individual if, through some chemical or structural change in his or her brain, that individual no longer had S as a characteristic. Similarly for the E-type brain. We can imagine how a person might argue that if she did not have autism, she would not be the same individual; she would be somebody else, even though she would be the same person if she were an inch taller or if she hated the taste of maple syrup. However, Baron-Cohen never discusses essentialism. He never makes any claims about whether I would still be me if I stopped being a systemizer or an empathizer, and he never discusses individual essentialism.

Instead, Baron-Cohen seems to be claiming that the differences between male and female brains are basic and fundamental with great significance. But in what way? He is making at least three claims. First, he argues that the differences between male and female brains are biologically based in nature. This might seem obvious—how could brains differ in some way *other* than biologically?—but it is not. For one thing, *environments* can cause biological differences in organisms. Some of these biological differences are then permanent. Environmental exposure to certain chemicals that mimic estrogens, for example, can cause physiological changes in animals—including a change in the animal's sex. Water temperature determines the sex of some amphibians under certain conditions, although the primary mechanism for sex determination is genetic.[47] Recently, it was discovered that female sharks, which normally reproduce sexually, can begin to reproduce parthenogenically when kept in tanks isolated from male sharks.[48] Such a shark is biologically parthenogenic, but its sexual features are not based in the nature or essence of the animal in the sense that Baron-Cohen seems to be using. There is no "essential difference" between the parthenogenic female shark and the non-parthenogenic female one; they are morphologically similar at the start, but dissimilar environment triggers the change in biology.

One might argue that men and women have different brains (in Baron-Cohen's sense) because of the environments they are exposed to. Smiling at girls more, for example, might change their brains to make them more E, and in turn cause behavioral differences. But Baron-Cohen appears to be arguing that in typical developmental environments, *including fetal environments*, male and female brains develop differently. They do so because of the different hormones that are found in the uterine environment. In particular, he is claiming that natural variations in fetal testosterone produce average differences in mental traits between the sexes; and, since on average males are exposed to more fetal testosterone than are females, males have more of the mental traits associated with fetal testosterone. In short, he is arguing that male brains and female brains are *organized* differently because of their naturally different development. This organization is not temporary, but permanent, and has lasting consequences for behavior. Most crucially, occurring *in utero*, it is not subject to the influences of culture. While Baron-Cohen claims that these differences are natural and biological, he does not claim that they are immutable, the way having an X and a Y chromosome throughout one's cells is immutable. It might be possible to eliminate or reduce the differences between female and male brains and the associate behavioral differences, either through behavioral interventions or through biomedical treatments.

Second, he also argues that these differences, while average, have significant and measurable behavioral implications. Higher levels of fetal testosterone, more typically found in the amniotic fluid surrounding male fetuses, predict a more S-type brain, and lower levels surrounding female fetuses predict a more E-type brain. He makes the extremely controversial claim that we can observe differences between female and male babies in the very first hours of life: "from birth, females look longer at faces, particularly at people's eyes, whereas males are more likely to look at inanimate objects."[49] The behavioral differences, he argues, are significant and measurable: both statistically significant (in the sense that the observed differences are not produced by chance) and large. They are not miniscule, insignificant differences between male and female brains.

Third, he argues that not only is the sex difference significant, but also that it is important. You might think that this is a distinction without a difference. But when something is significant, it is more than just a little bit; it is not trivial; it is substantial. So, for example, men tend to be significantly hairier than women, on average. However, one might argue that while there is a significant sex difference in average hirsutism, it is not an important difference; it doesn't matter much in the sense that it does not have important consequences. Baron-Cohen is claiming that the difference here is important in the sense that it has substantial consequences for the functioning of males and females. The preferences, hobbies, habits, and social roles of women are as different as they are because of these significant differences in biology. (It can, he argues, explain the small number of women in certain fields of science.) Moreover, the average brain differences can explain pathologies such as ASD, which are sexually dimorphic in their prevalence. When so many more males have ASD, and ASD is a significant impairment, this is an undeniably important difference.

Thus Baron-Cohen argues that certain differences between male and female minds are biologically based, measurably significant, and highly relevant to our functioning. This is what he appears to mean by "the essential difference." Understood this way, however, one might object that this still does not seem to be "the essential difference" in the ordinary sense of a single trait that makes males the kinds of beings that they are and females the kinds of beings that they are—a Kripkean essence. Calling something "the essential difference" seems much stronger than the interpretation I have offered here. However, because Baron-Cohen never explicitly states that E and S are the single most important traits of men and women, or that E and S are *definitive* or *constitutive* of men of women, the use of the term 'essence' is misleading. The E/S theory is not really a claim about essences. The E/S theory is actually a claim about average differences between the sexes that are said to be biologically based, significant, and have important consequences.

FETAL T AND THE COMMON CAUSE ARGUMENT

How is the "essential difference" or E/S theory relevant to autism? What is the relationship between the claimed average differences in male and female brains, the claimed average differences in the behavior and functioning of typical males and females, and the differential prevalence of ASD among males and females? What causal claim is he making? At times he seems to argue that average behavioral differences between the sexes can "help us to understand" autism.[50] This sounds as if basic sex differences in the brain explain why autistic people are the way they are, and why there are more males with autism than females. At other times, he seems to argue that facts about ASD help to explain why typically functioning men and women are as different as they are. Men are from Mars and women are from Venus, we might say, because men are a little bit autistic. Misunderstandings occur when we don't recognize that there are average differences between what men are good at and find interesting (systems) and what women are good at and find interesting (people). Men do not interpret and respond to emotions the same way that women do, and they enjoy machinery more. And we should therefore not be surprised when the systemizing found in autism is expressed in the general male population as greater mathematical ability: hence the disproportionate number of men in the STEM (Science, Technology, Engineering, and Mathematics) disciplines, particularly mathematics, physics, and engineering.[51] Nor should we be surprised that women, who are less likely to be systemizers and more likely to read and respond to people's emotions appropriately, are found in the caring and helping professions, such as teaching and nursing.

Baron-Cohen's main argument appears to be as follows. Sex differences in mental traits and the symptoms of ASD are both the result of a *common cause*: differences in the brain that begin *in utero*, triggered by fetal testosterone. Brain differences can explain observable behavioral and psychological differences between typically functioning men and women. At the same time, he argues, they also explain the particular symptoms of ASD, the higher prevalence of ASD among boys and men, and the correspondingly lower rate of ASD in girls and women.[52] More men are autistic and more men are mathematicians and engineers for the same reason: fetal testosterone.

Schematically, the argument can be represented as follows:

1. Fetal testosterone is causally relevant to the symptoms of ASD.
2. Fetal testosterone is causally relevant to certain mental traits: higher systemizing and lower empathizing.
3. Both ASD and the mental traits of higher systemizing and lower empathizing are more common in males: they are "male-prevalent."

4. ASD is simply a more intense version of the male-typical mental traits produced by fetal testosterone: they are part of the same broader phenotype.
5. If one set of symptoms is simply a more intense version of another set of symptoms, and they are produced by the same cause, then they are the same phenomenon.
6. ASD = EMB: Therefore, ASD should be understood as the Extreme Male Brain.

This argument asserts that two phenomena *A* and *B* have a common cause; that both *A* and *B* are male prevalent; and that *A* and *B* are different intensities of that same phenomenon. It concludes that because of this, *A* and *B* should be understood as essentially the same thing. The assertion of a common cause, male prevalence, and the interpretation of mental traits as autistic traits are jointly used to make the case that ASD and the male brain are essentially the same thing. As I shall argue below, this argument has a valid structure, although male prevalence should not be used as evidence for EMB. Rather, if EMB is true, it would be an explanation of male prevalence—male prevalence does not itself support EMB.

This raises the question of *causal mechanism*: how does fetal testosterone produce average sex differences and which ones? How could it contribute to the developmental disorders of autism? Most scientists accept that sex hormones, including testosterone, estrogen, and estradiol, have two different kinds of impact on mammalian tissue: organizational and activational. Hormones organize tissue when they create different morphologies (e.g., when they play a role in the development of testes in typically developing boys). They play an activational role when they trigger certain events, such as puberty.[53] Baron-Cohen argues that fetal testosterone is particularly important because it *organizes* the brain early on *in utero*, in addition to activating body and brain changes later in life. Estrogens also play a role in both organization and activation, but as Baron-Cohen notes, this class of sex hormones makes the activational/organizational distinction problematic, because the organizational effects of estrogen continue for a very long time.[54] More importantly, higher levels of testosterone in the developing fetus are, he argues, correlated with more "male typical patterns of behavior."[55] Some of this behavior, he claims, is the *same behavior* seen in autistic people where it is present to a greater degree. Since ASD is a biologically based developmental disorder that by definition develops before the age of three, Baron-Cohen speculates that the same mechanism—fetal testosterone—that produces sex differences in behavior also produces autistic traits.

Why are sexually dimorphic behavioral features and autism not possibly a deficiency or preponderance of estrogen or estradiol? After all, both males and females manufacture androgens such as testosterone as well as the other sex hormones. Testosterone is not the only hormone that organizes or activates. Briefly, Baron-Cohen finds no evidence that average differences in fetal estrogen correlate with either sexually dimorphic mental traits or ASD, or any other developmental disorders. Boys typically experience a surge in testosterone *in utero* that rises briefly at birth and then dissipates until puberty. Girls do experience a surge in estradiol shortly after birth, and it remains relatively high. Baron-Cohen says "there is little evidence for an effect of estrogen on rough-and-tumble play or reproductive behaviors," while there is more evidence that testosterone affects the expression of these behaviors. Even in a case where the placenta produces a very high level of estrogen, this estrogen is bound to alphafetoprotein in fetal blood, making it impossible for the estrogen to enter the fetal brain;[56] AFP disappears at birth. In addition, in the case of males born with no androgen receptors (Complete Androgen Insensitivity syndrome, or CAIS), their appearance is phenotypically female; their physical appearance, especially in the case of a complete lack of receptors, is female. So it appears that testosterone alone can play a role in masculinizing both phenotypic presentation as well as behavior.[57] If there is a probable common cause among the sex hormones for autism and sexually dimorphic behavior, testosterone appears to be the most likely suspect.[58]

Baron-Cohen does not claim to know the actual mechanism through which fetal testosterone produces dimorphic effects on the brain. So far, he has relied on correlational studies involving amniotic fluid, cord blood at birth, and salivary or serum levels of testosterone in adults.[59] His conceptualization of autism as "extreme male brain" was first published in 1997, when not many correlational studies were available. By 2004, he was able to use eleven correlational studies to discuss the effects of testosterone on behavior, and the results of those studies were quite mixed, as I shall discuss below.

There are some serious problems with this hypothesis. Baron-Cohen cites no studies or data correlating fetal testosterone and *autism*. Further research in this area is ongoing. Neuroscientist Lisa Eliot suggests the opposite conclusion, arguing that "if autism is caused by extreme testosterone exposure, then you would expect to find that boys with the highest prenatal testosterone levels are the ones who end up being diagnosed with the disorder, while boys with lower prenatal testosterone exposure would be diagnosed much less often. This is not the case."[60] Another problem involves the case of those who lack androgen receptors. One would expect to find that those XY persons with CAIS, who, due to a genetic mutation on the X chromosome lack receptors for testosterone entirely, would never have ASD. However, *no one has demonstrated or even reported this*. This is perhaps in part because CAIS is relatively rare, making the prevalence of autism in that population more difficult to study reliably.[61] In other words, there is no research showing that higher fetal testosterone levels *in either sex* increases the probability of the subject receiving a diagnosis of autism. The causal claim that fetal testosterone is causally relevant to autism or ASD is speculative in the absence of this research.[62]

Moreover, even in "idiopathic autism" (i.e., autistic features not caused by a known inherited genetic disorder such as Fragile X or tuberous sclerosis, or some of the genes on chromosomes 15, 22, and 7) many genes have been implicated.[63] In particular, *de novo* mutations seem to contribute to a significant percentage of the cases of autism—upwards of 10 percent.[64] These mutations (like the mutation responsible for Rett syndrome) are not inherited but are spontaneous germ-line anomalies. Since specific genetic anomalies, inherited or not, raise the probability of receiving a diagnosis of autism, it appears that fetal testosterone could at best be a *partial cause* of ASD. Baron-Cohen himself has suggested that the higher levels of fT (fetal testosterone) that produce autism have an inherited genetic basis.[65] Baron-Cohen does not dismiss the heritable genetic component, although he acknowledges it mostly by pointing out that parents and grandparents of those with ASD are more likely to have "autistic traits," rather than pointing to the specific genetic mutations that have been implicated to date.[66] Given the research implicating such a wide range of *de novo* mutations, is it possible that fT is implicated in all of most of ASD produced by these? Whether a genetic factor is inherited or not may ultimately become diagnostically significant, if not dispositive. In fact, it appears that when autism is associated with an inherited genetic disorder (such as Fragile X) and or a *de novo* mutation (such as Rett syndrome), individuals with that disorder are "undiagnosed" with autism (or, more accurately, reclassified according to "diagnostic substitution" and not regarded as appropriate research subjects for studies of autism proper. By such diagnostic substitution, individuals are "sub-typed" out of the class of people with ASD. Indeed, if this practice continues, the class of persons with ASD may be typed more finely until either the disorder no longer exists, or exists exclusively of a subgroup of individuals with *de novo* mutations and some other triggering factor.).

Nevertheless, it is possible that we may find evidence to support the claim that higher levels of fT will be at least one factor in some cases of autism. If so, will that vindicate the Common Cause Argument? As I aim to show, even a positive correlation between fetal testosterone and ASD diagnoses does not justify interpreting autism as the Extreme Male Brain.

IS THE COMMON CAUSE ARGUMENT A GOOD ARGUMENT?

Let's look at the argument in detail.

Premise 1: Fetal Testosterone and Autism

As I mentioned above, the first premise of this argument lacks support. There is no evidence *as of yet* that higher levels of fetal testosterone (fT) play a causal role in the development of autism. Baron-Cohen points out that there is some evidence that 2D:4D digit ratio (the ratio of the length of the second finger to the length of the fourth finger) is on average lower in males and is lower in people with autism than it is in (normal) females. Citing his own study on prenatal hormones and 2D:4D, he (controversially) postulates that the ratio of fT to fetal estrogen is negatively associated with this ratio. Yet this is not direct evidence that fT causes either male-typical 2D:4D or autism. There could, for example, be a confounding factor that produces both higher ratios of fT/fE and lower 2D:4D.

However, future research, such as that being conducted in the Longitudal Foetal Testosterone Project (at the Autism Research Centre, University of Cambridge), could vindicate such a causal role, even if only in a subgroup of people with ASD. So let us provisionally grant that Premise 1 might be true. If it is true, however, we would need to know whether all or some of the symptoms of autism are produced by higher levels of fT. In this case, for the purposes of confirming Baron-Cohen's theory, *we would still need to know that the specific traits of hypersystemizing and hypoempathizing said to be characteristic of ASD are generated by higher levels of fT—not simply the diagnosis itself.* Premise 1 has not been established.

Premise 2: Fetal Testosterone and Sexually Dimorphic Mental Traits

But what about the second step of the argument: that fT is responsible for male-typical mental traits? Most of Baron-Cohen's research seems to be aimed at providing evidence for *this* hypothesis, not Premise 1, which is about ASD in particular. Do higher levels of fT correlate with more male-typical mental traits—and, more importantly, are these mental traits weaker versions of those identified in ASD?

Baron-Cohen and others have argued that higher levels of testosterone in amniotic fluid are a good proxy for fT, and that amniotic fluid levels do indeed correlate with male-typical behavior. Cordelia Fine has pointed out that, while this is possible, we do not actually know this.[67] Baron-Cohen denounces Fine as an "extreme social determinis[t]" and defends this claim by pointing out that actually trying to extract blood from fetuses to directly test their testosterone levels would be unethical.[68] However, Fine did not suggest that Baron-Cohen should be faulted for failing to conduct such research; she only argues that his claim that amniotic fluid levels are a good proxy for fT is really just a guess. Rebecca Jordan-Young makes an even broader critique of the research associating fT and future gender behavior.[69] The relationship between the two is simply not well understood. In the absence of further evidence, this claim is only a conjecture, not a confirmed hypothesis. However, let us also provisionally grant that amniotic fluid levels are indeed a good proxy; we may, in the future, devise an ethical way of substantiating this claim.

Yet many questions arise from this premise; I cannot address all of them here. First, how strong is the evidence for the existence of sexually dimorphic traits identified by Baron-Cohen *et al.*? Second, how significant are the average differences identified? Third, how strong is the correlation between amniotic fluid testosterone and the average differences? Fourth, should such differences be understood as differences in systemizing and empathizing? Fifth, are the sexually dimorphic traits most reliably identified plausibly construed as weaker expressions of autistic traits?

The biggest problem with this premise in his argument, itself the conclusion of a very complicated argument, is this: the evidence that Baron-Cohen presents for sexually dimorphic mental traits is not evidence for the S/E dimorphism that is central to Baron-Cohen's argument. Stating the claim in general terms such as "sexual differences in cognition" masks the question of whether the evidence that supports sexually dimorphic traits is evidence for sexually dimorphic performances on tests of S and E. And it does not appear to do so.

Take the very first study that was said to show such dimorphism at a very early age: the test conducted by Baron-Cohen's graduate student. This study is rife with problems. The sample size was rather small at 102. The study was conducted over ten years ago, yet it has never been replicated. There is a substantial chance that the researchers knew the sex of at least some of the test subjects, and on top of it all, newborn infants have very poor eyesight,[70] making it implausible that the newborns of either sex could see the face *as a face*. But even worse, it does not seem to show that boys tend to systemize or that girls are more empathetic, on average. Looking at geometric shapes is not a tendency to systemize. And looking at faces is not empathizing. Even the claim that girls are (somewhat) more interested in faces is suspect, since girls could be more neurologically developed (Baron-Cohen and many others insist that they are) and therefore more able to recognize faces and find them salient. It shows, at most, a slight tendency among girls to look at faces sooner after birth than do boys. This is simply not anything like the empathizing interest and skill said to be a typically female trait. And all of this assumes that the experiment could be repeated without the problems and with the same results—a very big "if" indeed.

Much of Baron-Cohen's research purports to show that fT positively correlates with "autistic traits."[71] The experiment just cited does not try to show this; it only tries to show an innate average difference between the sexes in a behavioral/mental trait: the amount of time spent looking at a representation of a face, rather than a geometric shape, at a specific postnatal age. Should the above results be replicated, it would still not tell us *why* girls looked at the representation of a face slightly longer. Even if future research shows that fT levels are negatively correlated with looking at such representations of faces, it will not show that fT is correlated with autistic traits, because the above experiment does not show that such behavior is an autistic trait. Yet Baron-Cohen cites this study as an example of innate differences in empathizing behavior—a female-typical mental trait.[72]

In sum, there is not very strong evidence that there are significant dimorphisms in the specific cognitive and affective traits targeted by Baron-Cohen (and others), and in any case, those traits do not seem to amount to differences in systemizing and empathizing.

Premise 3: Male Prevalence of ASD

Interestingly enough, this claim gives the most intuitive plausibility to the EMB hypothesis, and yet turns out to be the least relevant. It is true that diagnosis rates of autism are significantly higher for males than for females at all levels of impairment, but especially for those with "high-functioning autism" or Asperger's. However, this does not provide support for the idea that autism is an extreme form of the typically male brain. There are many disorders that emerge early in development that are sexually dimorphic. The best known of these are X-linked disorders found in males, such as Fragile X and hemophilia. However, there are many other disorders that are sexually dimorphic and not linked to either sex chromosome, some of which are more prevalent in women (e.g., Graves Disease and many autoimmune disorders), and some of which are more prevalent in men. There is no reason to think that we should use sexually dimorphic prevalence as the basis for giving a disease a special status as particularly characteristic of or "essentially" male or female. So why is ASD's male prevalence not only often cited as evidence for EMB, but is usually offered as the *first* piece of evidence?[73] The answer is that male prevalence should not be offered as evidence for EMB, because it is not evidence. Rather, male prevalence is something that *requires* explanation. While he appears at times to think otherwise, the most charitable interpretation of Baron-Cohen's line of reasoning is that male prevalence is explained by the theory of autism as encompassing both clinical and nonclinical populations as expressions of a broader phenotype: the phenotype of the Male Brain, characterized by hypersystemizing and hypoempathizing. "Male prevalence" belongs below the conclusion line, not above it. Indeed, in his most recent writing, Baron-Cohen has offered EMB as the most plausible *explanation* of male prevalence.[74] The other candidates he considers are *de novo* mutations on the X chromosome as well as mutations on the SRY region of the Y chromosome. Male prevalence does call out for explanation. It is misleading to use it rhetorically as evidence that EMB is true. EMB can only explain male prevalence if EMB is true.

Premise 4: ASD and Male-Typical Traits Are Part of the Same Broad Phenotype

If Premise 4 is correct, it would help to explain male prevalence (Premise 3). The problem, however, is that it is hard to see how, on the basis of evidence offered by Baron-Cohen and others, Premise 4 is actually correct. There are several reasons to doubt that it is.

First and probably most fundamentally, there is no single accepted or even dominant theory as to what autism is. There is substantial disagreement as to how to conceptualize ASD, despite the relatively clear diagnostic criteria of the *DSM-V*. Many symptoms, such as extreme sensitivity to noise or other sensory inputs (especially touch), repetitive behaviors (such as hand-flapping and "stimming"), and seizures are not listed as "core" diagnostic symptoms, despite their pronounced co-occurrence with other autistic symptoms. Many people with ASD are mentally retarded (possibly as many as 50 percent), and yet the EMB pays no attention to this, focusing as it does on people with Asperger's who by definition have normal or above-normal IQs. EMB focuses on just two purported symptoms: hypersystemizing (which Baron-Cohen interprets as a version of the "restricted interests" criterion) and hypoempathizing (which Baron-Cohen interprets as the basis of the "impairments of social communication" criterion). But should we see autism as high S, low E?

There are other major accounts attempting to characterize the major or "core" deficits of autism. Executive functioning, central coherence, mind-blindness, and "Intense-World" theory all propose a fundamental way to understand the disorder. Like Baron-Cohen's account, each is brain-based, neurodevelopmental, and attempts to account for the core symptoms of autism. Intense World theory also proposes to account for common but "non-core" symptoms. Furthermore, each is grounded in brain and behavior research: observation and brain imaging of live human subjects, *post mortem* brain tissue samples from those with autism (although there are not large amounts of tissue from ASD subjects available), and research on rats, mice, and monkeys.

The heterogeneity of autism and its syndromic presentation has defied efforts to identify a single mechanism or set of mechanisms for onset and development. As Geschwind puts it, because of this heterogeneity in presentation, "it is not surprising that no unifying structural or neuropathological features have been conclusively identified."[75] In other words, no one can credibly say that we know what autism is, and we do not yet have a candidate for a major causal mechanism for its development. We cannot say that we really know *what the phenotype for autism is*. Therefore we cannot claim that autism is at the extreme end of the phenotype, and that typical males fall closer to that end of the phenotype than do typical females.

Premise 5: The Sameness Condition

Under what conditions can we say that *A* and *B* are the same thing? If *A* and *B* do not share all of the same properties, they are clearly not identical. However, under certain conditions, we might say that *A* and *B* are different versions or expressions of the same thing. The word "expression" is misleading, because it suggests that there is unique chromosomal or genetic cause of autism diagnoses and that different genetic factors (e.g., different numbers of repeats or deletions on a chromosome, or epigenetic factors) would explain the differences between *A* and *B*. No one, certainly not Baron-Cohen, makes this argument. In this case, in order to defend the Sameness Condition Baron-Cohen must be arguing that the symptoms of ASD are simply more intense versions of typically male traits. The concept of color saturation provides a good analogy here. Two colors can be the same, in the sense that we would all agree that they are the same color, respond to them as "red," and perhaps the measurable wavelength of the light would show that they are both predominantly the same (e.g., 650 nanometers). However, one may be more saturated than another, in that less of the light reflected off of the object would be 650 nanometers; that wavelength would be less dominant in a less saturated sample of the color. Yet we say they are the *same hue*.

In the case of a mental trait, we might consider the ability to perceive sound. A person might be completely unable to perceive sound audibly (although able to feel vibrations), and another might be unable to perceive sounds unless they are very loud. Another might be able to hear within a normal range for humans, except when there is a lot of background noise, making it difficult to listen to a conversation in a crowded room. Still another might be able to detect lower-frequency sound waves, but not high-frequency sound. Some people are deaf in one ear, but not both. All of these perceivers might be said to *share the condition of deafness*.

Notice that the condition of deafness does not depend upon a common cause. One might be deaf because of a congenital condition, because of an inherited condition, or because of trauma to part of the brain or inner ear. One might become deaf as a result of repeated exposure to loud noises or simply because of old age. What deaf people share is a functional deficit in the capacity of hearing. The profoundly deaf and the slightly deaf share the same condition, but to different degrees.

On the face of it, the condition of deafness would seem to support the general version of the Sameness Condition. However, classifying all of the above disorders as the same disorder could be misleading. Someone who cannot hear because of a brain tumor may lack functional hearing, but it is unclear that it is correct to say that such a person has the *same condition* as someone who lost her hearing due to a high fever in early childhood, even if the prescribed remediations were exactly the same. Thus it is unclear that symptoms alone would allow us to say that *A* and *B* are the same condition.

Two such people might have much in common. Yet it is not at all clear that they "have the same thing," in the way that two people with Down syndrome have the same thing: three copies of chromosome 21, rather than the typical two copies.[76]

Even two people with Down syndrome might be said to not share the "same thing," in that some people with Down syndrome do not have a trisomy throughout their entire genome (mosaicism), and some people with Down syndrome have a partial duplication of chromosome 21, or a translocation of part of a chromosome.

What about the "common cause" implicit in the Sameness Condition? Must the symptoms be more or less intense versions of each other *and* have the same cause, as in the case of Down syndrome? This seems too strong. If one person becomes deaf because an early trauma to part of the ear, and another becomes deaf due to genetic causes, they are still both considered deaf. Similarly, if one person has ASD produced by, say, exposure to valproic acid, and another has ASD clearly not produced by exposure to any toxin *in utero*, they still share a diagnosis of ASD.

The Sameness Condition seems, as a general rule, too strong. Diseases are usually understood functionally, often without an established etiology. However, even if some features of autism seem like "darker hues" of some stereotypical male behaviors, that doesn't mean that they *do* have a common cause. We cannot assume without better arguments that the S/E paradigm is useful for understanding the etiology of autism. If autism and male-typical mental traits have a common cause, that would not show that they are the same thing. Similarly, if ASD and male-typical mental traits are different shades of the same hue, establishing a common cause is not necessary. However, neither the claim of a common cause, nor the claim that ASD and male-typical mental traits are different intensities of the same phenomenon, has been established. The main problem is not the common cause, but the issue of whether male-typical mental traits are well understood, and whether they are sufficiently similar to autistic traits so that we can see them as different shades of the same phenomenon. I do not think this has been established.

CONCLUSION: WHY EMB NOW?

From all of this I conclude that there is no sound basis for regarding autism as a "male" disease, or as a form of an Extreme Male Brain. It is male-prevalent, but so are many other diseases. The symptoms and causal mechanisms that lead to a diagnosis of ASD are heterogeneous and still poorly understood. In addition, the average differences between male and female brains, and average differences in the cognitive and affective traits in the typical population simply do not clearly line up with differences between those with ASD and those without. As one group of researchers puts it, "The autistic brain functions differently, sometimes more like men, sometimes more like women, but we should consider that it might actually function in its own unique way."[77]

So how is it the EMB has come to be so widely referenced and enthusiastically endorsed, especially by researchers and lay people *outside* of the field of autism research? First, developing brain science has led us to become more confident that we can understand not only what the brain looks like, but also how it works, and how it is the source of our behavior, both in clinical and nonclinical populations. Autism is known to be a brain-based developmental disorder, and autism research is rapidly expanding as well as one of the more intensively funded areas of research. Second, popular books about sex differences, from John Gray's *Men Are from Mars, Women Are from Venus* to Louanne Brizendine's *The Female Brain*, claim to identify significant biologically based differences in the behavior, interests, and abilities of men and women. Given the male prevalence of ASD, Baron-Cohen was able to forcefully articulate his theory in ways that resonate with popular understandings of sex differences, making EMB a widely accepted understanding of autism. EMB is not really a scientific hypothesis, so much a piece of philosophy that emerged out of scientific research, and it capitalizes on popular theories of sex difference.

However, the influence goes both ways. EMB supports a social agenda that is quietist about the lack of parity in the STEM professions. It tells us not only that male prevalence in autism is natural, but so is male prevalence in these fields. The uncritical acceptance of EMB will lead to more funding to confirm it. Experiments that aim at shoring up EMB will get funding, and the proponents of EMB are more likely to orient their research around confirming it than disconfirming it. And research funding that goes toward shoring up EMB is funding that is not, for example, going toward showing what happens in the brain stems of people with ASD *in utero* (as the Intense World Syndrome account would indicate). It is also funding that is not going toward developing techniques of remediating the worst symptoms of autism or newer, more effective biomedical interventions. Brain science, psychology, and our interest in gender differences in humans led to EMB. And EMB will lead to more research that aims at confirming scientific claims that would support it. EMB's connection with gender will garner attention and allow us to ignore more heterogeneous findings of autism research.

The stakes are high. Funding is limited, and putting our scarce resources into a dubious scientific agenda that is attached to a quietist social agenda is dangerous. While he claims to have no social agenda, Baron-Cohen argues that not only is the male prevalence of autism a product of biology, but so is the male prevalence in math and science. There is no good argument that autism is just an extreme version of typically male traits, and yet Baron-Cohen and others are happy to conclude that male-dominated science, math, and engineering is largely natural. If we push for parity between men and women in the sciences, it is argued, then we are free to do so, but we are working against nature. This is a powerful disincentive to pursue equity in the STEM disciplines, and it contributes to the already powerful stereotype threat that women in STEM must face as they move through their careers—or drop out of them. Although it is tempting to move from basic scientific research to more general, grand, and popular claims about men and women, this is a temptation that should be resisted. Such extraordinary claims required extraordinary evidence—evidence that simply has not been produced.

REFERENCES

Aldridge, M. A., Stone, K. R., Sweeney, M. H., & Bower, T. G. R. 2000. Preverbal Children with Autism Understand the Intentions of Others. *Developmental Science* 3 (3):294.

Amaral, D. G., Bauman, M. D., and Schumann, C. M. 2003. Review the Amygdala and Autism: Implications from Non-human Primate Studies. *Genes, Brain & Behavior* 2 (5):295–302.

American Psychiatric Association (APA). *Diagnostic and Statistical Manual of Mental Disorders*, ed. IV and V. http://www.dsm5.org/proposedrevision/pages/proposedrevision.aspx?rid=94.

Auyeung, B., Baron-Cohen, S., Ashwin, E., Knickmeyer, R., Taylor, K., and Hackett, G. 2009. Fetal Testosterone and Autistic Traits. *British Journal of Psychology* 100 (1):1–22.

Auyeung, B., Baron-Cohen, S., Ashwin, E., Knickmeyer, R., Taylor, K., Hackett, G., & Hines, M. 2009. Fetal Testosterone Predicts Sexually Differentiated Childhood Behavior in Girls and in Boys. *Psychological Science* 20 (2): 144–48.

Badcock, C. R. 2009. *The Imprinted Brain: How Genes Set the Balance between Autism and Psychosis.* London: Jessica Kingsley Publishers.

Badcock, C., and Crespi, B. 2008. Battle of the Sexes May Set the Brain. *Nature*:1054–55.

Barbeau, E. B., Mendrek, A., and Mottron, L. 2009. Are Autistic Traits Autistic? *British Journal of Psychology* 100 (1):23–28.

Baron-Cohen, S. 1995. *Mindblindness: An Essay on Autism and Theory of Mind.* Cambridge, MA: MIT Press.

Baron-Cohen, S. 2003a. *The Essential Difference: The Truth About the Male and Female Brain.* New York: Basic Books.

Baron-Cohen, S. 2003b. They Just Can't Help It. *The Guardian* (April 17, 2001), August 1, 2011.

Baron-Cohen, S. 2005a. The Essential Difference: The Male and Female Brain. *Phi Kappa Phi Forum* 85 (1):23–26.

Baron-Cohen, S. 2005b. Testing the Extreme Male Brain (EMB) Theory of Autism: Let the Data Speak for Themselves. *Cognitive Neuropsychiatry* 10 (1):77–81.

Baron-Cohen, S. 2007. Sex Differences in Mind: Keeping Science Distinct from Social Policy. In W. M. Williams, and S. J. Ceci (Eds.), *Why Aren't More Women in Science?*, 159–72. Washington, DC: American Psychological Association.

Baron-Cohen, S. 2008. Autism, Hypersystemizing, and Truth. *Quarterly Journal of Experimental Psychology* 61 (1):64–75.

Baron-Cohen, S. 2009. Publish and Be Distorted. *New Scientist* 201 (2701):26–27.

Baron-Cohen, S. 2010. Delusions of Gender—'Neurosexism,' Biology, and Politics. *The Psychologist* 23 (11):904–5.

Baron-Cohen, S. 2011. Inside the Mind of a Man. *New Statesman* 140 (5033):38–39.

Baron-Cohen, S., Auyeung, B., Ashwin, E., and Knickmeyer, R. 2009. Fetal Testosterone and Autistic Traits: A Response to Three Fascinating Commentaries. *British Journal of Psychology* 100 (1):39–47.

Baron-Cohen, S., and Hammer, J. 1997. Parents of Children with Asperger Syndrome: What Is the Cognitive Phenotype? *Journal of Cognitive Neuroscience* 9 (4):548.

Baron-Cohen, S., Knickmeyer, R. C., and Belmonte, M. K. 2005. Sex Differences in the Brain: Implications for Explaining Autism. *Science* 310 (5749):819–23.

Baron-Cohen, S., Leslie, A. M., and Frith, U. 1985. Does the Autistic Child Have a "Theory of Mind?" *Cognition* 21 (1):37–46.

Baron-Cohen, S., Lombardo, M. V., Auyeung, B., Ashwin, E., Chakrabarti, B., and Knickmeyer, R. 2011. Why Are Autism Spectrum Conditions More Prevalent in Males? *PLoSBiol,* 9(6), e1001081.

Baron-Cohen, S., Lutchmaya, S., and Knickmeyer, R. 2004. *Prenatal Testosterone in Mind: Amniotic Fluid Studies*. Cambridge, MA: MIT Press.

Begley, S. 2009. Pink Brain, Blue Brain. *Newsweek* 154 (11):28–28.

Blatt, G. J. 2010. *The Neurochemical Basis of Autism from Molecules to Minicolumns*. Berlin, NY: Springer.

Brizendine, L., 2006. *The Female Brain*. New York: Morgan Road Books.

———. 2010. *The Male Brain*. New York: Broadway Books.

Ceci, S. J., and Williams, W. M. 2007. *Why Aren't More Women in Science?: Top Researchers Debate the Evidence*. Washington, DC: American Psychological Association.

Crespi, B., and Badcock, C. 2008. Psychosis and Autism as Diametrical Disorders of the Social Brain. *The Behavioral and Brain Sciences* 31 (3):241.

Dreger, A., Feder, E. K., and Tamar-Mattis, A. 2010. Preventing Homosexuality (and Uppity Women) in the Womb. Message posted to http://www.thehastingscenter.org/Bioethicsforum/Post.aspx?id=4754.

Eliot, L. 2009. *Pink Brain, Blue Brain: How Small Differences Grow into Troublesome Gaps— And What We Can Do About It*. Boston: Houghton Mifflin Harcourt.

Ellis, H. D. 2005. Book review. *Cognitive Neuropsychiatry* 10 (1):73–75.

Fine, C. 2010. *Delusions of Gender: How Our Minds, Society, and Neurosexism Create Difference*, 1st ed. New York: W. W. Norton.

Frith, C. D. 2004. Schizophrenia and Theory of Mind. *Psychological Medicine* 34 (03):385.

Geschwind, D. H. 2009. Advances in Autism. *Annual Review of Medicine* 60(1):367–80.

Gray, J. 1992. *Men Are from Mars, Women Are from Venus: A Practical Guide for Improving Communication and Getting What You Want in Your Relationships*. New York: HarperCollins.

Grice, D. E., and Buxbaum, J. D. 2006. The Genetics of Autism Spectrum Disorders. *Neuromolecular Medicine* 8 (4):451–60.

Hallmayer, J., Cleveland, S., Torres, A., Phillips, J., Cohen, B., Torigoe, T., Risch, N. 2011. Genetic Heritability and Shared Environmental Factors Among Twin Pairs with Autism. *Archives of General Psychiatry.*

Hayes, T. B. 1998. Sex Determination and Primary sex differentiation in amphibians: Genetic and Developmental Mechanisms. *Journal of Experimental Zoology* 281 (5):373–99.

Hill, A. 2009. Doctors Are Failing To Spot Asperger's in Girls. Guardian News and Media.

Holtcamp, W. 2009. Lone Parents: Parthenogenesis in Sharks. *Bioscience* 59 (7):546–50.

Jordan-Young, R. 2010. *Brain Storm: The Flaws in the Science of Sex Differences*. Cambridge, MA: Harvard University Press.

Keller, F., and Ruta, L. 2010. The Male Prevalence in Autism Spectrum Disorders: Hypotheses on Its Neurobiological Basis. In G. J. Blatt (Ed.), *The Neurochemical Basis of Autism: From Molecules to Minicolumns*, 13–28. Berlin, NY: Springer.

King, M., and Bearman, P. 2009. Diagnostic Change and the Increased Prevalence of Autism. *International Journal of Epidemiology* 38 (5):1224–34.

Kripke, S. A. 1980. *Naming and Necessity*. Cambridge, MA: Harvard University Press.

Kunzig, R. 2004. Autism: What's Sex Got To Do With It? *Psychology Today* 37 (1):66–76.

Locke, J., Yolton, J. W., and Yolton, J. S. 1989.*Some Thoughts Concerning Education*. New York: Clarendon Press; Oxford: Oxford University Press.

Lutchmaya, S., Baron-Cohen, S., and Raggatt, P. 2002. Foetal Testosterone and Eye Contact in 12-month-old Human Infants. *Infant Behavior & Development* 25 (3):327.

Manning, J. T., Reimers, S., Baron-Cohen, S., Wheelwright, S., and Fink, B. 2010. Sexually Dimorphic Traits (digit ratio, body height, systemizing–empathizing scores) and Gender Segregation between Occupations: Evidence from the BBC Internet Study. *Personality & Individual Differences* 49 (5):511–15.

Minio-Paluello, I., Lombardo, M. V., Chakrabarti, B., Wheelwright, S., and Baron-Cohen, S. 2009. Response to Smith's Letter to the Editor 'Emotional Empathy in Autism Spectrum Conditions: Weak, Intact, or Heightened?' *Journal of Autism & Developmental Disorders* 39 (12):1749–54.

Pease, B., and Pease, A. 2000. *Why Men Don't Listen & Women Can't Read Maps: How We're Different and What To Do About It.* New York: Welcome Rain.

Pinker, S. 2008. *The Sexual Paradox: Men, Women and the Real Gender Gap.* New York: Scribner.

Same Difference: How Gender Myths Are Hurting Our Relationships, Our Children, and Our Jobs. 2005. *Future Survey* 27 (6):21–22.

Skuse, D. H. 2000. Imprinting, the X-chromosome, and the Male Brain: Explaining Sex Differences in the Liability to Autism. *Pediatric Research* 47 (1):9–16.

Smith, A. 2009. Emotional Empathy in Autism Spectrum Conditions: Weak, Intact, or Heightened? *Journal of Autism & Developmental Disorders* 39 (12):1747–48.

Turkheimer, E. 2010. The It Strikes Back. *PsycCRITIQUES* 55 (24): No Pagination.

Valla, J. M., Ganzel, B. L., Yoder, K. J., Chen, G. M., Lyman, L. T., Sidari, A. P., Belmonte, M. K. 2010. More than Maths and Mindreading: Sex Differences in Empathizing/Systemizing Covariance. *Autism Research* 3 (4):174–84.

Wheelwright, S., Baron-Cohen, S., Goldenfeld, N., Delaney, J., Fine, D., Smith, R., Wakabayashi, A. 2006. Predicting Autism Spectrum Quotient (AQ) from the Systemizing Quotient-revised (SQ-R) and Empathy Quotient (EQ). *Brain Research* 1079 (1):47–56.

Witt, C. "Feminist History of Philosophy." *The Stanford Encyclopedia of Philosophy (fall 2008 edition), Edward N. Zalta (ed.).*

Witt, C. 2011. *Feminist Metaphysics: Explorations in the Ontology of Sex, Gender and the Self.* New York: Springer.

Zimmerman, A. W. 2008. *Autism Current Theories and Evidence.* New York: Springer.

NOTES

This chapter has benefited from comments from John Collins, Cathy Frierson, Sarah Richardson, Julia Rodriguez, Paula Salvio, and Charlotte Witt, as well as audiences at the University of New Hampshire Law School's Implicit Bias Seminar and the University of New Hampshire Philosophy Department.

1. Baron-Cohen 2003.

2. I will use ASD to refer to the group of three developmental disorders of PDD-NOS, Asperger's, and autistic disorder, as described in the *DSM-IV*. Current experimental research into autism and ASD typically excludes subjects with primary diagnoses that are often associated with autistic symptoms—e.g. diagnoses such as Fragile X, Prader-Willi, and tuberous sclerosis; they also exclude subjects whose autism was subsequent to exposure to environmental agents such as valproic acid, thalidomide, and rubella (Grice and Buxbaum 2006).

3. See, e.g., Pinker 2008; Brizendine 2006 and 2007; Pease and Pease 2000.

4. Baron-Cohen 2008, 78.

5. Keller and Ruta 2010, 15.

6. Crespi and Badcock 2008.

7. Baron-Cohen 2007.

8. Baron-Cohen 2010a, 904.

9. Turkheimer 2010.

10. Baron-Cohen 2008.

11. Hallmayer *et al.* 2011, E1.

12. Zimmerman 2008.

13. Markram, Rinaldi, and Markram 2007.

14. Geschwind 2009.

15. Russell 1997.

16. Frith 1989; Happe and Frith 2006.

17. Baron-Cohen *et al.* 1985; Frifth and Happe 1994.

18. Amaral *et al.* 2003; Baron-Cohen *et al.* 2000.

19. Markram, Rinaldi, and Markram 2007.

20. King and Bearman 2009.

21. See http://www.dsm5.org/proposedrevision/pages/proposedrevision.aspx?rid=94 for *DSM-IV* and *DSM-V* and APA's rationale for the changes.

22. Witt 2008.

23. Locke, John. 1692. *Some Thoughts Concerning Education.*

24. Mill, John Stuart. 1869. *The Subjection of Women.*

25. Richardson 2010.

26. Baron-Cohen 2003, 185.

27. Baron-Cohen 2003, 122.

28. Baron-Cohen 2003, 127.

29. Crespi and Badcock 2008.

30. Crespi 2009.

31. Baron-Cohen 2003, 171–76.

32. Baron-Cohen 2008, 68.

33. Baron-Cohen, 1995. The Sally-Anne test (Wimmer and Perner 1983) evaluates whether a subject will can distinguish between the subject's own belief about the location of an object and another person's. Briefly, the subject watches two actors (in the original experiment dolls were used), Sally and Anne, as Sally places an object (e.g., a marble) in a basket as Anne watches. Sally then leaves the room, and Anne subsequently moves the object to her own box. The subject is asked, "Where will Sally look for the marble?" In some studies, children with autism more often predict that Sally will look in the new location, whereas lower IQ but nonautistic children (e.g., children with Down syndrome), accurately predict that Ann will look in the first location. This is supposed to show that at least some autistic children—those who are functional enough to respond the question—have deficits in the ability to theorize about other minds. Not everyone thinks this test is a good test of "theory of mind." See Bloom and German 2000.

34. Minio-Paluello *et al.* 2009.

35. Baron-Cohen 2008, 68.

36. Baron-Cohen 2008, 65.

37. For example the *DSM-IV* states: "A total of six (*or more*) items from (1), (2), and (3), *with at least two from* (1), *and one each from* (2) and (3)" (emphasis added) (APA).

38. Baron-Cohen 2008, 66; Baron-Cohen does not make the static–dynamic distinction, but I add it in order to clarify.

39. Baron-Cohen 2008, 65.

40. Baron-Cohen 2008, 66.

41. Baron-Cohen 2005, 95–104.

42. Baron-Cohen 2005, 1.

43. Baron-Cohen 2007, 169.

44. Kripke 1980.

45. Baron-Cohen 2005, 1.

46. Witt 2011.

47. Hayes 1998.

48. Holtcamp 2009.

49. Baron-Cohen 2007, 165.

50. Baron-Cohen 2003.

51. Baron-Cohen 2007.
52. Auyeung, Baron-Cohen *et al.* 2009.
53. Goya and McEwen 1980.
54. Baron-Cohen, Lutchmaya, and Knickmeyer 2004, 9–11.
55. Auyeung *et al.* 2009.
56. Eliot 2009, 28.
57. Baron-Cohen *et al.* 2004, 17–19.
58. However, estradiol, which is produced by testosterone through aromatization, has not been ruled out, and some have argued that "oestrogen, rather than testosterone, is the critical hormone to understand the skewed sex ratio in autism" (Keller and Ruta 2010, 20).
59. Baron-Cohen *et al.* 2004, 50.
60. Eliot 2009, 81.
61. Zimmerman 2008, 191.
62. Zimmerman 2008, 201.
63. Durand *et al.* 2007.
64. Geschwind 2009, 370.
65. Auyeung *et al.* 2009.
66. Baron-Cohen 2005, 154.
67. Fine 2010, 108.
68. Baron-Cohen 2010, 904.
69. Jordan-Young 2010.
70. Fine 2010, 112–17.
71. Auyeung *et al.* 2009.
72. Baron-Cohen 2003, 56.
73. Auyeung *et al.* 2009; Crespi and Badcock 2008.
74. Baron-Cohen *et al.* 2011.
75. Geschwind 2009.
76. Even two people with Down syndrome might be said to not share the "same thing," in that some people with Down syndrome do not have a trisomy throughout their entire genome (mosaicism), and some people with Down syndrome have a partial duplication of chromosome 21, or a translocation of part of a chromosome.
77. Barbeau, Mendrek, and Mottron 2009, 27.

Chapter Four

I Think, Therefore I Am. I Am Verbal, Therefore I Live.

Nick Pentzell

In 2006 I was introduced to arguments about theory of mind and how it relates to autism. It was astonishing to me as a person on the autism spectrum that we had not been involved in this academic discussion. Encouraged by my friend and former professor Dr. Anna Stubblefield, who suggested I approach the subject for the Society for Disability Studies conference that year, I broached the topic by analyzing several scholarly papers and reacting in the context of my own experience. [1]

Theory of mind involves imagining what a person other than oneself might think in a given situation. A typical test involves a candy box. The subject is asked what she or he expects to find in the box; she or he replies "candy" and is shown it contains pencils. Next, the subject is asked what a stranger would expect to find in the box. "Candy," of course, is the correct answer. Often, this test is given to three- and four-year-olds, which is usually the dividing ages for what proponents claim is the acquisition of theory of mind: three-year-olds answer "pencils," while four-year-olds answer "candy." Many autistic children, four years old and older, continue to answer "pencils," thus apparently indicating they have not acquired a theory of mind that can comprehend how another might think.

Frith and Happé, in "Theory of Mind and Self-Consciousness: What Is It Like to Be Autistic?," explain that most autistics appear not to acquire a theory of mind. Confident that for many years I have been able to pass their theory of mind test, I tried to think back in my own past to a time I might have failed it. I must explain to you that it was not until I was thirteen years old that I acquired the means to communicate with words via facilitated communication. Up until then, I was diagnosed as severely mentally impaired and autistic. I spoke a few words inconsistently, but no one suspected I was capable of understanding much more than rudimentary language. Facilitated communication (FC) is an alternative and augmentative form of communication whereby one person (a facilitator) provides physical support and resistance to the hand or arm of another person (FC user) who has physical and/or neurological differences that make it difficult to type accurately on a communication board or keyboard. The backward pressure against the FC user's hand makes it possible for her or him to point to letters without wobbling or jerking; the touch of the facilitator also pulls the FC user into a state of body consciousness so that he or she can focus on typing. Before I was introduced to FC, on the Vineland Adaptive Behavior Scale my communication abilities tested at an age equivalence of one to twelve months. A little more than a year after I began communicating via FC, I had begun my academic education as an inclusion student in a fifth grade classroom of the local public school.

Before I began communicating with language, my mode of thinking was drastically different. As I remember it, I did not have much control over thought. I had impressions and, sometimes, images. I understood most of what was said to and around me. Phrases, often from television, floated through my mind and lodged in my memory. I knew how to get food or show when I needed something. I was impressed with educated people and loved *Wheel of Fortune* and *Jeopardy* on television; people like my father, a college professor, who knew facts and information had a power I desired. I had deciphered a number of written words and understood that writing was a representation of speech, but my snippets of coherence were not something I could shape or hold onto. Feelings, impulses, fears, and overwhelming sensations interrupted and fragmented my processes of thought.

Imagine yourself sitting in a room with other people, listening to someone speak, focusing on what is being said to you. Perhaps, on a subliminal level you are aware of the room's temperature, the feel of your clothes on your skin, the smells of the people in the room around you—their movements as they shift or scratch and their moods and energy, the colors and textures in your visual field, the brightness or pulsating of the room's lighting, the sound of air handlers—of coughing, squeaky chairs, background noise from the hall or other rooms, and maybe electrical or plumbing sounds. If you have attention-deficit disorder, some of these stimuli may be distracting. If you have a migraine, it might be painful. If you are on recreational drugs, the stimuli may be fascinating and entertaining. If you are autistic, it may be some or all of the above. The more you are aware of all of this sensory stimulus, the more you are probably feeling uncomfortable, irritated or upset, nervous or out of control of the environment and situation, and too overloaded to hold onto thought. Amplify this sensitivity several times over and you might withdraw "into your own world," develop odd behaviors like rocking or fidgeting with an object as a means of calming yourself or blocking out stimulus, echo words or phrases as a mantra, or become to all appearances autistic. In the relative quiet of your room later on, you might be able to recall bits and pieces of what was said in the midst of sensory and emotional chaos. Over the years you might even develop an amazing retention of passively absorbed information.

But if you have no means of communication and have motor-disturbance problems that slow your reactions so that people are always missing your attempts to show you understand, if you are bored by baby talk and the simple tasks people offer you as education and have given up on participating or are angry at being controlled, if your body is neurologically damaged and you are horribly uncoordinated and have little or no speech—well—you will be a jumble *inside* yourself and, *outside*; it will be difficult for you to have gotten the practice and interaction that most babies/children/adolescents/adults receive in developing organized thought. It doesn't surprise me that many autistic children, even those who can speak or have Asperger's, flunk theory of mind tests. At age four I was too lost in sensation to respond to, let alone pass or fail, such a test. I think just maneuvering through a day's stimuli prevented me from thinking from other people's points of view. It seemed, somehow, everyone else was different from me; they weren't so crippled by the world around them. I couldn't edit any of it out. I couldn't imagine what it was like not to be overstimulated. I really couldn't have cared whether people expected candy or pencils when they opened a box.

Opponents of theory of mind, like Gallagher in "Understanding Interpersonal Problems in Autism: Interaction Theory as An Alternative to Theory of Mind," have pointed out flaws in theory of mind theory and, alternatively, have taken into account neurological and sensory-motor issues of people on the autism spectrum. Gernsbacher and Frymiare, in "Does the Autistic Brain Lack Core Modules?," have cast "doubt on arguments that the autistic brain is missing the core modules responsible for understanding theory of mind and for processing faces"[2] and have demonstrated that, although in trials 50–80 percent of autistic subjects have failed theory of mind tasks, the ability to pass these tests is linked with an individual's linguistic development. They believe that theory of mind is not innate nor is it linked to a specific neural mechanism. Once one masters the grammar of "sentential complement constructions, in which a complement clause is embedded in the matrix clause"[3] "such as 'what will Jesse think is inside the box before I open it,'"[4] one is able to pass theory of mind tests.

I have always had a thinking mind. However, my thinking has not always been organized. The structure of my language has structured how I think. Remedial language allows a person to communicate about wants and needs. However, linguistic fluency shapes understanding and how one thinks. It allows a person to plan, dream, analyze, criticize, change, shape, influence, and control the world around her or him; to play, joke, and be ironic; to create, express, and approach things artistically. A grasp of language puts my life in my hands. I can be who I most intimately and truly am.

When I first made use of language with FC, it was an effort to spell out words. It still is, because it is tedious. Then, however, it required me to think in a new way. I frequently typed initials, abbreviated words, or began spelling and faltered when I didn't know if I was doing it correctly. My facilitators were good at providing prompts, corrections, guesses, and education. I was fishing for information. At first, I was stubbornly against silent "e"s and refused to use them. I saw no reason why the letter "r" should not do for "a-r-e." I began with one-word communications and, as language became more comfortable, added more words to create sentences. After a little over three months, I accidentally constructed my first poem, and I made up my own jokes:

> HOW IS A MAP OF MICHIGAN LIKE A WALRUS? I DONT NO BUT IT
> LOOKS LIKE A HEAD OF MOST ORDINARY PEOPLE JUST TANPERD
> [tampered] WITH.I WENT TO A LATE SHOW OF FRANKENSTEIN AND
> I SEE NO PEOPLE IN THE THEATRE.
> SO I SAY WHERE IS EVERYONE? AND THE MONSTER SAYS I DONT
> NO BUT I JUST SEE A MONSTER INSIDE THE MOVY THEATRE. I
> GUESS THE PEOPLE LEFT ME.

I was a wise guy at school and told my teachers the cafeteria food was "slop." Politely, or mouthing off, I was able to tell the people around me when I needed my environment modified to reduce stimulus so I could participate. I loved large words: "I need sustenance" for "I'm hungry." I could plan the effect of my communications. I could show my intelligence. I could play with language.

I could learn how other kids thought and what they were able to do. I came home from school and told my stepmom—stretching the limits of reality in my statements in order to discover just what it was that they actually did—that "real" kids did this or that. ("Who are you? Pinocchio?" she asked.) As I began doing these things myself, I guess I became real, and, instead, I told my mom about "kids." I began watching situation comedies on television, now able to relate to the characters more and to follow a sustained plot. Muppets and cartoons had been a fun stimulus before, but, once I was able to follow the conversations and situations more closely, I wanted complexity. I progressed from black-and-white 1960s reruns, which were less visually distracting, to more visually difficult programs in color. I learned about how others thought and felt from TV, from the stories and novels my parents read to me every night, from the people and situations of which I was now a part. With language, I could take the steps I had missed in learning about other people, and I could accurately imagine how they might think and react.

Experience was one thing, but Gernsbacher and Frymiare point out that grammatical complexity is another. There are certain grammatical constructions that seem to create relationships that, for me, are spatial in nature. I can respond better when I see these written down; hearing them, the sentences lose conceptual shape. But, it is not a matter of the tangibility of the written word. For me, the conceptual structure requires a physical orientation involving a visual element. For example, let's say you said, "Simon visited his mother after he went to the store, then he stopped by Yolanda's house to borrow her lawn mower. What did he do first?" Even though I understand he went to the store first, my immediate response is, "Simon visited his mother," because it is at the beginning of the sentence and my mind jumps to the order in which the sounds and the images they created were patterned. To pattern the order of the time sequence, I need to be able to visually arrange the pieces, either as written words I can see or point to or, if I am listening, as places on the table in front of me or on my arm that I put in sequential order by touching them as I comprehend the meaning of the sentence: "Simon visited his mother" (touch) "after he went to the store" (touch to the left of the original place), "then he stopped by Yolanda's" (touch to the right of the original place). When you ask the question about what Simon did first, I can touch that place and recall the image of the action.

As posed by Gernsbacher and Frymiare, the question in the theory of mind test—"What will Jesse think is inside the box before I open it?"—has three parts: what Jesse thinks, before the box is opened, and the opening of the box. These are not arranged in the order in which they occur. Without my visual/touch indicators, with which I arrange these actions sequentially, it is possible that I would answer that he thinks "pencils," NOT because I believe this is the answer but because this is the last image in my mind: "…before *I open it*." You open the box and I see pencils! In a second I will realize that my mind has retrieved the wrong information, but the image is strong and has jumped impulsively to the forefront.

Perhaps I am explaining the manner in which all of us learn to sort out this sort of complex sentence structure, and maybe my thought patterns are not as well-exercised as yours, so my effort is more conscious. Regardless, whatever the mastery of the candy box test actually demonstrates, I believe several things. Sensory overload inhibits *anyone* from thinking about much more than surviving its barrage. People on the autism spectrum (children and adults) have an awareness of how other people think and react but (as with the general population) the depth of their understanding is related to the depth of their involvement in interpersonal relationships. Language fluency increases one's degree of interaction, as well as the sophistication of one's thinking and understanding. Moreover, the use of language shapes thought, makes patterns of thinking more apparent, and—in organizing thought so that it can be analyzed—gives the thinker the tools to control sensation, interaction, and (ultimately) to use thought to create a meaningful, livable life.

REFERENCES

Frith, Uta, and Francesca Happé. 1999. Theory of Mind and Self-Consciousness: What Is It Like to Be Autistic? *Mind & Language* 14(1):1–22.
Gallagher, Shaun. 2004. Understanding Interpersonal Problems in Autism: Interaction Theory as An Alternative to Theory of Mind. *Philosophy, Psychiatry, & Psychology* 11 (3):199–217.
Gernsbacher, Morton Ann, and Jennifer L. Frymiare. 2005. Does the Autistic Brain Lack Core Modules? *The Journal of Developmental and Learning Disorders* 9:3–16.

NOTES

1. An earlier version of this chapter was presented as part of the "The Power of Communication" panel at the "Disability Goes Public" conference, by Society for Disability Studies, June 2006. That talk was later published online as Pentzell, Nick. 2008. *The Autism Perspective* 4(3):86–89.
2. Gernsbacher and Frymiare 2005, 13.
3. Gernsbacher and Frymiare 2005, 6.
4. Gernsbacher and Frymiare 2005, 7.

Chapter Five

A Dash of Autism

Jami L. Anderson

It seems that for success in science and art a dash of autism is essential.

—Hans Asperger

Some months ago I was sitting on an examining table, working my way through hundreds of questions about our son's developmental progress while my husband and he amused one another. We were all waiting (and *had* been waiting for almost two hours) for a neurologist to arrive. Our son had recently suffered a series of terrible migraines and we had been referred to this neurologist to see if there were any prophylactic treatments available for young children to prevent migraines as there are for adults. I filled out question after question concerning early developmental progress: how old was he when he first sat? stood? crawled? walked? ran? The questionnaire was ridiculously long; by page ten, I was peevish, by page fifteen my answers bordered on science fiction. I had noticed both "migraine" and "autism" listed on the top of my son's forms and I began to suspect that all of this paperwork had far more to do with the neurologist's interests in my son's autism than with a genuine concern for his migraine problems. Finally an intern came in and asked yet *another* round of questions very similar to those on the forms. One of the questions was "When did he start talking in full sentences?" At that very minute our son was signing[1] a song he knew, showing off to anyone who would pay any attention to him. I have long ago become so tired of that question, a question fraught with so much emotional baggage,[2] I asked, rather snappishly, "Does sign language count as talking? He *signs* complete sentences." The intern stared at the form, mumbled, "I'm not sure," and then wrote something down on the chart. But what did he write if he did not know what the question meant? So this is how research on autism is done by neurologists at world-renowned university research centers, I mused. Then, the moment we were all waiting for: the neurologist arrived. Within a minute he told us that there was nothing he would give us for the migraines—our son was far too young for migraine medication. But he did suggest that we get lab work done to test for autism. Both my husband and I asked what purpose that would serve. After all, we know he is autistic. The neurologist smiled condescendingly and replied "There is a new genetic test. It was not around when your son was first diagnosed. It will help us find a cure for autism." He must have been expecting whoops of joy and our lack of interest seemed to annoy him. He turned to me[3] and said, rather peevishly, "It is a *simple test*— blood work, no more, and you are done. They check the DNA. (dramatic pause) It is very important." Getting what can be at best described as complete indifference from us as we organized our bags and coats and readied to leave (while our son continued to sign, sing and lark about the room) he tried again, speaking very slowly and pointedly, "You do want to *CURE AUTISM*, don't you?" I was surprised to find myself thinking, "No. I do not."

YOU WANT TO *CURE* AUTISM, DON'T YOU?

I certainly would not have come to that conclusion six years earlier. Not because I had well-considered views about autism but because I had not given the matter any serious thought and would have been parroting the generally held view of most people: that autism is a sad affliction that causes much suffering for the child, the parents and fellow family members and therefore we must, as a society, do all that we can to eradicate it. I would have thought that such a view was enlightened and reasonable. Before coming to the realization that I do not believe that autism needs to be *cured*,[4] I have taken what seems like an acid trip through therapy-hazed madness.[5] I will start at the beginning, which seems to me like many lifetimes ago, but which is not my son's full lifetime ago.

It seems almost impossible that just under six years ago I knew next to nothing about autism. I had heard the term "autism" but knew almost nothing of what the term meant, knew no one who is autistic (or so I thought), knew nothing of what it was like to live in this society with that label. What I knew (and what can hardly be counted as 'knowledge') came almost entirely from an NPR story I heard one morning. It concerned a father who was describing the hardship and pain he suffers from having a daughter who is autistic. What struck me was the heartache he described when he thought of the years laying before him, empty of any affectionate or loving physical contact with his daughter whom he described as "extremely touch adverse." I am not sure what the ostensible purpose of that 'news' story was, but I do know I have at many times thought of that father's professed suffering, and the public presentation of an autistic child as a profound disappointment for a parent.

Some months later, my husband and I were in a neurologist's office[6] and were being presented with the news that our son, then about twenty-eight months old but not yet talking, was, according to the neurologist "without a doubt PDD-NOS." I felt both sick with shock yet utterly bewildered, having never heard of that condition before. The neurologist then did us the favor of translating: **P**ervasive **D**evelopmental **D**isorder, **N**ot **O**therwise **S**pecified. None the wiser, he explained: PDD-NOS is a subcategory of the Autism Spectrum Disorder[7] which "makes up an umbrella." (At this, he waved his hand in a wide arc and for a split second I almost *did* see an invisible umbrella there, suspended, in the room.) He must have talked for a few minutes more, though I have no memory of what he said. While he talked, I watched my son walk around the small examining room, happily making playful overtures to engage with my husband. My son's tactic was (and still is) to place himself right in front of a person, stare intently into their eyes without blinking,[8] and then to implant his intentions into their mind. More than once I've concluded that, if anyone has telepathic powers, he does, as I often find myself inexplicitly bending to his will, persuaded by the sheer force of his stare. The neurologist ended his emotionally flat patter with a perfunctory, "So, any questions?" In retrospect, it was almost funny. Any *questions*? Had I the power to formulate any *thought*, one question I surely would have asked would have been, "What the hell are you *talking* about?" I do not remember what either of us said but it must have been something about our son's prognosis, because I do very clearly remember him saying, "His symptoms will eventually disappear but he will always be autistic." He then wished us good day and left the room.

SO WHAT NOW?

I do not remember the next couple of months very well. Both my husband and I had the astonishing good fortune to be on sabbatical for the whole of that academic year; I am sure neither of us would have been able to teach any classes or attend a committee meeting without falling apart had this diagnosis come during any other year. I had been in the middle of writing a book for which I had a contract with a publisher, but I could no longer concentrate on it. I could not bring myself to care about much at all.[9] I could not comprehend the total misfit between what I thought I knew "autism" to be—children who were aloof, distant, touch-averse head bangers—and what I knew my son to be—ebullient, joyful, hilarious, cuddly, funny, energetic, loving, and with a wonderful and spontaneous sense of humor. It did not fit. It could not fit. The diagnosis was simply impossible. Indeed the whole idea of a category such as PDD-NOS was *ridiculous*—"not otherwise specified" simply stank of "we do not know what the hell we are talking about." And every time I thought of the neurologist's words "his symptoms will completely disappear but he will always be autistic," my mind reeled—what could that even *mean*? If that was the case, why should we care? Why would autism even *matter*?

Not too surprisingly, we could not stop talking about it (with each other, never with anyone else), arguing about it, obsessing about it. After stewing about it for months, we both, independently, devoted all our energy to researching autism. You would think becoming genuinely educated about autism would be relatively simple given how many people in this society are researching, talking and writing about autism. Yet when I entered the world of autism, I entered a colossal, mad, cacophonous circus, one filled with a bewildering number of barkers, each frenetically promising a "complete cure" or "total recovery" all the while warning us to avoid the charlatan in the next tent whose treatments were a hopeless waste of money if not deadly dangerous. In addition to the hundreds, if not thousands of therapies, herbal and medicinal remedies and treatment plans available, there are millions of products parents can buy (if one can afford the hyperventilation-inducing prices) that are designed just for autistic children: special clothing, bedding, toys, school supplies, books and other education supplies, occupational therapy gadgets, videos and CDs—all of which are designed to alleviate, if not eliminate, the symptoms and signs of autism. Product after product features a parent professing that, after purchasing this or that device, their little Johnny or Susie is now "symptom free," "his old self again" or "completely recovered." Some of those things are useful and some are simply fun [10] but a good deal of the stuff is stupefying nonsense. Here are some bullshit autism cures worth mentioning: [11]

Autism Herbs: For a touch of the Orient, you can try Chinese Herbal Medicine such as Special Brain's Powder. Here is one story: "Joe is 8 years old…[w]hen he first came into our centre [he was] jumping and screaming all over the place and zero communication and eyes contact. He is in his own world, very scared and frustrated, until he hits himself on the head continuous…" But with just 30 days of treatments, two sessions per day, using this Special Brain's Powder Joe was "almost 100% recovered!!!" and Joe and his parents "…went home with a HAPPY HEART!!! NO MORE MEDICINE, WORRY, STRESS, FRUSTRATION, SLEEPLESS NIGHT." [12]

Adult Stem Cell Therapy: One group of audacious clinicians at the Stem Cell Institute claim to treat autism with Adult Stem Cell Therapy. Adult stem cell research is not currently approved by the United States Food and Drug Administration (FDA) nor is it "considered standard of care for any condition or disease." Furthermore, "for most diseases no prospective, randomized clinical trials of adult stem cells have been performed, therefore no guarantee of safety or effectiveness is made or implied."[13] Nonetheless it is being offered as a viable treatment for children with autism. Interestingly (alarmingly?) the treatment is not performed within the borders of the United States but in Panama City, Panama, after one's application—and one's credit line—has been approved.

Testimonials from the parents of survivors of this process attest to the wonders of it: Nine-year-old Kenneth started adult stem cell treatment and within two days his parents saw improvement. "[H]e's more aware of his surroundings. He even remembers birthdays, days of the week and he can tell time. We've just been waiting for the new things and the gains to stop coming and they're not stopping. They're coming every day."

James developed severe autistic symptomatology one month prior to his sixth birthday.

> The anguish and pain we felt as our family watched him disappear into the abyss of thoughtlessness is indescribable…The initial round of stem cells significantly improved my son's cognitive skills….Each day we see many subtle improvements like consistently smiling for pictures, allowing his sibling to blow out her birthday candles or understanding that Sunday comes before Monday.

One parent writes of her daughter, "Emma is progressing beyond my wildest dreams."[14]

Dr. Wong's Secrets: This manual is chock-a-block full of secrets that will not only teach you how to "defeat" autism but promises a child that will "spring out of bed at 6 a.m. every day to go to normal school, free, refreshed and ready for all the beautiful moments in life you thought autism had stolen from them forever." Dr. Wong warns that his Secrets are not for every parent, though. They are not for those "who don't have an open mind or who are negative people."[15] The subtext of Dr. Wong's "Miraculous Cures Manual" is clear: if the cures do not work, the cause of the problem is not the therapy but with the "negative" parents with closed minds.

Clay Baths: Just one part of the mind-boggling discussion of the benefits of "detoxing" autistic children, clay baths are said to "draw out" the harmful metals, chemicals and other contaminants in the toxic bodies of the autistic child. Amazingly, all symptoms of autism fade in just minutes as these enthusiastic parents testify:

> I am absolutely amazed that after a few short baths with…clay, my son's behavior has changed quite noticeably

> Our 2 ½ year old son, who is autistic, increased his vocabulary from 4-5 words
> to 20 words

> Keven lost his baby speech at the age of 18 months, right after his vaccina-
> tions....A couple of days ago my son Keven came downstairs and told me he
> was back. So I asked him, "Back from where Keven?", and he said, "I was
> very far away from you but now I am closer to you." All the while he pointed
> to his head. "While you were far away from me, where you happy Keven?"
> And his reply was, "I was alone and afraid." This from a child that walks the
> same shadow with me from the moment he was diagnosed. [16]

After acknowledging that Food and Drug Administration (FDA) regulations
disallow claims that taking a clay bath will *cure* autism, they do assert that
"many parents of autistic children have seen their child's symptoms reverse
or go away entirely."[17]

Hyperbaric Chamber Therapy: In short, this is the medical use of oxygen at a
level higher than atmospheric pressure.[18] Apparently someone has decided
that autistic children would benefit from spending their hours inside hyperbaric machines.[19] What exactly hyperbaric oxygen therapy (HBOT) could
possibly offer an autistic child is unclear and the various web page discussions are often filled with obfuscatory explanations of autism and the reasons
why HBOT will help. Here is a typical example:

> HBOT increases the oxygen tissue concentration which increases cerebral
> blood flow to an area thus enabling the body to restore brain tissue metabolism
> of oxygen and nutrients, helping restoration of any areas which are suffering
> from hypoxia. New blood and oxygen begin to stimulate an area, especially
> one that has viable, recoverable brain cells that are "idling neurons" not know-
> ing what to do instead of function normally.[20]

These parents write of their son, Christian, since he underwent his forty
sessions of HBOT:

> His expressive ability with language is outstanding. He actually talks on the
> phone and carries on a two-way conversation. His replies are no longer just
> one word. His desire to use language is much more pronounced. His teachers
> are amazed and very happy with the changes. They report that he is much
> better at "talking with" the other children and interacting in general.[21]

If parents are serious about this (and their wallets cooperate), they can pur-
chase their own HBOT chamber for home use. Some HBOT chambers are
big enough to hold both the parent and the child (as photos on the website
attest) though one may wonder about the wisdom of needless HBOT treat-

ments if one did *not* have "idling neurons." Prices for personal HBOT chambers range from $5,995 to $15,995.

Packing: Packing therapy involves "wrapping someone in damp sheets for one hour sessions while the therapist encourages them to notice other sensations."[22] Many therapists claim that autistic children benefit from packing. What is typically *not* acknowledged is that the only "packing study" to use autistic children used just six children, and only two of those children were autistic. What is also never made clear is how much or in what way the autistic children benefitted from the packing. That is, in what respect their *autism* improved from the packing and how long lasting these benefits were. As a parent with finite resources, I would want to know: could that hour my child spent wrapped in cold, damp sheets have been have been more productively spent? It seems to me that the study sample was *far too small* to draw any conclusions about autistic individuals, who are a very diverse collection of people and therefore it would be absurd to conclude that this study revealed anything conclusive about autism or the therapeutic benefits of packing for autistic children.[23]

Holding: Innocuous enough sounding, holding theory is defined as an intervention in which the caregiver or parent "holds the child very closely and very tightly while speaking in a comforting manner. The caregiver may not release his/her hold until the child 'surrenders' and spontaneously looks into the caregiver's eyes. The caregiver then returns the child's gaze and exchanges affection."[24] If the child is particularly reluctant to make eye contact (some children may refuse for hours) parents or caregivers are instructed to resort to "poking" or "prodding of the child's torso and armpits" which is termed "tactile stimulation" by advocates of this approach.[25] Defenders of holding therapy claim that autism is not a genetic condition but a "disorder of attachment" which can be repaired by forcing the child to experience and acknowledge the control and authority of an adult.[26] There no evidence that this treatments helps autistic children.[27]

Magnets: Magnetic power is, apparently, essential for maintaining health (or so it is professed on many websites). Thus, the logic goes, a simple magnet sleep pad engineered to mimic the Earth's magnetic field of 4,000 years ago (a more natural and healthy level, *obviously*) will immediately reduce if not eliminate all symptoms of autism. One parent attests:

> Our daughter...has high functioning autism and was not sleeping through the night for 7 years! Once we received the sleep pad she has slept all night and wakes up a much 'happier' child. When she does not sleep in her bed we

notice a negative difference in her behavior.... We see such a significant improvement in her behavior that I wouldn't want to give up the magnetic pad![28]

Also available are magnetic bracelets, jewelry, body wraps (both firm and
flexible), magnetic insoles, magnetic water, as well as products for one's
pets.[29]

Aversion Therapy: Aversion therapy exposes an individual to a stimulus
while simultaneously subjecting him or her to a form of discomfort. The
purpose is to cause the individual to associate the stimulus with unpleasant
sensations in order to stop the specific behavior.[30] So, for example, if an
autistic child fails to make eye contact with someone, or "flaps excessively,"
or fails to use age-appropriate sentence structure, he or she would be subjected to such "discomforts." Judge Rotenberg Education Center (JREC), a
live-in school for children who exhibit "autistic like behaviors"[31] uses aversion therapy exclusively, including electric shock, the forced inhaling of
ammonia, withholding food and reduced calorie diets to treat autistic (and
"autistic like") children.[32] JREC uses a "Behavior Rehearsal Lesson" to treat
particularly recalcitrant autistic children: The child is restrained and told to
misbehave and if the child attempts to pull away, he or she is shocked. If he
follows the order and misbehaves, he or she is shocked. I am not sure what
the child will learn from this, other than that the staff at JREC are real
bastards, but some parents approve, indeed enthusiastically. Here are a few
testimonies from parents who praise the Center:

"My son has been [psychotropic] free for 9 years and he is improving."
"It does work! It stops him from being in a padded cell, on drugs."
"[I]s it more humane to drug my son until he can barely stay awake?"[33]

The JREC web site describes the Center as having a "colorful and attractive
school building."[34] I would hope so given that parents are paying over
$730,000 a year for each child despite the Center's long history of lawsuits,
recent criminal charges brought against the founder of the Center[35] and an
inadequately trained staff of over 900, most of whom have only a high school
diploma.[36]

Exorcism: Some parents believe that autism is the result of a "generational
curse" visited upon the child for the sins of the parent. Others believe autism
to be a sickness curable by the "laying on of the hands." Either way, what the
autistic child needs is a healthy dose of exorcism.[37]

It is tempting to laugh at these "treatments" and conclude that any parent
who subjects their child to such experiences is a fool at best. I would never
recommend any of the above as a therapy option for autism (indeed would

strongly discourage them), but I can believe that after being informed of an autism diagnosis for their child and then being inundated with *hundreds* of suggestions of therapies, parents can, in a state of half-witted desperation, convince themselves that giving the highly implausible a whirl is better than doing nothing at all. And given what I think of as the Culture of Autism that pervades our society (how autism is presented to parents by so-called experts, how it is portrayed in the media, online, on billboards[38]), it is not at all surprising, really, that parents feel tremendous pressure to try therapies, even highly dubious ones, for their autistic child.

The primary commandment of the Culture of Autism is "Early Intervention." Picking a therapy plan and getting it underway after diagnosis is *not* akin to deciding whether or not to renovate one's bathroom—something that one can put off year and after year because of the expense and inconvenience. Parents are told that autism is like cancer,[39] a problem that you simply do not mess around with. Indeed, once you are handed the diagnosis, you are told to *run*, not walk, to the nearest therapist and begin a therapy program *yesterday*. Once we were given our son's diagnosis we found that every highly recommended therapist within one hundred miles of us was booked solid for months, some for almost *two years*. I felt rage and frustration because, after being told that we had waited far too long to get our son diagnosed,[40] we were now being put off for possibly two years. What the *hell*? Aren't we in the middle of an autism *epidemic*? What kind of doctors are these people that they do not work evenings and weekends?[41] Miraculously, there was a cancellation[42] and we were able to jump the queue, securing an appointment with a highly regarded child developmental psychologist in our area near us after waiting only a few weeks.

Selecting and committing to a therapy program is not the end of one's difficulties; rather, it is only the beginning. Because (you are told), if you are going to go into the ring with autism, you have to *combat* it,[43] defeat it,[44] be ready to fight it with every resource you have[45] and, if you do not give up—maybe, just *maybe*, you just might not see *regression*.[46]

Susan Wendell writes of the guilt-ridden burden felt by individuals with impairments or illnesses when friends and family members offer, surely motivated by kindness and love, endless advice about new treatments, perhaps something they saw on a talk show or advertised on the Home Shopping Network. Wendell writes,

> To turn down a suggestion is to risk the judgment that you do not want to get well. To pursue every suggestion is a full-time job (with a price tag instead of a pay-cheque). For people with life-threatening illnesses, pressures from their loved ones to seek a cure can consume their remaining time in medical and quasi-medical quests.[47]

Wendell correctly points out that a plethora of therapies does not make the ill or impaired person's life better and richer—it makes her situation profoundly worse, for at no point is she permitted to come to terms with her illness or condition and learn to live with it. Because there is always something else to buy, to try, there is always another battle to fight. And these battles are *exhausting*. Wendell's astute discussion concerns adults who are placed in the situation of having to make crucial therapy decisions without complete information regarding their own future outcomes. What is so stressful for a parents of children diagnosed with autism is that they must make therapy and treatment decisions on behalf of their child who is completely vulnerable and cannot (at the age these life-changing options are being foisted upon the parents) play a role in the decision-making process. It is absolutely terrifying.[48] Lest the parents lose energy, conviction, or confidence, there always seems to be a therapist nearby to spur them on. The first time we met with our son's child developmental psychologist[49] he said, "It's all on you: if you provide him with all the resources he needs, he *may* become a self-sufficient contributing member of society, perhaps even a brilliant scholar. If you *fail* him, he'll end up living out his days in a group home." I genuinely believe his remarks were motivated not by hostility (though they certainly provoked hostility in me) but by the desire to prompt us to take seriously our task as our son's caretakers, to inspire us to do *everything* we could so that we would keep him safe from the horrors of institutional life which, just a few decades ago,[50] was the most probable outcome for an autistic child.[51]

Although we did settle on a reasonably noninvasive therapy plan with the child developmental psychologist,[52] I cannot say I felt any sense of relief because I had no time to relax, ever.[53] If I was not actively engaging with our son in some sort of therapeutic activity or taking him to a therapist of some kind or other, I discovered that we had to make sure that he was protected at all times from those that might try to hurt him. Because, it seems, there is no shortage of people willing to inflict serious injuries upon autistic children. We discovered when our son was very young, just three and far from being able to verbalize his thoughts, that special education schools are not safe places for autistic children. One day I arrived to pick him up a few minutes early and, standing outside the schoolroom door, could hear the teacher screaming inside. When I turned the knob (but found it locked) the yelling inside suddenly stopped. A few seconds later the teacher opened the door and, looking flustered, she said to my son, (rather saccharinely, it seemed to me), "Look who's here! It's your mommy!" My son, who is normally a vivacious and happy boy, was standing rigidly in the corner, facing the walls—a behavior I had never seen him engage in before. That was the last day he attended that class. I have no idea what was going on in those classes. I think, I hope, my son has forgotten, which means I never *will* know.

Two years later, we tried a different program and a different teacher. Our son, by then five years old, was still not verbal but fairly competent with sign language and this teacher was wonderful[54]—but her paraprofessional ("para-pro") was a nightmare. To give but one example: if a child touched or accidentally bumped into a classmate while walking down the hallway on the way to the bathroom, the child lost his or her privilege to use the bathroom. The next year, when he was moved to a "real" elementary school when he was in kindergarten, his special ed teacher, despite acknowledging that he could easily handle a "mainstream" class such as art, kept him in special classrooms all day long. My husband and I thought that trying out one nonacademic mainstream course would have facilitated transitioning him to academic mainstream classes when he was older. Our son's teacher agreed with our plan, yet we noticed that our son was not being moved into any mainstream courses but instead was still spending every day in her special ed classes. One day, in March or so, with most of the school year gone by, we told her that we were fed up with the delays and that we wanted him to be mainstreamed in art immediately.[55] She furtively looked over her shoulder and whispered, "I *really* don't think that's a good idea. That teacher is really *abusive* to the 'special' kids. He will *not* be safe there. But PLEASE don't tell anyone I said that." I have had special ed teachers tell me the "low down" of our public school district in school parking lots, after work hours ended, in strictest confidentiality, because they feared repercussions. They were horror stories indeed.

Is it a consolation that these tales of woe are not limited to our school district but fairly typical? Not really. Every parent of every autistic child has good reason to be terrified for his or her child's safety at the hands of others. Although students with impairments make up just 14 percent of the nationwide student population, students with disabilities make up 19 percent of those receiving corporal punishment.[56] Autistic children, perhaps because they are often nonverbal and are therefore particularly vulnerable, are among those children *most likely* to receive corporal punishment in public schools.[57] Punishment methods include paddling, hitting with belts, rulers, pinching, slapping, grabbing, dragging across floors, being locked alone in an empty room for hours on end, and being slammed into a wall.[58] Restraints include duct taping an autistic child to a desk, taping their mouth shut, holding them in a "basket hold" or other restraint position designed for adult psychiatric patients.[59] The consequences of these practices can be devastating to autistic children.[60] On top of any immediate physical injuries, parents report their children to be too traumatized to go back to school, too afraid to go to stores for fear of seeing teachers or a principal, and report the onset of self-injurious behavior, nightmares, bed-wetting, crying and "meltdowns."[61]

As disturbing as the fact that teachers brutalize autistic children is the fact that the children's behaviors that prompt the violence are: failing to answer a question posed by a teacher, talking repetitively on a favorite theme, rocking and wiggling in a chair, fidgeting in class, spinning while walking down a hallway, and taking shoes off during class.[62] Each of these behaviors is entirely consistent with a diagnosis of autism and therefore typical for an autistic child to engage in. Thus, being punished for any of these actions is, I think, a violation of the American Disabilities Act and is, therefore, against federal law.[63]

The hostility does not end there. Among the madding crowd I found parents of autistic children, many of whom lamented their fate, griping about how violent their autistic children are and how burdened their lives are since their child "became" autistic. In her notorious essay "The Monster Inside My Son," Ann Bauer refers to her twenty-one-year-old son in the most dehumanizing terms: a "gnashing beast," "the warty monster from a Grimm fairy tale," and "a night creature."[64] In it, too, she describes his behavior as "senseless," "rampaging," and "full of rage"—he is an "unspeakably violent" problem that cannot be reasoned with and who is beyond understanding. When a friend misunderstands the nature of her son's "illness," she chooses not to clarify, allowing the friend to assume the son has "something like leukemia." Bauer writes, "I wanted to tell her I would hack off my right arm in return for something *as simple as cancer*. The flickering beauty of a sad, pure, too-early death sounds *lovely*. Instead I nodded, silent and dumb."[65] So Bauer would rather have a child dying of cancer than her son who has autism? Hundreds of people commented in response to this essay, and all but a small handful offered their overwhelming support of Bauer. Many wrote that they found Bauer's essay "brave" and "honest," an "important" insight into how "painful" and "heartbreaking and home wrecking" autism is.

Autism Every Day, a documentary film sponsored by Autism Speaks, contains the much–commented upon moment in which Alison Tepper Singer states, in front of her autistic daughter, that confronting the challenges of searching for satisfactory schooling for her autistic daughter has prompted her to consider driving off a bridge (thus killing herself *and her daughter*).[66] And lest one conclude that Singer's dramatics are just so much talk, stories of parents who kill their autistic children enter the news with pathetic regularity. Karen McCarron, a physician, smothered her two-year-old autistic daughter with a plastic bag on May 3, 2006, just four days after the release of the film *Autism Every Day*. In July, 2010, Saiqa Akhter killed her five-year-old son and her two-year-old daughter because they were both autistic. In her now famous 9-1-1 call, she explained why she strangled both her children with a wire (after her attempts to poison the children failed because the children would not take the poison), "They're both not normal, not normal. . .They're autistic. Both are autistic. . .I don't want my children to be like that. . .I want normal kids."[67] Newspapers articles, attempting to make sense of Akhter's actions, typically include interviews of social workers who explain the high stress parents of autistic children are under. Apparently the feeling, even hope, for death among parents of autistic children is not unusual. But, these social workers tell us, death is not the solution—additional therapy is.[68] Just recently, Elizabeth Hodgins shot her adult son, George Hodgins, who was twenty-two years old, because (apparently) she tired of him living at home.[69] George, who was described as "a delight" by his teachers, did not speak or communicate much. Heather Jauch, the Hodgins' neighbor for five years, said Elizabeth Hodgins had just a few days before the killing mentioned that she found the thought of caring for George for the rest of her life simply overwhelming.[70]

Jean Lewis, a director of FEAT,[71] an organization for parents and family members dedicated to "early autism treatment," warns that, without treatment, "[K]ids *like this* are usually institutionalized by the time they're adolescents. They're living in restraints, living in diapers. They have to have their teeth removed because they bite."[72] The belief that autistic children will bite, hit and assault others—and therefore extreme forms of violence can justifiably be used against them to prevent their inevitable attacks—is quite widespread. Initially, one of my son's teachers resisted quite strongly to allowing him into her classroom despite the fact that his previous teachers had provided him very positive recommendations and that he would be accompanied by a "personal assistant" at all times.[73] At one point during our conversation she asked, "Can you *guarantee* that he will never harm the other children?" Considering what I have seen so-called "normal" children do to one another in school hallways and on playgrounds (both during my own childhood and while observing my older son's earlier school years), I found this question astonishing. "Can you guarantee that none of those children will ever, at any time, harm *my* son?" I asked. Of course *neither* of us could make any such guarantee because *no one* can make guarantees regarding the future behavior of any person. Any human is capable of engaging in violent behaviors (in one circumstance or another) including, of course, children. Whether or not the person is autistic is simply irrelevant.

But the correlation between *autism* and *violence* is never irrelevant to the parents of an autistic child. Because even if they know that their child is not prone to being violent, they know that the Culture of Autism is thoroughly soaked with the idea that their autistic child *is* inherently violent—is a "monster" that threatens every classroom and will continue to be a burden for the rest of their life. Is it any wonder, then, that parents of autistic children propel themselves into a frantic search for therapies and treatment programs for their child, if only to save him or her from the malevolent and punitive actions of others. Even more understandable is that parents press researchers to find the Holy Grail of autism: a Cure.

CURING AUTISM

It is generally accepted that there is, at this time, no way to cure or prevent autism. This fact is regarded by most as a great tragedy and, therefore, there is a tremendous demand being made on researchers to find a cure for this complex neurological condition.[74] But there are two, very different, ways to conceptualize the notion of "cure" and in the frenzied conversations about autism, they get muddled, either unintentionally or, perhaps, not.

One way to conceptualize "cure" is as therapy. I will refer to this as the Therapeutic Cure (TC) model and on this account a cure is a beneficial treatment for the patient that eliminates or ameliorates the harms of the disease, disorder or condition. Modern medicine is rife with examples of cures that fit the TC model. For example, in 1999, The World Health Organization established a goal cure rate of 85 percent of the tuberculosis patients in Russia; these patients were treated with antibiotics. The achieved cure rate was 80 percent.[75] In contrast, diabetes is typically managed with insulin. Because insulin does not *end* the medical condition of diabetes, insulin is not a *cure* but instead a treatment.

It is difficult to conceptualize what a therapeutic *cure* for autism would be. This is because autism, it is claimed, affects every neurological process of an autistic individual. Dawson *et al.* write:

> Few aspects of neurology have not been proposed as being atypical in autism. For example, regions of reported neurofunctional atypicalities range from the brainstem to the inferior frontal gyrus, while reported neuroanatomical atypicalities range from increased white and gray matter volume to more densely packed cells and increased numbers of cortical minicolumns. Neurofunctional connectivity has been suggested to be atypical, and neural resources may be atypically allocated or rededicated. Virtually every fundamental human cognitive and affective process, singly or as part of an overarching model, has been proposed to be dysfunctional or absent in autism.[76]

Indeed, if we are to believe what is published,[77] the entire "autistic brain" is neurologically atypical. Moreover, these neurological atypicalities begin being structured well before birth. Thus, the only plausible therapeutic cure would seem to be gene therapy.[78] However, Jill Boucher writes,

> Given the complexity of the genetic factors that may contribute to autism and the unknown environmental factors that influence the processes of brain-building, and brain function set in motion by the genes, gene therapy effecting a complete cure is probably only a remote possibility. Equally, the complexity and variability of the neurobiological bases of autism suggest that completely curing all cases of autism by altering patterns of brain chemistry, growth and function is also only a remote possibility.[79]

Boucher's skepticism is reasonable given what we are proposing gene therapy to accomplish. Despite the fact that parents may not see symptoms or "signs" of autism until a child is two or even three years old (or even later), early triggers begin building relevant brain structures very early in development—perhaps during the earliest stages of fetal development. Moreover, since brain development is influenced by environmental factors (such as maternal diet and health, as well as countless other factors), it seems reasonable to hypothesize that environmental factors heavily influence how autism is expressed in each individual. Thus, to cure each and every single autistic person would require not merely understanding the myriad genetic markers that initially *trigger* autism, but would also require addressing the resultingly varied brain structures of each autistic person after being influenced by environmental factors.

But let us set aside all those worries.[80] Even if gene therapy *could* work for *all* the various autistic individuals (who express their autistic symptoms in an astonishing variety of ways), gene therapy would effectively "rewire" each autistic person's brain—their entire neurological structure—so that it was no longer neurologically atypical. I suppose the underlying assumption of gene therapy is that treatment would cease when the autistic person (a) would no longer exhibit any external signs of autism (would no longer *act* autistic); (b) would no longer have the neurological structures of an autistic individual (would no longer have what is rather bizarrely and entirely misleadingly referred to as an "autistic brain") which we are meant to believe is verifiable with an MRI; (c) would no longer cognize[81] as an autistic individual; and (d) would no longer have the emotional responses (such as social anxieties) typical for an autistic individual.

If it really *was* possible to cure autism using gene therapy, the implications of undertaking such a treatment program are grotesque, given that the identity of a person is intimately connected to their brain structures. Indeed, the autistic person's very being—who they are (their memories, their desires, wishes, hopes, plans) and what they can become—would be altered by this so-called *cure*. Surely such a neurological treatment is deeply unethical. Researchers have concluded that insurmountable practical obstacles have ensured that searching for a therapeutic cure for autism is simply a nonstarter. However, given the ethical implications of a therapeutic cure for autism, especially in the form of gene therapy, I think we should be profoundly grateful for those practical obstacles.

There is another way to conceptualize cure. Rather than conceive of a cure as therapy as TC does, you strive to eliminate the disease at all costs without regard for the health or well-being of any specific patient. I refer to this as the Negative Eugenics Cure (NEC) model. With NEC, the disease, disorder or condition is considered so deleterious, that preserving the person with the disease or condition has a lower priority than the priority of eliminating the disease or condition. There are two approaches the NEC model could adopt to curing autism:

1. Genetic counselors could provide couples who have an autistic child but who are considering having another child with information about the statistical chances that any additional children they may conceive will be autistic. Depending upon the information they receive and how they feel about autism the parents may select to not have additional children and, therefore, remove themselves from the "gene pool."[82]

2. Genetic screening is the other possibility, which itself provides two moments for testing, either with preimplantation genetic diagnosis (PGD) or with an amniocentesis test during pregnancy. The idea of PGD is that, were many embryos created and each screened for autistic markers, and only *some* tested positive (but some not), the parents are then in the position to decide to choose to implant those embryos that tested positive for autism *or not*. Likewise, with the amnio, the DNA strand of the fetus is tested for autism markers and, if it tests positive, the mother is in a position to decide whether or not she wants to abort the fetus.

Criticisms of genetic screening for diseases and disorders are not new but worth mentioning briefly. Amnio tests are not 100 percent reliable; they yield a large percentage of false positives (up to around 5 percent for some conditions) and women may, as the result of a false positive, choose to abort a child they otherwise want.[83] And, very significantly, even if the test accurately identified autistic markers, what parents really want to know is "how serious the autism is" because, as I have stated above, given the class stratifications within the autism spectrum, there is a clear valuation within the autism spectrum, with a strong preference for Asperger's (or "Aspies" as they are sometimes known) over the so-called low functioning autistics.[84] Of course, what parents should be told (because it will be true), is that there is no possible way to predict the future wellbeing of a child based on knowing the genetic markers. Given that environmental factors affect autism and, given how readily some autistics respond to occupational and speech therapy, for example, there is simply no possible way to know at the embryonic stage how successful any specific child will be—or, just as importantly, how generously society will respond to that same child when as an adult he or she is looking for employment or housing. What social supports will be in place? What opportunities will be—will have been—in place for that person to make use of and most benefit from? If a would-be parent is risk averse (as is likely otherwise why genetically screen the embryos for autism?), then it is highly likely that she will implant the embryos that do not test positive for autism.[85]

Of course, at this point in time, a conversation about genetic screening for autism is purely theoretical because, although it is generally agreed that there is a strong genetic basis for autism, one's genetics do not entirely determine one's autism. Early reports on twin studies claimed a heritability rate of 90 percent for autism, but now it is generally agreed that those reports were "overstated."[86] Nonetheless, the bulk of current research seeking a cure for autism is focused on genetics—and the inevitable outcome of that research, if successful, is clear: genetic screening. On February 23, 2005, Joseph Buxbaum of the Autism Genome Project at the Mount Sinai School of Medicine predicted that there would be a prenatal test for autism within the next ten years.[87] In response to Buxbaum's statement, disability rights advocates created an Autistic Genocide Clock set for a ten-year countdown.

AN ANTI-CURE PERSPECTIVE

At some point I had had enough. I simply could not stand what had happened to our family since the therapists had, in effect, moved in. Every time our son sat for an hour or two, drawing eggplants over and over (no matter how artistically), I thought "perseveration" and felt slightly sick inside. Every time he toe-walked or flapped, I thought, "regulation problems," and felt the burden of the need to schedule in occupational therapy hours. Every time he beetled up to his room in search of a book or toy but did not return, presumably having become lost in the joy of playing with his other toys, I would think, "executive dysfunction," and felt terrible distress. Fortunately, amazingly, I discovered autistic writers, thinkers, artists, and activists, each of whom is critical of the idea that autism is a disorder in need of a cure.

Jim Sinclair is credited with founding the anti-cure movement in the 1980s.[88] The first foundational claim is that autism is an essential feature of the person, not a contingent feature. Moreover, essential features should be respected much in the way we treat other essential features of persons, like their race identity or sex or sexual identity: with respect. Having a disease such as multiple sclerosis or a condition such as asthma would be, according to Sinclair, a contingent, *non*essential feature of a person. Therefore, were a person to be cured of multiple sclerosis or asthma, their essential nature, that is who they are as a person, would not be changed. However, unlike asthma or multiple sclerosis, autism is an identity and thus to cure autism (were that even remotely possible) would be to alter the identity of the person. In his seminal essay, "Don't Mourn For Us," Sinclair argued:

> It is not possible to separate the autism from the person. Therefore, when parents say, "I wish my child did not have autism," what they're really saying is, "I wish the autistic child I have did not exist and I had a different (non-autistic child) instead." Read that again. This is what we hear when you mourn

over our existence. This is what we hear when you pray for a cure. This is what we know, when you tell us of your fondest hopes and dreams for us: that your greatest wish is that one day we will cease to be, and strangers you can love will move in behind our faces.[89]

Sinclair is credited with introducing the language which many autistic activist organizations promote today, the preferred language of "I *am* autistic," (or "He or she *is* autistic") rather than "I have autism" (or "He/she *has autism*").

This debate is no trivial matter and emotions can get heated. Consider this discussion in a *New York Times* editorial, which describes the agonies felt by some parents distressed by their recalcitrant autistic children. One parent, Kit Weintraub, lamented her eight-year-old son's choice to be Mickey Mouse for Halloween when normal eight-year-olds wanted to be Frodo from *Lord of the Rings*. Weintraub complained, "I worry about when he gets into high school, somebody doesn't want to date him or be his friend," she said, "It's no fun being different." Her son, it seems, continues to display "signs" of autism (such as a stilted manner of speaking and, as stated above, the unacceptable preference for Mickey Mouse over Frodo) which, it seems to Weintraub, is evidence of a need for additional A.B.A. treatments.[90]

In her widely circulated blog, *A Mother's Perspective*, Weintraub, mother of two autistic children, writes:

> My children *have autism*; they are not "autistics." What's the difference? The difference is that autism refers to a neurological disorder, hereditary in nature. Autism, according to the vast majority of medical experts today, causes *severely abnormal* development, and without appropriate treatment it can condemn those affected to a life of isolation and dependency. "Autistics" is a rather new politically-correct term that I find troubling; it is a label that attempts to define people with autism as members of an elite group of human beings who differ from the rest of us only in terms of their unique talents and their superior way of experiencing the world.[91]

Weintraub is clearly concerned. But why? On the one hand, she is convinced that all autistics are severely abnormal yet, on the other, she seems worried that merely the use of a new-fangled term will elevate autistics to an elite corps. Many autistics, adults and teenagers, scorn the views held by parents like Weintraub.[92] To the anti-cure perspectivists, Weintraub's allegiance to normalcy reveals not only a profound lack of empathy for the autistic person's interests and values (which is ironic since nonautistics are allegedly naturally capable of empathy), but also a spectacular intellectual dullness.

Which leads us to the second foundational claim of the anti-cure movement, that society should appreciate and protect *neurodiversity*. The term "neurodiversity" was coined by autistic Judy Singer in the 1990s.[93] Valuing neurodiversity means, at a minimum, accepting that autism has an organic basis. More significantly, it means regarding autistic individuals *as fully persons* rather than as broken beings in need of repair. It also means that rather than regarding autistic neurological structures as "defective" or "disordered," one should regard autistic neurology as worth valuing because each neurological structure contributes to the collective variety of human neurological diversity, in much the same way that each human culture contributes to cultural diversity and each of the hundreds of human languages makes a valuable contribution to human linguistic diversity.[94]

Although one could endorse neurodiversity simply for its own sake, in a reaction against sameness, singleness, or narrowness, others argue that autistics create original art, literature, music and are creators of scientific innovation that have cultural worth.[95] Joseph Straus claims that recent contributions made by autistic writers, artists and musicians make talking of "autistic culture" coherent. Straus argues that autistic culture has three characteristics:

Local Coherence: Although typically pathogized as "obsessive compulsive" or "getting lost in the details and an inability to attend to the whole," Strauss describes the autistic artist (whether he or she is a musician or painter, say) as one who *attends to minute detail* and preference for complexity rather than confusion.

Fixity of Focus: In medical models, autistics will be described as ritualistic if not bordering on being paralyzed by rigidity or sameness. Strauss describes artists as expressing this as a preference for a neatness and orderliness in style and design, often providing them with a capacity to engage in a calm constancy that allows them to engage in repetitive activities over and over again—which may be necessary for completing complicated craft or artistry that requires a tremendous attention to detail.[96]

Private Meanings: Autistic thinking is usually described as idiosyncratic. Autistic artists are often very private, not only in the way they think but also in how they think. Because they are not "caught up in social niceties" they are free to defy social conventions, often with profoundly liberating ways. Autistic art, comedy, literature, and music is *avant garde*, though not self-consciously so. As Gunilla Gerland writes, "This apparent disregard for the convention appears to be brave. In fact, I had absolutely no idea that there were such things as conventions."[97]

Strauss claims that as more and more autistic individuals self-identify as autistic and make their membership in the autistic community known, this fledgling community will become even more vibrant than it already is.[98]

AND, SO…?

What does all this mean? For all my railing against the therapeutic industry, I will hereby admit that I have gained one invaluable insight from our son's child developmental psychologist. During one meeting with him, we were talking about something (I can't remember specifically what now), some behavior of our son's that would be classified as "perseverative" in text-books. Because I had already internalized the Culture of Autism, I was fret-ting about the "meaning" of our son's seemingly meaningless behaviors and, most likely, pressing him for a future date when the behavior would, with enough therapy, magically go away. He then asked me if I had ever tried engaging in the so-called "perseverative" activities that my son enjoyed so much *alongside* my son—such as lining up plastic toys, lying on the ground and staring at the sand as it ran through his hands, throwing giant rocks into a pond or pool over and over. I stared at him in bewilderment. "No," I said, "I haven't." "Well," he smiled (reminding me a bit of the Cheshire cat in *Alice in Wonderland*), "Perhaps you should. *He* is clearly having the time of his life. Maybe if you join him, you will find out *why* he is doing what is doing and *why* it makes him so happy." This suggestion shocked me for a number of reasons. Not only did it force me to realize the obvious, that my son had *reasons* for his behaviors (he was not merely a collection of pathologies as the *DSM-IV* implies), but that he may have *good* reasons for what he does. Indeed, it may be the case that, were I to give his preferred activities a try, *I* may find pleasure in them as well. But also surprising and deeply disappoint-ing, was how vividly I realized how utterly dull and adult, how painfully normalized, I had become. I had a view of myself as a radical outsider and yet here I was fretting about my son becoming normal. Where was that coming from? I was never normal when I was growing up and I had never *wanted* to be normal. Why did I think I wanted my son to be normal? What was I *thinking*? I suddenly remembered a conversation I had with my hus-band years earlier, when our son was first diagnosed, while I was reading something which claimed that with "aggressive intervention an autistic child can live a normal life" and my husband said something to the effect of "But what if they don't *want* a 'normal life'?"

Shifting perspective to a toddler's and, later, preschooler's interests was fascinating and liberating. And it certainly allowed me to rediscover some parts of my own long-lost childhood. When three and four years old, our son was particularly interested in throwing rocks in our pond (over and over), lining up toys, "water play"[99] and jumping on the trampoline.[100] But he really loved anything that was messy—slimes, doughs, mud, wet sand, glue—any viscous gelatinous substance (even better if it stained fabric) was highly appealing. And he reveled in those globs, pulling, pushing, shoving, kneading them into his mouth, up his nose, into his eyes and hair; he was living it all the way. Although I was never able to *completely* share his zestful enthusiasm for bodily encounters with slimy substances, I do admit that I was able to overcome my discomfort for having 'icky hands' and was able to enjoy playing in mud, sand and slime with him. Playing in the mud with him also dislodged a happy (and completely forgotten) memory of me taking a mud bath when I was very young and felt no revulsion for wallowing in mud.

I will not pretend that raising a child with autism is easy. Yet despite the difficulties, some parents of autistic children are voicing their concerns for the search for a cure for autism. Virginia Bovell, parent of autistic son, Danny, writes,

> To cure my amazing son Danny would be to suggest that there is something dreadfully wrong with him, perhaps even something we, as parents, couldn't live with—but nothing could be further from the truth. If someone took away Danny's autism, it would also take away so much of who he is. And I am certain that many parents of autistic children would agree, because how can I ever tire of watching my son's face light up with joy as he kicks leaves in the park on his way to school? It's a simple pleasure, but Danny—thanks to his autism—has access to a kind of rapture we, as 'normal' people, cannot imagine. He has a level of pleasure way beyond the rest of humanity, and just the simplest of things—sitting behind me on our new tandem bicycle, bouncing on a trampoline or seeing his grandmother—set him off giggling with pure joy. His enjoyment of life stems from simple things, but that is one of the things that make him so special—and to me, curing him would be to take away all that characterizes my beloved son.[101]

Ken Bruce, parent of autistic son Murray, states, "I believe the world would be a better place if every family had experience of a child with autism."[102] I do not believe Bruce is wishing that every family have a child that is autistic. Rather, I think he is claiming that living with and coming to genuinely understand one's autistic child—developing an empathetic affection for that child, grandchild, sibling, cousin, loved one—makes you a genuinely better human being. And, were every nonautistic person able to have a genuinely caring and affectionate connection with an autistic person, the world would be a far better place. I agree with him.[103] The difficulties I face do not stem primarily from my son's autism, but from (initially) my complete lack of understanding of autism, from the lack of social supports we had to scramble to find for him and ourselves,[104] from the fact that our public school system is completely unable to educate autistic children,[105] and the lack of adequate federal regulation to protect vulnerable parents from rip-off artists and charlatans selling dangerous medications, "herbal supplements" and "alternative remedies" that are endangering autistic children.[106]

When the worries of raising an autistic child seem too much, perhaps it helps, if only slightly, to think of Hans Asperger's words of more than sixty years ago, "We are convinced, then, that autistic people have their place in the organism of the social community. They fulfill their role well, perhaps better than anyone else could, and we are talking of people who as children had the greatest difficulties and caused untold worries to their care-givers."[107]

REFERENCES

Asperger, H. 1991. "Autistic Psychopathy" in Childhood, 1944, translated and annotated by U. Frith. In *Autism and Asperger Syndrome*, ed. U. Frith. Cambridge, UK: Cambridge University Press.

Boucher, Jill. 2009. *The Autistic Spectrum: Characteristics, Causes and Practical Issues*. Los Angeles: Sage Publications Ltd.

Dawson, Michelle, Laurent Mottron, and Morton Ann Gernsbacher. 2008. Learning in Autism. *Learning and Memory: A Comprehensive Reference*, J. H. Byrne (ed.-in-chief), H. L. Roediger, III (vol. ed.). New York: Academic Press.

Granpeesheh, Doreen, Jonathan Tarbox, Dennis R. Dixon, Arthur E. Wilke, Michael S. Allen. 2009. Randomized Trial of Hyperbaric Oxygen Therapy for Children with Autism. *Research in Autism Spectrum Disorders* 3(4):1014–22.

Lyons, V. and M. Fitzgerald. 2007. Did Hans Asperger (1906–1980) Have Asperger Syndrome? *Journal of Autism Developmental Disorders* 37(10):2020–21.

Straus, Joseph. 1997. Autism as Culture. *The Disability Studies Reader*, 3rd Edition, ed. Lennard J. Davis. New York: Routledge.

Sykes, N. H., and J. A. Lamb. 2007. Autism: The Quest for the Genes. *Expert Review Molecular Medicine* 9(24):1–15.

Wendell, Susan. 1996. *The Rejected Body: Feminist Philosophical Reflections of Disability*, 97–98. New York: Routledge.

NOTES

1. There is tremendous energy spent debating whether or not autistic children should be taught to sign and years earlier we were thrown right into the storm. One camp advises that prelingual autistic children will be "confused" by sign language and this confusion will delay the development of "normal" speech. The other camp advises that children should be taught to sign because it is a visual language and therefore it will be easier for them to learn sign than a verbal language and, so, it will both facilitate immediate communication and will also help verbal communication skills develop later on. With both sides promising that the wrong choice will ruin the child forever and that theirs is the only way, "to sign or not to sign" is just one choice among seemingly hundreds that parents of autistic children must make with almost no reliable empirical guidance available. We sided with the signing side and found resources for him to teach sign to himself (given that we do not know sign) and he LOVED IT. He learned it easily, quickly, and enthusiastically. Though he has just recently become somewhat verbally confident, he still signs every day, often while singing but especially if tired or when not feeling well. But I have come to the conclusion that signing is more than merely a useful tool that facilitates communication; signing is a game, a secret code, a special passage into a world of symbols that, for a child already giddy with delight at the patterns made by letters and with words themselves. Signing is simply a source of delight. For example, signing WATER is so much more than a means to get water: you make a "w" with your first three fingers and you tap your chin—but do you see what you did? Water *starts* with W and when you sign WATER it's like the "w" goes right into your mouth and turns into water as you tap your chin. If you think about the sign, you can almost understand a toddler's delight with signing—a toddler, that is, with a predilection for answering questions such as "What is that?" (when shown a picture of a

cat in a book) with "3-1-20" because C is the 3rd letter, A is the 1st letter and T is the 20th letter of the alphabet. The whole world becomes a visual symbol, a semiotic metaphor, a physically embodied manifestation of thought! What could be better? And signing is still one of his favorite interests, a hobby really, which he has tried to teach to me many, many times. And I *have* tried to learn, I really have. But there is no way I can keep up with him because his memory is far superior to mine. Anyway, he enjoys showing off what he knows and I do not think it is so terrible a thing that he can outshine his parents at something he loves to do so much. (Our son's predilection for coding, we were later told, is termed "hyperlexia." I was continually encountering resistance whenever I described my son in terms of his individual capacities or personality. Therapists were forever reminding me that he would do this or that because of the "autistic tendency for X" or because of the "autistic tendency for Y." Moreover, virtually everything we said about him would be redescribed as an autistic pathology. Yet, I happen to find hyperlexia (and other autistic "splinter skills" like photographic memory and phonographic memory) quite awesome.

2. By this point in our son's life I would guess I have spent at least one hundred hours filling out questionnaires for various psychologist and psychiatrists, therapists (of every sort imaginable), and special education teachers and support staff for special education schools and programs concerning his autism. All the questionnaires are the same and all have the same conceptual problems. And every time I have asked, "Does signing count as talking?" the test givers do not know. This is no trivial matter because if they are asking about verbal language development, then it should not. If they are asking about communication development, that is, about whether or not our son initiates and successfully creates complex sentences in any format whatsoever, then I would think it should count as language as a fully signed sentence is a form of social communication. So which is it? Bizarrely, I have been told (when I objected to filling in questionnaires with ambiguous questions) that these questionnaires must be completed entirely despite the fact that neither the person answering the questions nor the person giving the questionnaire understood the questions and that skipping questions is not allowed (on pain of what, one wonders—lost grant money?) and that those administering the questionnaires were instructed to give the stock answer: "Just fill in the bubbles the way you think makes most sense."

3. I am not sure why he decided to focus his attention on me since neither my husband nor I were giving any indications that we were the least interested in his proposal. Perhaps he had decided on a "divide and conquer" strategy that was to start with me.

4. Now the phrase "curing autism" sounds odd to me, comparable to curing homosexuality—not only a scientifically misguided project but highly ethically and politically suspect.

5. Although (as Orson Welles remarked) we are born alone, we live alone and we die alone, I did not experience this autistic therapy haze alone. While I was always among others and we survived these events together, nonetheless, we each made sense of them in our own way, very much alone. I am writing about my experiences from my point of view only.

6. This was the same neurologist to whom we were years later referred for my son's migraines. You would think that we would not have gone back to him that second time but I can only say the migraines our son had suffered were horrific and we were desperately hoping that "one of the very top neurologists" in the region would come through for us with something that would ameliorate the pain. No dice.

7. It is debatable that autism deserves the term "disorder" since common "splinter traits" that autistic individuals have are advantageous and highly valuable, such as superior memory. I prefer the name Autism Spectrum Condition (ASC).

8. Is it any wonder that one of his favorite books has always been Maurice Sendak's *Where the Wild Things Are*? And one of his favorite passages in the book is when Max tames the wild things by staring into their yellow eyes without blinking once. I've long been convinced that my son "tames" me, getting me to do his bidding by staring into my eyes without blinking once, and has been doing so since well before his first birthday. It is a powerful skill he has developed and he shows no sign of giving it up as he gets older.

9. To this day the chapter drafts sit, dusty on a shelf in my office. I really do not know if I will ever get back to it. It now seems like a book started by a different person.

10. For example, when our son was three, he did benefit enormously from having very heavy-duty, three-sided colored pencils (rather than standard crayons) to color with until his fine-motor skills developed sufficiently that he could use other writing implements more successfully. Crayons would simply break in his hands and he would get too frustrated to enjoy coloring. Now that he no longer needs those heavy-duty colored pencils, we no longer buy them—which is a relief because they are ridiculously expensive. But I do believe they are important for developing valuable skills. I am sold on mini-trampolines, too; they're great for developing balance and large motor skills and, even better, they're fun. Fortunately (if you do not need to buy the ones with safety bars on the sides) they are not too expensive.

11. I have many ways to waste time, surfing the web is only one. I hereby admit that one perverse web surfing interest of mine is "collecting" bullshit autism cures. Why I do this, I really do not know. I never slow to stare at car accidents and could not possibly care less about the train wrecks that are the lives of most celebrities. So why do I spend my very rare spare time imagining the horror shows that are playing out with sad regularity, like movie schedules at a local cinema, of rip off artists selling these useless if not dangerous treatments to depressed, terrified and misinformed parents who then inflict them upon their vulnerable autistic children?

12. http://www.autismherbs.com/.

13. http://www.cellmedicine.com/pages/patient-application/?menu=footer.

14. http://www.cellmedicine.com/testimonials/?catid=17.

15. http://www.newautism.com/.

16. http://www.clayforautism.com/.

17. http://www.clayforautism.com/. Hundreds of products are marketed to "detox" autistic children. Most are simply a waste of money; some are dangerous if not deadly. "Probiotic-Rx" (a "professional strength formula" that "represents an evolutionary leap in probiotic science") includes 10 vitamins, 8 minerals and 18 amino acids 6.5 times normal strength (though normal strength of what is not made explicit). "BioGuard" professes to restore the autistic child's "bions" to optimal function—whatever those are. These products cost hundreds of dollars per month and have no known efficacy in treating autism. http://www.helpyourautisticchild.com/products. On chelation websites, parents testify to self-medicating their autistic child with heavy doses of zinc, magnesium, calcium, mega-doses of vitamins A, B-6, B-12, D and E, taurine, cysteine, sulfate, methionine, selenium and copper. One site sells a FAR Infrared Sauna (FIR) Detoxification Therapy system that will allegedly "enhance your immune system;" this site implies a link between using this sauna and "recovering" from autism. Prices range from around $1,500 to just under $3,000 depending on the size and materials used (http://www.sunlighten.com/?gclid=CNuPx-vWza4CFULrKgod9mlG-g).

18. This treatment is alleged to be successful for individuals suffering from carbon monoxide poisoning.

19. Research conducted by the Center for Autism and Related Disorders (CARD) found that hyperbaric oxygen therapy has no significant effect on symptoms of autism. But why let the results of research stop you from subjecting your child to this treatment? See Granpeesheh et al. 2009; http://www.centerforautism.com/autism_publications/default.asp.

20. http://www.balancedhealthtoday.com/Hyperbairc-Oxygen-Therapy-Autism.html.

21. http://www.balancedhealthtoday.com/Hyperbairc-Oxygen-Therapy-Autism.html.

22. http://autism.healingthresholds.com/therapy/packing-therapy. One feature of autism (either a defining feature or common symptom) is sensory processing difficulties. The purpose of occupational therapy, one highly regarded form of therapy for autistic individuals of all ages, is to help autistic individuals better "organize" sensory inputs with their cognitive awareness. In short, it helps autistic individuals become more skilled at attending to sensory inputs as well as becoming more physically competent at both fine and large motor skills. Therefore wrapping an autistic child in cold, clammy sheets for an hour and instructing him or her to not focus on what I would imagine would be strong sensory inputs seems to me, then, completely counter to everything that I have learned from our son's occupational therapist and what she set out to accomplish during the four years she and our son worked together.

23. The alleged purpose of the study was to test the therapeutic benefits of packing in response to catatonia. The fact that two of the children were autistic was, actually, irrelevant to the initial purpose of the study. Only four of the six children benefitted from packing, and of

those four, two were autistic. Simply because two of the four children in this study were autistic and this study was widely reported, it has become practically "common knowledge" that packing helps autistic children and packing is considered a standard therapy procedure in many clinical settings (http://autism.healingthresholds.com/therapy/packing-therapy).

24. http://www.asatonline.org/intervention/treatments/holding.htm.

25. http://www.psychologytoday.com/blog/child-myths/200909/holding-therapy-and-autism.

26. Both claims are attributed to Bruno Bettelheim, who did not believe that autism had an organic basis but instead believed it was caused by "refrigerator mothers" who withheld affection from their children. In his book, *The Empty Fortress* (1967), which was immensely influential in the United States, he compared the world of the autistic child to someone in a concentration camp. Holding therapy—forced restraint—would, he claimed, force an attachment between the parent and a child. In fact, it usually caused panic and terror in the child (http://www.firstthings.com/article/2008/08/006-in-the-case-of-bruno-bettelheim-15). Temple Grandin, a self-identified autistic and author of *Thinking in Pictures*, developed what she calls the "squeeze box." See: http://www.time.com/time/arts/article/0,8599,1960347,00.html. This mechanical device is made out of two big pads that gently squeezes the person within the machine. The essential difference between holding therapy and Grandin's squeeze machine is that holding therapy is forced upon the person by someone else and is, therefore out of the control of the autistic individual—a potentially terrifying experience for the person being held. On the other hand, the "squeeze box" (or, as it is sometimes called, hug machine) is self-controlled and is therefore in no way anxiety-inducing (http://www.asatonline.org/intervention/treatments/holding.htm).

27. Indeed, there have been fatalities when overly enthusiastic parents have held down a resisting child and asphyxiated the child or caused the child to go into coronary arrest (http://www.psychologytoday.com/blog/child-myths/200909/holding-therapy-and-autism).

28. http://4optimallife.com/Magnetic-Sleep-Pads-For-Health.html.

29. http://www.magnetictherapy.co.uk/.

30. As with many therapies, the popularity of aversion therapy goes in waves. At one time aversion therapy was commonly used to treat homosexuality. Now, as a treatment for homosexuality, it is regarded by the American Psychological Association as a dangerous practice that does not work. Nonetheless, aversion therapy is still used on children and teenagers if they are suspected to be homosexual by their parents. These children may be "forced to smell ammonia, describe humiliating scenarios, or engage in other uncomfortable acts, while looking at nude pictures, listening to audio tapes describing sexual situations, or describing their own fantasies. In order to measure sexual response, devices such as penile plethysmographs and vaginal photoplethysmographs are sometimes used, despite the controversies surrounding them." In 1992, the Phoenix Memorial Hospital used these methods on children as young as ten. See http://www.ethicaltreatment.org/arizonarepublic.htm and http://www.ethicaltreatment.org/yankowski.htm.

31. http://www.judgerc.org/.

32. JREC pooh-poohs the idea of positive reinforcement and therefore does not use it. Ever. They also seem inordinately pleased that they use only "minimal psychotropic treatments" on the children. But is a parent's idea of minimal usage the same as theirs? Probably not, but there is nothing parents can do about it since parents must waive all rights to interfere with JREC treatment decisions concerning their child (http://www.judgerc.org/).

33. http://www.judgerc.org/.

34. http://www.judgerc.org/.

35. On April 29, 2010, the American human rights organization Mental Disability Rights International filed a request with the United Nations Special Rapporteur on Torture, stating they believed the residents at JREC were being subjected to human rights abuses because of the use of electric shock on children. JREC was court ordered to turn over their security videotapes to the court. However, before the court could view the tapes, those tapes were destroyed. So, in May 2011, Matthew Israel, founder of JREC, was charged with misleading a grand jury over the school's destruction of the tapes, as well as being an accessory after the fact. Dr. Israel resigned in a deferred prosecution plea deal with the Massachusetts State Attorney General's

office (http://articles.boston.com/2011-05-25/lifestyle/29582413_1_shock-case-criminal-case-face-criminal-charges). However, according to the JREC website, Israel resigned because it was "time for [him] to move over and let others take the reins" (http://www.judgerc.org/). Interestingly, some inmates of JREC have posted YouTube videos protesting their experiences at JREC. They are rather heartbreaking to watch—though one young man did receive enthusiastic offers of affection from several commenters. The protest videos—and their responses—are a fascinating and wholly unanticipated, but quite inevitable, outcome of JREC's boast of "A Computer for Every Student," I cannot help but think.

36. http://articles.boston.com/2011-05-25/lifestyle/29582413_1_shock-case-criminal-case-face-criminal-charges.

37. Exorcism can be risky business as Ray Hemphill of the Faith Temple of the Apostolic Faith Church in Milwaukee, Wisconsin, discovered in 2003 after he killed an eight-year-old autistic boy after attempting to exorcise the autism out of him, an activity that required wrapping the boy (who was known to be extremely touch averse) in sheets while three women, including the child's mother, sat on the boy's arms and legs while Hemphill sat on his chest and whispered aspersions at the devil into the boy's ear. After two hours of such efforts, the boy stopped breathing (http://www.cbsnews.com/stories/2003/08/25/national/main570077.shtml).

38. I have been driving past one annoying billboard sponsored by Autism Speaks once a week, sometimes twice or even three times a week, for the past five years. It features a doe-eyed young boy with the text, "Every 20 minutes a child is diagnosed with autism." Of course there is no reason to believe these children are being accurately diagnosed, but the billboard is sufficiently alarmist, and that is its purpose.

39. "Autism is like cancer" is an analogy that has been used in an Autism Speaks newsletter on their website. Its capacity to terrify parents into frenzied action is likely the reason that Autism Speaks is one of the largest autism organizations in existence, which has raised (they claim) millions of dollars to "fight" autism. They explicitly advocate curing autism though I cannot find statements on their website explaining the exact nature of the research projects they support, such as whether or not they support genetic research that would lead to prenatal genetic testing and, therefore, selective abortion (http://www.autismspeaks.org/).

40. We were asked *ad nauseam* "When did you first notice the signs?" Why don't they get it? We never saw "signs." Because we exhibit the same "signs"? I don't know. We would not have ever gone to that neurologist if other people—pre-school teachers, for example—had not suggested to us that we ought to "get advising." Sometimes I wish we never had gone, but had simply moved far away from civilization instead. The epistemic shift one undergoes when handed a label which, it turns out, is practically meaningless, is nearly impossible to explain. And we can never go back to being P.D. (Pre-Diagnosis)—those wonderfully Halcyon days when you view your child as wholly individual, with a completely open future, rather than utterly essentialized by a condition. Of course, the truth is that your (autistic) child is still wholly individual with as much an open future as any other (nonautistic) child, but I have found that others view autistic children (just as they view all others with impairments) as essentially autistic, and nothing more. Resisting the conception of our son as nothing more than autistic is yet another exhausting battle to wage.

41. These are the kinds of hostile thoughts I had going through my mind during those months. I have heard that adversity brings out the best in people. I cannot say that I saw that happen in myself, particularly.

42. "What an idiot! Apparently they don't care about their kid!" was my first thought about some anonymous parent. As I said, these were not my best moments.

43. Combat Autism Act of 2006, Pub Law No. 109-416 was signed into law by President George W. Bush on December 19, 2006. This act authorized the spending of about a billion dollars on autism research over five years. It also authorized the Director of the NIH to create an "Autism Czar"—that is the real title, I did not make that up—who would coordinate NIH-based research. Staying true to the theme of war and disaster, Jon Shestack, co-founder of Cure Autism Now (CAN), stated "This bill is a federal declaration of war on the epidemic of autism. It creates a congressionally mandated roadmap for a federal assault on autism" (http://abcnews.go.com/Health/Story?id=2708925&page=1, emphasis added). The five years are up. As far as I know, autism has not been combated, defeated, or cured.

44. Defeat Autism Now (DAN) is the name of a rather notorious therapy program, more so since an autistic boy died after being subjected to the treatment plan (http://www.defeatautismnow.net/, see also http://www.acsh.org/factsfears/newsID.624/news_detail.asp).

45. Indeed, parents of autistic children are encouraged to spend not only their available resources but to go massively into debt. What decent parent would prioritize their own financial future or secure retirement when their child needs expensive therapy now? Why even bother setting aside for a college for that child if skimping on therapy means that child will never have a chance to go to college—indeed may never have the chance to go to a "normal school" at all? At one "parent support group" I met a couple who decided to spend a small fortune (given their incomes as middle-school teachers at a local public school) on one of their autistic children. They decided it was worthwhile to pay over $40,000 for the father and his almost three-year-old autistic son to live for four weeks in a hospital facility just over one hundred miles away to learn healthful dietary regimens because the son was a particularly fussy eater. The mother had elected to stay home with the boy's autistic fraternal twin sister, who was a less fussy eater. At the time I thought the decision was madness. But, as years have gone by and I have thrown away what sometimes seem like a small mountain of uneaten food (the word "NO!" echoes in my mind), I think to myself, "How much money have I wasted on rejected food? And at what point will those dollars total 40,000?" But the better question is: Did the hospital stay work? And, even if it did for them, would it work for us?

46. "Regression" is a term parents of an autistic child are bombarded with over and over again. Every enthusiastic therapist, counselor, book, manual and educational pamphlet, psychiatrist and psychologist has horror story after horror story of the child who "regressed" inexplicably. Typically these children were progressing amazingly—talking, succeeding in school, learning perhaps two, maybe three languages! They were children any parent would dream of having and then—poof!—it all disappeared. They regressed! They were back to acting like toddlers, in diapers again, they "lost" their capacity to talk—they were lumps! The moral of the story is: Everything parents work for can be STOLEN by autism ALL OVER AGAIN in the blink of an eye! I am not sure what purpose these stories are meant to serve in the Autism Mythos except to terrify. And terrify they do. They reel you in, just as when the carnie barker captivates his audience with tales of wonder and intrigue, you find yourself—despite whatever Ph.D.-trained sensibilities you brought with you to the Tent of Wonders—suckered more easily than a child. Any parent who loves their child will do everything to stop regression from happening to their child.

47. See Wendell 1996, 97-98.

48. Never mind that many parents of autistic children have not had a good night's sleep in years since up to 80 percent of autistic children have difficulty sleeping (http://www.kennedykrieger.org/patient-care/patient-care-programs/outpatient-programs/sleep-disorders-clinic-and-lab). Our son did not sleep more than two-hour stretches until he was about five years old. I hardly remember the years between my pregnancy with him and when he was five or so years old when he started sleeping through the night regularly. What little I do remember is veiled with headaches, exhausted caffeine-addled nausea and an itchy-eyed stupor. Is it any wonder that parents of autistic children are especially vulnerable to con artists and charlatans?

49. This psychologist scorned the diagnosis of PDD-NOS given by the neurologist ten months earlier and instead diagnosed our son as autistic. There is, I now know, an informal caste system within the "umbrella" of autism diagnoses. Perhaps not too surprisingly, parents covet the diagnosis of "high functioning autism," which is sometimes regarded as synonymous with Asperger's. Yet some want to distance Asperger's from autism and treat it as a distinct category (class); autism, a lower class, is then divided into high- and low-functioning autism. For obvious reasons, no parent hopes for a diagnosis of low-functioning autism despite the fact that there is no evidence that early diagnosis correlates with later success (or lack thereof). Thus low-functioning autistic children may be "late bloomers" and, in their teen years, acquire language skills of a level that allows them not only to meet but to surpass the skills acquired by so-called high-functioning autistic children. PDD-NOS is sometimes regarded as synonymous with low-functioning autism and sometimes regarded as its own category, distinct from both Asperger's and autism (both high- and low-functioning). Our son has been diagnosed as PDD-

NOS, as mentioned earlier, by a neurologist and by one occupational therapist; low-functioning autistic by the speech therapist, occupational therapist, social worker, and case worker at the special education school he attended when he was pre-K (I was told that this was a "stock label" they gave all their ASD kids so that they would get maximal therapy services from the school district; I do not know if they were trying to console me because of the disheartening label or not); "way high-functioning autism"—whatever that means—by one play therapist; autism, as stated above, by the child developmental psychologist; and "autism but not like anything I've ever seen before" by another speech therapist he saw privately for about three years. After a while, it is difficult to take these labels seriously—except that they entirely determine access to therapy services, of course.

50. I write "decades ago" as if institutionalizing autistic children no longer occurs standardly, but unfortunately it still does, though far less often. Part of the motivation for "early detection, early intervention" is, we were told, to ensure that life-long institutionalization occur less often than it did in the 1950s and 1960s, so as to prevent the barbaric horrors those people experienced.

51. Of course, the fact that parents who institutionalized their autistic children were following the enthusiastic recommendations of psychologists and psychiatrists is something that therapists now do not draw attention to. The history of inconsistent claims about autism, the history of useless and dangerous treatments for autistic individuals defended by the American Psychiatric Association, and the barbaric abuses inflicted upon autistic individuals by psychologists and psychologists is not something therapists are completely upfront about. Perhaps if they were, parents of autistic children might start thinking that the science of autism is like the Wizard of Oz: just a tiny man behind a curtain pushing a lot of buttons to create the illusion that something really fantastic is happening.

52. By noninvasive I mean that it did not require any biomedical or pharmaceutical products, was in no way connected to A.B.A. (which relies too heavily on aversion therapy for my comfort), and was not cripplingly expensive. It did require learning some bizarre jargon that I never quite mastered and which I now suspect is complete rubbish, designed to (a) get papers published in psychology journals and (b) impress parents. It also required that we tolerate various "play" therapists in our home for three hour stretches while they (1) videotaped us, (2) "shared" with us critiques of the previous play session, and (3) had us make a plan for the next session. I found the play sessions draining and dreaded each and every one. Both my husband and I would desperately hope the play therapist would be a "no show" but, unfortunately, he or she always showed up. (To be fair, I really, really liked them as people and of course I got a lot out of these sessions; otherwise I would not have continued with them for over a year. I just hate therapy sessions and really do NOT enjoy being videotaped, nor do I enjoy having people analyze how I behave while playing with my son while being videotaped for THREE FUCK-ING HOURS!) At one point, because we were participating in a study funded by a grant and organized by our son's child developmental psychologist, we had three different play therapists, each coming to our house for three-hour sessions, almost every single Friday for six months. It was a kind of living hell.

53. As with many reputable therapy programs, the therapy plan we chose recommends thirty-five to forty-five hours of therapy for our son every week, divided up between my husband and me, our son's "personal assistant" (someone who has known him since he was an infant and has gone through the "therapy training" with us), a speech therapist, occupational therapist and music therapist. Music therapy is not typically considered "essential therapy" for autism but, like art therapy, if the child is interested in it and there is a really good therapist, I believe the benefits can be tremendous. Our son has developed an amazingly close relationship with his music therapist. Our son has perfect pitch, was able to read music at a really young age, and is fascinated with musical instruments, particularly the guitar and piano. So, putting all his interests and "splinter skills" together, weekly music therapy seemed the obvious choice for developing his large and fine motor skills, communication and social skills. What turned out to be particularly challenging for him was playing both treble and bass clef on the piano at the same time. But, since he is so highly motivated to succeed, he does not give up. As a result, he plays piano as well as any child his age; more importantly, though, he is inordinately proud of himself when he masters a song (especially holiday songs—Jingle Bells was a particular

favorite). Indeed his attention span with his music therapist is seemingly unlimited; the fifty minutes seem to fly by. Our son never fails to give him eye contact appropriately; he sits calmly in his chair the whole time; and converses (and jokes) with his music therapist about what they are doing. During the rest of the week, our son mentions at least once a day—sometimes many times a day—the number of days until the next music therapy lesson. (Life is a perpetual countdown in our house.) But that same boy, in his mainstream classroom, stares out the window, wiggles endlessly as if he has fire ants in his pants, can't bring himself to look his teacher in the eyes, and spends his time doodling or talking about busses, sharks, eggplants, or any other idea that pops into his head. His teacher asks me at every parent–teacher meeting, what she can do to "reach him." The only truthful answer is: "Be as amazing as a well-trained therapist." But what would be the point of saying that?

54. This teacher, who is a little hard of hearing, signed throughout the day, and worked very well with our son. They were a great team and he adored her. Three years have gone by since he was in her class and he still gets out photos of her and mentions her lovingly.

55. I only mention art here as an example. In fact, we ended up discussing all the possibilities and each one was as bad as the other. But even I knew that the mainstream math class was impossible because I could hear the thirty-odd children yelling and screaming at top volume in that classroom. Our son never would have been able to handle the noise levels of that room—I could hardly stand walking past it to get to his room to drop him off in the morning. Eventually I did reach my limit for the whole damn place and I pulled him out about three weeks before the end of the school year. It all just got too much—for me—not for him. The school was just too miserable and depressing and one day I decided that I could never go there again. By the time he was five years old, I had pulled him out of six separate schools mid-year or mid-program because the teachers, classrooms or schools were simply too horrific or dismal. His older brother, who has always been able to take advantage of "gifted" programs or college prep schools, has never had to go to the city's most mildewed and dilapidated buildings. Our autistic son is in a school now that is not part of the public school system and it has no special ed program. There are pros and cons to being part of a public school and there are pros and cons to being at a school that is largely ignorant of the "special ed" culture. If I had my druthers he would not go to school at all.

56. http://www.aclu.org/pdfs/humanrights/impairingeducation.pdf, page 2.

57. The Human Rights Watch and ACLU study only has statistics on corporal punishment and restraint rates in public schools because they are mandated to report to state and federal agencies. The report notes that it is reasonable to conclude that (a) actual rates are likely to be much higher than reported rates and (b) private institutions are likely to rely on corporal punishment and restraints as well (http://www.aclu.org/pdfs/humanrights/impairingeducation.pdf). According to this report by the Department of Health and Human Services Office of Inspector General, state hospitals fail to report about one-third of all "deaths by restraint." If state hospitals are massaging the numbers, why would private institutions, which are not required to report to anyone, broadcast deaths by restraint? (http://oig.hhs.gov/oei/reports/oei-09-04-00350.pdf).

58. Some schools have specially designed paddles for using on the children, many of whom are as young as four or five years old, made from baseball bats that have been shaved flat on one side with holes drilled into them so they hit harder (http://www.aclu.org/pdfs/humanrights/impairingeducation.pdf).

59. Using a restraint hold on a child that was designed for an adult is both painful and dangerous for the child. The child's body is too small and not only bruises easily but their bones, particularly their ribs, are much softer than an adult's. Numerous incidents of "death by restraint" have occurred in this country when inadequately trained adults have put a child in a restraint hold improperly and caused to the child to go into cardiac arrest if the basket hold is used, or asphyxiate if the prone position is used. Although hospital records are incomplete and private institutions are not required to submit "death by restraint" records to federal agencies, estimates place "death by restraint" rates of children in public schools during the years 1995–2005 at around 150 deaths (http://www.disabilityrightsca.org/pubs/701801.pdf and http://www.gao.gov/new.items/d09719t.pdf).

60. I suspect they would be to any child.

61. http://www.aclu.org/files/pdfs/humanrights/impairingeducation.pdf, 46–47.

62. http://www.aclu.org/files/pdfs/humanrights/impairingeducation.pdf.

63. At the time the Impairing Education report was written (in 2009) by the Human Rights Watch, twenty states had laws which permitted the use of corporal punishment in public schools. The Ending the Corporal Punishment in Schools Act (ECPSC) was reintroduced in Congress on September 22, 2011. ECPSC, were it to pass, would place a federal ban on corporal punishment in public schools. Since there is ample evidence that corporal punishment prevents all students, but students with impairments especially, from being able to take advantage of educational services being offered to them in the public school setting, the argument is that any instance of corporal punishment is a violation of both the American Disabilities Act and a violation of Title IX. Unfortunately, given how entrenched notions of authoritarianism within public schools are, particularly where the "worst offenders" seem to be, most people who track rates of child abuse do not predict that ECPSC will pass. Certainly no state laws that have attempted to eliminate or even moderate corporal punishment have ever passed in states that permit corporal punishment. In short, those teachers really want to keep hitting those children, especially children with impairments. See Alice Farmer, a researcher at Human Rights Watch, at *The Hill's Congress Blog* for regular Congressional updates (or lack thereof) regarding these matters.

64. http://www.salon.com/2009/03/26/bauer_autism/.

65. http://www.salon.com/2009/03/26/bauer_autism/ (emphasis added).

66. The film received severe criticism from disability activists. See, for example, Stuart Murray's *Representing Autism: Culture, Narrative, Fascination* (Liverpool University Press, 2008). Despite intense criticism of the film, a forty-six-minute version was given a special screening at the 2007 Sundance Film Festival. A special thirteen minute version debuted at a fundraiser named "A New Decade for Autism" on the Don Imus show on MSNBC and an additional seven-minute version has been created for YouTube (http://abcnews.go.com/GMA/AmericanFamily/story?id=2286321&page=1).

67. http://articles.nydailynews.com/2010-07-22/news/27070582_1_capital-murder-children-death-penalty.

68. http://www.cnn.com/2010/HEALTH/07/23/autism.death.mother/index.html.

69. Further insights into Elizabeth's motives will remain a mystery as she shot herself dead after killing her son George.

70. March 2012. http://www.sfgate.com/cgibin/article.cgi?f=/c/a/2012/03/07/BAVR1NH8B4.DTL

71. http://www.feat.org/FEAT/tabid/58/Default.aspx.

72. http://autismcrisis.blogspot.com/2006/11/dehumanization-specialists.html (emphasis added).

73. Bitterly disappointed with our experiences with parapros, we hire what we call our son's "personal assistant" to accompany our son while he is at school. She is really a communication facilitator, helping him when communication breakdowns inevitably occur while he is still not comfortable verbalizing his thoughts with people I think of as "non-familiars." He is a "chatty Cathy" with familiars but not with people he does not know, does not trust or when in new or stressful situations. He can communicate very effectively nonverbally (by writing notes, drawing pictures, and signing) and makes every effort to do so but, I have found, most people are very unwilling to attempt to understand his nonverbal communication efforts. Therefore I believe that a go-between is, at this stage in his life, vital to his success (and safety) at school.

74. There are always stories of "full recoveries" of autism but they are never verified by objective, independent observers and can be more reasonably explained three ways: (1) *Wrongful Diagnosis*—A mistaken diagnosis of autism was made by an overly anxious teacher or physician who believed, say, a nonverbal toddler exhibited "signs" of autism but, a year later after parents threw themselves into various kinds of treatment, those "signs" disappeared once the child started talking as he or she would have anyway; (2) *Wishful Thinking*—A child is autistic and has not actually changed remarkably but developed in ways perfectly compatible with an autistic diagnosis, but parents, therapists and/or teachers are so keen to see progress because of their commitment to a therapy or treatment program, they "see" astonishing progress that others would not (or do not) see; (3) *Quackery*—Individuals lie or exaggerate to

mislead others into believing that autistic individuals have "fully recovered" or have been "cured" when they have not.

75. http://www.who.int/topics/tuberculosis/en/.

76. Dawson *et al.* 2008, 759–72.

77. And I do stress *if*—research done on autistic individuals is often laughably unreliable.

78. Earlier, I mentioned one clinic that claims to be currently treating autistic children with gene therapy. Yet no reputable research institute is claiming that gene therapy is currently available as a therapeutic treatment for autism. At this point, there is simply no evidence that any available existing gene therapy programs could possibly offer any therapeutic results for autism.

79. Boucher 2009, 283.

80. Though apparently there are a just a few researchers who believe it is not completely implausible. See Hu-Lince, C., Craig, D., Huentelman, M., & Stephan, D. 2005. The Autism Genome Project: Goals and Strategies. Databases and Genome Projects. *American Journal of PharmocoGenomics* 5:233–46.

81. I will develop a fuller discussion of the cognitive and affective processes and capacities of autistic individuals later but it is claimed that autistic individuals think very differently from the way nonautistic individuals do. For example, it is often claimed that autistic individuals often fail to understand public associations but, instead, follow reasoning processes that rely on private associations which nonautistics cannot (or, in my experience, refuse to) understand. For example, in the United States a public association is that Christmas colors are red and green— those are the "correct" colors for that season, other colors are "not right." For an autistic individual, Monday may be square, the number eight may be itchy, October may be loud— anything goes. How one arrives at a private association simply depends on whatever private associations that individual has made between one concept and another. Private associations do not make sense to others but make perfect sense to the person who created them. For examples of autistic college students describing how they think and how they think about thinking, see *Aquamarine Blue 5: Personal Stories of College Students with Autism*, edited by Dawn Prince-Hughes (Ohio University Press, 2002). See also Daniel Tammet's *Born on a Blue Day* (Free Press: New York, 2006).

82. This seems like a fairly innocuous enough model if genetic counselors are neutral in presenting genetic information to parents. Yet a review of literature available presents the decision to not have "defective" children, children with "closed futures" or those who will live a "life not worth living," as perfectly reasonable, if not ethically obligatory. See Jeff McMahan, The Morality of Screening for Disability, *Ethics, Law and Moral Philosophy of Reproductive Biomedicine* 10 (1, 2005) :129–132; Dena S. Davis, Genetic Dilemmas and the Child's Right to an Open Future, *Hastings Center Report* 27 (2, 1997): 7–15; Julian Savulescu, Procreative Beneficence: Why We Should Select the Best Children, *Bioethics* 15 (Oct. 2001): 414–26. Given the current Culture of Autism, parents may feel pressured to not conceive if they already have an autistic child (or if there are autistic individuals in the family). At another parental support group, I met a young couple who had a four-year-old boy who had been diagnosed as autistic. They had just received the news that their two year old son was autistic. Interestingly, given that everyone there had a child who was autistic, everyone expressed sadness and various words of comfort. Clearly the assumption was that this was very, very bad news. One mother whispered, almost fearfully, pointing to the wife's very pregnant abdomen, "Aren't you worried that your unborn will be autistic, too?" She whispered the word "autistic" as if saying it too loudly might cause the fetus inside to suddenly turn autistic right there in the room. To my amazement the dad said, "Well, we thought about it but I just figure: we have the routine down by now. And the great thing about autism is, if 8 o'clock is bedtime, then that's it, that's when they go to bed. And if they like SpaghettiOs, don't buy 2 cans, buy 20!" He chuckled happily to himself while his wife smiled in agreement and rubbed her tummy bulge contentedly. Everyone else in the room stared at them speechlessly. Even the therapist hosting the counseling session was at a loss—and she was supposed to be offering us help for depression. What was so fantastic about their attitude was that it was a complete rejection of the presumption of negativity and grimness that hung over those group therapy sessions. I never saw two people more at ease in the world. I think of them often. I stopped going to those support groups because,

although occasionally there were amazing people like this couple, in general I found the sessions to be horrifically depressing because they reinforced the attitude that autism is nothing but a terrible grind.

83. See Hubbard, Ruth. 1990. *The Politics of Women's Bodies*, 193–95. Rutgers University Press: New Brunswick.

84. I attended a talk given by Judy Endow, a self-identified autistic who said that she is well aware that she is "merely" a "brown eyed" autistic rather than one of the "blue eyed" Aspies in the autism community, which is an interesting insight for an autistic person to have, given that autistics are alleged to be incapable of understanding social cues. Her very biting social commentary—critical of both the autistic community and "neurotypical society"—was in turns thought provoking, funny and poignant. Autcom Annual Conference: October 15–16, 2010, Milwaukee, WI.

85. Although given how amusing life can be, doing so is no guarantee that the parent will not end up with an autistic child because these tests are, as discussed, unreliable, providing both false positives and *false negatives*.

86. Sykes and Lamb 2007, 1–15.

87. http://www.msnbc.msn.com/id/7013251. "If we get to the point where we have 10 genes that predict risk *to some significant degree*, then there is a prenatal test," Buxbaum stated. (emphasis added). The room for error is obvious when put so baldly.

88. Along with fellow autistics Kathy Lissner, Grant and Donna Williams, they formed Autism Network International in 1992, the first organization run "by and for autistic people." One of the fundamental principles of ANI is that autism should not be cured. See www.autreat.com.

89. http://nymag.com/print/?/news/features/47225/.

90. http://www.nytimes.com/2004/12/20/health/20autism.html.

91. http://www.asatonline.org/forum/archives/mother.htm (emphasis added). Organizations concerning autism neatly divide into two camps: those run and organized entirely by individuals who are autistic and those run and organized by individuals who are not autistic. The tone, politics and goals of the two are entirely different. I have yet to discover an organization that was established entirely by individuals who are not autistic (such as Autism Speaks) that permits autistic individuals to have any influence on how the organization is run or to help set the agenda of the organization.

92. http://www.nytimes.com/2004/12/20/health/20autism.html. The slur "curebie" refers to any person who is a particularly weak-minded slave to conformity; it is usually someone who is in favor of finding a cure that will eliminate autism and, thereby, narrow neurodiversity. But it may also specifically refer to someone who is attempting to "train" any evidence of autism out of their child through behavior modification therapies (such as A.B.A., which relies on aversion therapy) so that they appear normal and can "pass" as nonautistic. Thus, just as with race and sexual identities, individuals have much to gain and lose with the politics of autistic identities. No wonder Kit Weintraub says of the anti-cure movement in that same *New York Times* editorial, "I'm afraid of this movement."

93. Singer is an autistic sociologist. The first published use of the term is credited to Harvey Blume's use in an article in *The Atlantic*. Blume writes, "Neurodiversity may be every bit as crucial for the human race as biodiversity is for life in general. Who can say what form of wiring will prove best at any given moment? Cybernetics and computer culture, for example, may favor a somewhat autistic cast of mind" (September 30, 1998, http://www.theatlantic.com/magazine/archive/1998/09/neurodiversity/5909/).

94. At this point, the conversation becomes difficult and, not too surprisingly, neurodiversity advocates divide. Some believe that conversations about neurodiversity really makes no sense when talking about "low-functioning" autistics and should apply to high-functioning autistics, such as Aspergers, only. The idea is that the neurology of high-functioning autistics is worth preserving, but low-functioning autistics really do need to be "cured" (that is, genetically eliminated). See Jaarsma, P. and Welin, S. 2011. Autism as a Natural Human Variation: Reflections on the Claims of the Neurodiversity Movement. *Health Care Analysis* 20 (1):20–30. Yet, as has been mentioned several times, carving nature at the joints is tricky business and distinguishing between "high-functioning" and "low-functioning" autistics is no-

toriously difficult. (And where are the PDD-NOS's in this conversation?) As I have also previously pointed out, early diagnosis is no indication of later success. The further problem with this separatist line of reasoning, which should sound familiar to anyone who knows race or gender identity theories, is that from what genetic researchers have so far concluded, genetic markers for autism are not only highly complex, they give no indication whatsoever of how autism will be realized (or expressed) in a person. That is, there is simply no way to (reliably) eliminate the "low functioning" autistics but save all the "high functioning" (valuable) Aspies—either we screen for them all or we screen for none. In other words, the high functioning autistics (or, Aspbergers) want to essentialize themselves as inherently different from the low functioning autistics, but there is no genetic or neurological essential difference between the two groups. The difference is in name, and socially constructed privilege, only. Interestingly absent from the conversation is the question of why neurodiversity would not commit one to advocate the mass production of autistic individuals. Perhaps because the standard question is so often about the elimination of autism, the question of increased autism populations does not arise. And, perhaps since most people accept the myth that autistics are asocial (indeed, antisocial) they probably cannot imagine autistics sexually reproducing—yet, have children they do! See Kathleen Seidel's brief discussion of her attitudes regarding parenting in *New York Time Magazine* (June 2, 2008), http://nymag.com/news/features/47225/. Advocates of neurodiversity are not committed to the (rather silly) idea that autistics ought to be created *en masse*. Rather, neurodiversity ought to be regarded as a way to establish protection for individuals who are members of a group with a minority status, not as a means to coerce individuals within a minority group to reproduce to "bulk up" the population or maximize the neuro-variety of that minority group.

95. It is increasingly common for long-dead scientists, literary "geniuses" and innovators to be forensically diagnosed as autistic. Almost every philosopher has been diagnosed as autistic. Certainly Jeremy Bentham, John Stuart Mill and Immanual Kant would get diagnosed today as "classic cases." Instead they were allowed to get through their childhood label-free and live perfectly successfully. I have also recently read arguments that Charles Ludwig Dodgson (Lewis Carroll), Thomas Jefferson, Charles Darwin, and Emily Dickinson have been labeled as autistic though there are skeptics.

96. *Threads* magazine featured an article by Alice Korbach who knits beaded purses on sized 00000 needles, using 6 mm beads. She has to design the patterns in advance, stringing 5,760 different colored beads onto the silk thread at one time, so that when they are knitted they end up making the colored pattern. If she miscounts one too many, one too few, the whole pattern will be off. (*Taunton Press* (August/September 1989): 24-29). Althea Merback knits "conceptual clothing." One Fair Isle sweater, which is smaller than a quarter and complete with inset pockets, and cabled pleats, took her over 500 hours to complete. Some of her cardigans— "micro sweaters"—are 1/144th scale and smaller than a dime. *KnitKnit: Profiles + Projects from Knitting's New Wave*, ed. Sabrina Gschwandtner (Stewart, Tabori & Chang: New York, 2007, 134–37). "Fixity of focus" is essential for both such artistic endeavors.

97. Straus 1997, 541–44.

98. Straus 1997, 548–49.

99. That is occupational therapy speak for "turning on the garden hose and having a wildly good time in the backyard."

100. We splashed out on a big trampoline (with a safety net—we've seen The Simpsons!) and the feeling of flying through the air, suspended, motionless, just before you start to fall is truly thrilling. It makes me almost giddy. But it really is hard on "old knees," sad to say. Our son is older now and his interests have turned primarily to swimming and biking for "big muscle" activities and reading and drawing for quiet time activities—all of which are easier on my knees and involve a lot less clean-up. But I do miss playing in the mud once in a while.

101. http://www.dailymail.co.uk/femail/article-1081698/I-wouldnt-change-autistic-boy-world-An-admission-son-ex-wife-author-Nick-Hornby.html.

102. http://www.dailymail.co.uk/femail/article-1206734/Ken-Bruce-Why-I-believe-world-better-place-family-experience-child-autism.html.

103. Although some have argued, rather poorly in my opinion, that autistics are nonmoral persons because they lack empathy, I think, a better moral litmus test that autistics could pass

(and many nonautistics would often fail) is the honesty test. In the autistic world, justice and morality are founded on such categorical imperatives as keeping promises and being honest— not in playing favorites, maintaining social networks, or "working the system."

104. Our insurance does not cover any autism therapy. Another bit of advice our child developmental psychologist gave us, "If you want good therapy, pay out of pocket." We were discussing the virtues of private therapy versus public school therapy services, and I think he is right but how many people can foot that bill since a good speech therapist (in our area, at any rate) charges $75 for forty-five minutes per week and speech therapy is a several-year-long commitment? Never mind all the other therapies that are needed to be paid for out-of-pocket as well. Is it any wonder the headlines read that parents of autistic children are paying on average $40,000 per year for services? When I read that I snorted, thinking that that was so much "antiautism scare talk," until I did the math and realized that that is pretty much exactly the amount we were paying for private therapies, including our son's "personal assistant" to accompany him at school. If insurance does cover therapy, as it does in some states, it will be A.B.A., a type of therapy I am opposed to since it relies on aversion therapy and the evidence of its success is highly dubious.

105. Michelle Dawson *et al.*, argue that cognitive literature is completely incapable of explaining autistic learning. For example, autistics are said to learn passively, a style of learning not favored by nonautistics. Moreover many autistics, such as our son, are "hyperlexic" which will give them "extremely advanced decoding skills." Discussing a boy with the reading skills of a twelve-year-old but a "mental age" of less than two, they argue, "[E]xisting cognitive accounts are inadequate to account for the development of literacy in this child" (Dawson *et al.* 2008, 759–72). And a typical public school curriculum cannot accommodate such a child, and a teacher has no idea how to educate such a child, either.

106. To protect myself from chicanery, my automatic defense against something, like an "alternative remedy" is to dismiss it. But since there is most likely at least one product or device that might be useful, this is not an optimal approach. (I already mentioned the unbelievably expensive, but really good three-sided pencils that we would never have bought if they had not been suggested by our son's occupational therapist.) How many other little gems are there out there lost in the dross of inadequately regulated crap?

107. During WWII, Hans Asperger opened a school in Vienna for children with "autistic psychopathy" where he cared for several hundred autistic boys, shielding them from the infamous T-4 policies which certainly would have slated them for extermination. Asperger wrote over 300 publications, mostly about autism; unfortunately, most were destroyed during a bombing. None were translated into English until after his death (Asperger 1991, 37–92). Asperger's positive outlook for the autistic children is interesting, especially when compared to other researchers who were working with autistic children in other countries during that era, most notably Leo Kanner. After the war ended, Asperger became director of a children's clinic in Vienna. Later, in 1964, he headed the SOS-Kinderdorf in Hinterbrühl, and was responsible for helping poor, orphaned children who required medical care. Many have speculated that Asperger was "on the spectrum": he was known to be devoted to the children he cared for, able to "just know" what they needed even if they could not adequately verbalize their needs, yet he was well known to be uneasy among adults. Dr. Fred Stone, a pediatric psychiatrist described meeting Asperger at a conference in Vienna, "He was on duty "welcoming" people--actually, he didn't welcome anybody, he just sat at the door of the lecture theater...I couldn't engage him. I think that those who claim that he may have been suffering from the same syndrome that would later bear his name could be right" (Lyons 2007). Asperger's birthday, February 18, is International Asperger's Day and is observed by various autism organizations as an unofficial International Holiday.

Chapter Six

Knowing Other Minds: Ethics and Autism

Anna Stubblefield

I once had a conversation with a fellow philosopher, in which I mentioned that I am interested in autism and the problem of knowing other minds.

He replied, "Oh yes, isn't it fascinating how autistics lack a theory of mind and can't empathize?"

"Well," I said, "that's actually not true, but it precisely illustrates my point. When I say I am interested in autism and the problem of knowing other minds, the problem I'm referring to is how people who are not autistic have failed to empathize with people who are."

There are days when I feel that if I see one more puzzle piece ribbon on the back of a car or one more Internet post about the "enigma" or "mystery" of autism, I am going to have a meltdown. I feel this way because autistic ways of experiencing the world—which have been amply explained by many people labeled with autism—seem to me perfectly comprehensible. (Maybe that's because the people labeled with autism I know are friends I spend time with, not "patients" or "subjects" only encountered in clinics or labs.) Yet the supposed puzzle of autism has been used as a justification for the massive and widespread oppression of autistic people by neurotypicals (people not labeled with autism). So I really had to bite my tongue when I encountered a book characterizing people with autism as "among them, but not of them," the subtitle of Deborah Barnbaum's *The Ethics of Autism.*

Barnbaum does not deny moral status to autistic people, but she denies them moral agency, thereby relegating them to the realm of what Tom Regan calls "moral patients."[1] She does so because she accepts the notion—put forward by Uta Frith, Francesca Happé, and Simon Baron-Cohen, among others—that the "core deficit" of autism is a lack of theory of mind. According to this thesis, autistic people do not grasp that other people have minds with intentional states: to autistics, other people are simply objects. Furthermore, according to this thesis, because we supposedly learn to recognize and refer to our own intentional states through interaction with others in which we grasp their intentions, autistic people lack the ability to recognize their own minds.

If the "no theory of mind" hypothesis of autistic deficit is correct, then autistic people present conundrums for philosophical theories of personhood and moral agency. Barnbaum's book is primarily an exploration of two of these supposed problems. First, there is widespread agreement among contemporary moral theorists that "relationships with other human beings are an essential contributor to well-being for humans."[2] If people with autism lack a theory of mind, then they lack the ability to have genuine relationships with other people. But if they are thereby cut off from a crucial aspect of being human, that calls into question their humanity and hence their personhood status. Second, major Western ethical theories require that moral agents possess a "theory of mind." Barnbaum discusses Humean sympathy, the desire to maximize pleasure and minimize pain for all that undergirds utilitarianism, the ability to recognize others as ends in themselves that is crucial to Kantian deontology, and the sensitivity to moral obligations and context required by theories involving prima facie duties. If people with autism lack a theory of mind, they cannot employ any of these approaches to moral reasoning, which suggests that they cannot function as moral agents at all.

Yet these supposed challenges presented by autism to moral theory evaporate if the "no theory of mind" hypothesis is incorrect, and in that case, Barnbaum's thorough and detailed analysis is, at best, a waste of time and effort. Barnbaum's failure is instructive in this regard, because it provides, within the discipline of philosophy, an example of how the fascination with the supposed "puzzle" of autism has led to so much professional and societal investment that people are unwilling to let go of theories that emphasize the difference between "us" and "them." There is sufficient evidence—that I will present below—to call into question both the "no theory of mind" hypothesis about autism and the more general belief that autistic people and neurotypical people are unfathomable to each other. But there is also a question here of perception: people can fail to see what they do not want to see. Those who are invested in the belief that autism is a puzzle, because they have built research careers and organizations upon the foundation of that belief, may resist evidence to the contrary. Two neurotypicals—one who believes that autism is a puzzle and one who empathizes with autistic people—can spend time with the same person with autism and respectively see a different person.

I stated above that Barnbaum's book is "at best" a waste of time and effort. If that were the only point to be made, I would not bother writing this chapter. But the belief that autistics cannot empathize and that they are irredeemably strange to the "rest of us" reinforces attitudes that have led to past and ongoing harm to people labeled with autism. This harm includes:

Segregation

- In 2007-2008, only 34.5 percent of children labeled with autism attended general education classes for at least 80 percent of the school day.[3]
- As of 2006, the number of people with developmental disabilities still living in institutions (defined as residential facilities housing sixteen or more people) nationwide was 101,416 (the relevant statistics are not broken down by disability label, so this number includes people labeled with autism but also those with other developmental disabilities).[4]

Denial of basic human rights, including:

- Denial of or overwhelming barriers to access to communication, literacy, postsecondary education, employment, and self-determination.[5]
- Torture through abuse, withholding of food and seclusion as forms of "behavior modification," and physical restraint.[6]
- Murder, including, as only a few recent examples, the deaths of:

—Michael Renner-Lewis III, age fifteen.[7]
  In 2003, following a seizure, Renner-Lewis was restrained by school personnel in a prone position (face-down on the floor) for nearly an hour and died of asphyxiation.

—Hansel Cunningham, age thirty.[8]
  In 2005, Cunningham had run into the backyard of the group home in which he lived and removed his clothes, after biting a staff member who was trying to restrain him. The staff member called 9-1-1 and three police officers shot Cunningham twice with a stun gun, sprayed him with pepper spray, tackled and handcuffed him, and then injected him with a sedative. He died on the way to the hospital.

—Jonathon Carey, age thirteen.[9]
  In 2007, Carey was riding in a van with two staff members and another resident from the institution where he lived. They stopped at a bank, where one staff member went inside. Carey got up from his seat after having been told to sit still and the remaining staff member pushed

him face-down on the seat and then sat on him to restrain him. Carey died from asphyxiation about fifteen minutes later.

I want to be clear that I am not accusing Barnbaum herself of condoning these horrors. Barnbaum emphasizes that neurotypicals have moral obligations to people labeled with autism and argues that they should be included in the moral community.[10] But her reiteration throughout the book of how different they are and how they cannot understand us and we cannot understand them[11] reinforces the stereotype of autistic people as alien. Due to the premise on which it is based, Barnbaum's book is ultimately a denial of autistic humanity. It is not sufficient to suggest that "we" have moral obligations to "them" as beings who are not like us. To call into question autistic humanity is to call into question the human rights of people labeled with autism, and that is neither accurate nor morally acceptable.

My argument will proceed as follows. First, I present the "sensory and movement differences" explanation of autism as an alternative to the "lack of theory of mind" explanation. Second, I discuss flaws in the theory of mind tests that are the basis of the "lack of theory of mind" thesis. Third, I argue that proponents of the "lack of theory of mind" explanation have engaged in circular reasoning that has led them to discount evidence that the "lack of theory of mind" hypothesis is incorrect. Fourth, I demonstrate that Barnbaum, in her commitment to the "lack of theory of mind" hypothesis, misrepresents—by omitting details that demonstrate empathy and morality—the self-descriptions of the people labeled autistic whose "voices" she includes in her book. I conclude that those who deny empathy and moral agency to people labeled with autism are engaged, presumably unintentionally but with nonetheless egregious results, in an insidious version of blaming the victim that ignores the ways in which most neurotypicals and our society at large have failed to empathize with and protect the rights of the people our society labels as autistic.

WHAT DOES IT MEAN TO SAY THAT SOMEONE IS AUTISTIC?

The answer to this question is "it depends on who is talking." The American Psychiatric Association's *Diagnostic and Statistical Manual of Mental Disorders, Fourth Edition* (*DSM-IV*), which establishes the "official" criteria for diagnosis used by mental health professionals, defines autism in terms of qualitative impairments in social interaction and communication along with restricted, repetitive, and stereotyped patterns of behavior, interests, and activities. It is important to note, however, that autism is a concept that has been "developed and applied, not discovered."[12] There is to date no known, objectively diagnosable etiology for autism. Neurologists have identified some observable differences between the brains of subjects labeled with autism and neurotypical subjects, but those differences are not diagnostically useful nor is it understood how they relate to the behavioral criteria invoked in the *DSM-IV* with enough specificity to be useful.[13]

Furthermore, the *DSM-IV* criteria are not merely descriptive. Rather, they are judgmental. For example, one of the "symptoms" that can lead to a diagnosis of autism based on the *DSM-IV* is "apparently inflexible adherence to specific, *nonfunctional* routines or rituals" (my emphasis). But who is to say whether a routine is functional or not? As Stephen Shore and numerous other people who have been labeled autistic have observed, the routines in which people labeled autistic engage often do serve important functions for them. For example, many people labeled with autism report vestibular and proprioceptive challenges: they lose track of their sense of balance and the location of their body parts. Running in circles, rocking, or flapping hands can provide vestibular and proprioceptive input that helps them. Most people engage in repetitive behaviors that help us focus or calm anxiety: foot jiggling, pen tapping, hair twirling, doodling, nail biting, gum chewing. Neurotypical people consider these repetitive behaviors to be "normal" and they are not perceived as nonfunctional or as symptomatic of a deficit. Less typical behaviors such as fiddling with a string of beads, flapping one's lips with a finger, or pacing around in a roomful of people who are seated are labeled as "abnormal," although they serve the same purpose.[14] Thus, to define autism as it is defined in the *DSM-IV* is to make a judgment call about a set of behaviors that can be interpreted in multiple ways.

There are currently two broad approaches to interpreting and explaining the characteristics that are linked with autism via the *DSM* definition. The first explains the behaviors labeled as autistic in terms of sensory and movement differences. This approach to understanding autism is based on reports by people labeled with autism and their support providers that "disturbances of sensation and movement are a constant concern, frequently constraining the ability to communicate, relate to others and participate in life. Organizing and regulating sensory information and movement in order to participate in social relationships may be frustrating for people with such differences. These differences can involve difficulties initiating and executing movements or difficulties with stopping, combining, and switching sensation and movement, including speech, thought and emotion, making social relationships and many other activities very challenging and even overwhelming."[15] In this model, autism involves both differences in how sensory and proprioceptive stimuli are received and processed by the brain and also interruptions in motor response and intentional control of movement.

The second approach explains the *DSM-IV* autistic "symptoms" in terms of deficits in higher order mental functions: either a lack of theory of mind, weak central coherence, or weak executive function. Barnbaum navigates debates among advocates of these theses by suggesting that there is a substantial phenomenological overlap among them. Furthermore, because, according to Barnbaum, "the claim that persons with autism have tremendous difficulty ascribing intentionality to others is empirically proven, and is consistent with the other two theories," she takes the lack of theory of mind explanation of autism as the jumping-off point for her discussion of the ethical implications of autism. [16]

According to the lack of theory of mind explanation of autism, people who display the characteristics that earn them a label of autistic under the *DSM-IV* criteria do so because they lack a core module in their brain that allows neurotypical people to ascribe intentionality to others. If someone lacks a theory of mind, he is unable to understand the thoughts and feelings of other people—he is unable to attribute mental states to others to predict their behavior. According to proponents of this thesis, a lack of theory of mind explains the social and communication impairments associated with autism and is supported by the performance of people labeled with autism in psychological experiments. [17]

REASONS TO QUESTION THE LACK OF THEORY OF MIND THESIS

Just as it is important to understand that there is no such "thing" as "autism"—because to diagnose someone as autistic is simply to observe that he or she displays a certain number of a list of characteristics—so, too, it is important to recognize that the idea of a "theory of mind" is a metaphor. Researchers who advocate the lack of theory of mind thesis have not actually identified a specific brain mechanism for attributing mental states to others. [18] They infer the existence of such a mechanism from studies that supposedly test the ability of subjects to recognize false beliefs in others. One classic version of a "false belief task" is the Smarties test. In this task, the subject is shown a Smarties candy box. The subject is asked "What do you think is in the box?" and the subject responds "Smarties." Then the subject is shown that the box actually contained pencils. Next, the subject is asked "What did you think was inside the box before I opened it?" If he identifies the actual content of the box (pencils) rather than the expected content (candy), then he fails the first phase of the false belief test: he has supposedly demonstrated that he lacks a theory of his own mind.

In the second phase of the Smarties test, a fictional or real character (e.g., Bill) is introduced who has not seen the actual contents of the box. The subject is asked "What do you think that Bill will think is inside the box before I open it?" If the subject again answers "pencils" rather than candy, he has failed the second part of the false belief task: supposedly demonstrating that he lacks a theory of others' minds. [19]

In a 2005 paper, Morton Gernsbacher and Jennifer Frymiare argued that autism cannot accurately be defined as a lack of theory of mind because in all the studies that use false belief tasks, some of the subjects labeled with autism passed the tests (in one study, 50 percent passed). [20] Furthermore, they observed that the syntax of the questions asked of subjects in the false beliefs tasks—a complement clause embedded in a matrix clause—is among the most complex in English. They hypothesized that the false belief tasks measure a subject's ability to process and respond to a question involving convoluted grammar rather than his possession of a theory of mind. [21]

In 2007, Colle et al. responded with a nonverbal version of the false belief task. In this study, subjects were introduced to a task in which an experimenter placed a piece of candy inside one of two identical boxes. This action was performed behind a screen out of sight of the subject. But a second experimenter, referred to as a communicator, had been, through a series of pretests, introduced to the subject as someone who would watch where the candy was being placed and correctly indicate to the subject which box the candy was in, so that the subject could retrieve the candy. In one third of the trials of the task, the communicator would leave the room and the experimenter, in view of the subject, would switch the identical boxes around, so that when the communicator returned to the room and pointed to the box that she believed held the candy, she would be pointing to the wrong box. Subjects passed the test if, when asked after the switch to point to the box with the candy, they pointed to the box that the communicator had not indicated.

Subjects labeled with autism performed less well than control subjects on this test, although there was not complete failure on this test among the subjects labeled as autistic. The control group, however, only achieved about 50 percent success. Although this task avoided the use of questions involving complex syntax, it still required mentally processing a complex sequence of logical reasoning: "If the communicator is pointing at Box A and he always points at the box that he believes has the candy, but he doesn't know as I do that the boxes were switched, then the candy must really be in Box B." It remains debatable whether failure on this task demonstrates a lack of theory of mind.

A recent study demonstrated no lack of theory of mind skills in adolescents and adults labeled with autism. The authors argue that, although the main function of a theory of mind is to master social situations, developmental psychology studies have not explored how people apply their theory of mind skills to social interactions. The false belief studies that support the lack of theory of mind hypothesis about autism compare older children with autism (about nine to fourteen years of age) to typically developing young children (four to six years of age) and assume an "idealized, and in some respects erroneous" theory of mind ability in typical adults. Yet studies have shown that typical adults do not display a perfectly accurate theory of mind. [22]

In Begeer's study, subjects were asked to perform an interactive task. The subject and an experimenter playing the role of "director" sat on opposite sides of a grid with sixteen open slots. Five slots were occluded so that the director could not see what was in them, but the subject could. The director turned away and another experimenter placed objects in the slots. Some objects that the director could see were similar in kind (e.g., spoon) to an object in an occluded slot that only the subject could see. Others were similar in name (e.g., a cassette tape and a roll of adhesive tape). [23]

The director then asked the subject to move a specific object to an empty slot. The subject passed the test if, when asked to move the spoon or the "tape," he moved the spoon or the "tape" that the director could see, rather than the spoon or the "tape" that was invisible to the director. Subjects labeled with autism and the control subjects were identical in their ability to take the director's knowledge into account when interpreting what she requested. [24] Note that in avoiding logical complexity of the sort demanded by the nonverbal false belief test ("if this and this and not this then that"), the test more directly gets at what it means to possess a theory of mind: "Because the director does not know what objects are in the slots she cannot see, the object she is asking me to move must be the one that she can see."

Furthermore, prior to the Begeer study, the validity of the false belief studies was also challenged by people who identify as autistic. For example, during a panel discussion at Autism Europe's Congress 2000, Jared Blackburn noted that accurate performance in the false belief studies depends on "verbal ability, attention, information processing, and other capabilities that may be impaired in the subjects." Katja Gottchewski observed that it is not improbable that autistic children, who, based on self-reports and observation by others, have difficulty keeping up with the quick flow of typical social interactions, [25] might assume that other people can actually read each other's minds (a theory of mind that would explain why others can follow nuanced interactions that they cannot), and hence would believe that the character who has not seen the pencils in the Smarties box would nonetheless already know that that is what is inside. She also suggested that a person labeled with autism might be more likely to entertain reasons why the character who is supposed to have a false belief might actually have a true belief (e.g., he participated in the test before, or he was spying when the box was opened and the pencils were revealed) and that asking subjects to say what the character is *likely* thinking rather than *definitely* thinking might have yielded better results. [26]

In a paper presented at the Society for Disability Studies in 2006 (and published in this volume), Nick Pentzell observes that, as a child, he was too lost in sensation to respond to, let alone pass or fail, such a test. I think just maneuvering through a day's stimuli prevented me from thinking from other people's points of view. It seemed, somehow, everyone else was different from me; they weren't so crippled by the world around them. I couldn't edit any of it out. I couldn't imagine what it was like not to be overstimulated. I really couldn't have cared whether people expected candy or pencils when they opened a box.[27]

WHY THE LACK OF THEORY OF MIND INTERPRETATION OF AUTISM IS PERNICIOUS

Researchers who support the lack of theory of mind explanation of autism have responded to challenges to their theory with circular reasoning that renders their hypothesis unfalsifiable.

In their 2007 review of cognitive theories of autism, Rajendran and Mitchell observe that when adolescents and adults labeled with autism demonstrated the ability in some studies to pass both first order and second order theory of mind tests, advanced tests were designed that they could not pass. This seems like overcommitment to a hypothesis that has not stood up under experimentation.

> The development of advanced tests could be viewed as a post hoc response in finding data anomalous to the theory of mind hypothesis that some individuals with autism pass tests of false belief. In Baron-Cohen et al's (1985) seminal study, the aim was to use what was regarded as a definitive test of theory of mind (i.e., an unexpected transfer test of false belief) to discover whether or not individuals with autism have an impaired theory of mind. Subsequent studies using advanced tests have turned this logic on its head: they seem to be premised on the assumption that individuals with autism do have an impaired theory of mind, implying that tests which do not reveal this must be insensitive or unsuitable.[28]

Furthermore, reconceptualizations of the theory of mind, such as the Enactive Mind hypothesis, come across as grasping at straws to try to prove that people labeled with autism lack a theory of mind. In one study, the researcher showed both adolescent and adult subjects labeled with autism and same-age control subjects a silent animation involving geometric objects "interacting" with each other. The subjects were then asked to describe the animation. The control subjects searched for social meaning in the animation: "What happened was that the larger triangle—which was like a bigger kid or bully—had isolated himself from everything else until two new kids come along and the little one was a bit more shy, scared, and the smaller triangle more like stood up for himself and protected the little one." Autistic subjects, on the other hand, simply described the movement of the objects: "The big triangle went into the rectangle. There were a small triangle and a circle. The big triangle went out. The shapes bounce off each other. The small circle went inside the rectangle. The big triangle was in the box with the circle. The small triangle and the circle went around each other a few times."[29]

This study is supposed to demonstrate that people labeled with autism lack a theory of mind. Another interpretation, however, is that describing the movement patterns of the shapes—rather than attributing psychosocial characteristics to them—demonstrates a refreshingly clearheaded refusal to engage in unwarranted anthropomorphizing.

Although Rajendran and Mitchell are accurate in pointing out the circularity in the theory of mind studies, they do not explicitly question the assumption that the best interpretation of autism will be a cognitive explanation, rather than the sensory and movement differences explanation. None of the theory of mind studies takes into account that sensory and movement challenges are a more straightforward explanation of the differing performances of subjects labeled with autism compared to control subjects. Why? A contributing factor is that neurotypicals learned about the sensory and movement challenges experienced by people labeled with autism from the latter, through self-reports, including published autobiographies, that began appearing in the 1980s. These contradict the lack of theory of mind hypothesis, which concludes that people who lack a theory of mind cannot accurately report on their own mental states.

Frith and Happé addressed this challenge to the lack of theory of mind hypothesis by arguing that the "highest functioning" people on the autism spectrum do often demonstrate the ability to laboriously develop a theory of mind at a much later age than it is seemingly spontaneously acquired by developmentally typical children. But they suggested that autobiographical accounts be approached with caution, as reconstructions were based on later acquired abilities that were not present at the time. They also focused on "reading between the lines" for what is not included in the accounts, rather than taking the accounts at face value. [30]

Victoria McGeer contended in response that there are methodological problems both with Frith and Happé's extension of the theory of mind account to self-awareness and also in their unwillingness to fully accept the validity of self-reports by people labeled with autism.

According to McGeer, "One of the striking and recurrent themes commonly sounded by so-called expressive autistics is not just how difficult it is for them to understand the nuances of normal human behavior, but also how strongly they experience a problem of not being understood themselves." She notes in particular the frustration expressed by some people with autism that their supposed lack of empathy is given as the best explanation for their difficulties in social interaction, rather than the failure of neurotypicals to understand people on the autism spectrum. [31]

McGeer observed that autobiographical writings by people labeled with autism are explicitly intended as an attempt to educate neurotypicals about what it is like to be autistic. She argued that this project has two motivations. One is straightforwardly practical: to improve the quality of interactions between people on the autism spectrum and neurotypicals, particularly parents, teachers, and other professionals. The second motivation, as McGeer described it, is "not without practical import, but is itself poignantly non-instrumental and strangely at odds with the standard conception of autistic 'aloofness,' not to mention autistic lack of self-consciousness. It expresses a basic human desire to be known and accepted by others for what one is: abnormal, perhaps, but importantly human nonetheless."[32]

In her paper, McGeer acknowledged that questions of people's frustrations or desires to be acknowledged as human beings are arguably orthogonal to the cognitive science aim of uncovering the mechanisms behind autism spectrum symptoms. She argued in response, however, that in the case of autism, the concerns expressed by people labeled with autism about bridging the gap between themselves and neurotypicals, and their frustrations at not being understood, suggest a sophisticated understanding of themselves and others that is at odds with the theory of mind hypothesis.[33]

McGeer's second methodological concern was that autobiographical accounts by people labeled with autism provide an important check to conclusions that may be overly influenced by theoretical preconceptions. For example, it has been argued that repetitive behaviors in people labeled with autism should not be understood as obsessive-compulsive behaviors, because obsessive-compulsive behaviors stem from anxieties, and people on the autism spectrum cannot, because they lack a theory of mind, experience themselves as having anxiety.[34] Yet self-reports from people on the autism spectrum confirm over and over that their repetitive behaviors are responses to (and often ways to calm) anxieties, and their autobiographical accounts make it clear that experiencing high levels of anxiety is a common symptom of life on the autism spectrum. Happé acknowledged that, for some people on the autism spectrum, this may be the case, but refused to acknowledge it more generally.[35] But this seems to be a case in which evidence that is worth following up on if we are to have a better understanding of autism is dismissed or interpreted as an "exception to the rule" because commitment to the theory of mind theory requires dismissing the evidence.

As McGeer argued, the benefit of self-report from people labeled with autism as a check against conclusions that rest on theoretical preconceptions

> is lost if the going theory systematically calls into question the reliability of autistic self-report. Worse, it is hard to see how such a theory will not license researchers to manipulate the data in a way that comes perilously close to compromising standards of scientific objectivity. Thus, however much they

couch their proposals as purely "speculative," and despite the care they take in elaborating their view, the special interpretive strategies they adopt to compensate for autistic "introspective incapacity" (such as focusing on what is not said) practically ensures discovering these reports to be riddled with "signs" of the very disability their theory predicts.[36]

Furthermore, as McGeer acknowledged, one of the most important contributions of self-reports from people labeled with autism has been about the extent to which they experience sensory challenges (and also movement challenges, which she does not discuss) that arguably interfere with the kinds of interactions with people that figure in the development of communication and social skills. Dismissing self-reports by people on the autism spectrum of their sensory (and movement) challenges blocks pursuing what could be a very fruitful avenue of research for understanding human communicative and social development.[37] Temple Grandin expresses frustration with researchers who "are more interested in studying emotions rather than studying sensory problems...Severe problems with sensory oversensitivity wrecks the lives of many people on the spectrum. The most miserable individuals are the ones with such severe sensory problems that they cannot tolerate a restaurant or office. Socializing is impossible if your ears hurt from normal noise."[38]

In the 2003 second edition of her book, *Autism: Explaining the Enigma*, Frith concedes that autobiographical writings by people labeled with autism "leave no doubt about the extensive self-knowledge of autistic people."[39] But she suggests that,

Perhaps there is an awareness that is *all* self and does not include the reflection of the self in other selves....Could it be that individuals with autism who acquire a conscious theory of mind, first and foremost attain knowledge of their own mind? This would mean that they can possess detailed knowledge about themselves, but not about others. If so, we could explain why the autobiographies of autistic people go into remarkable detail about their own inner states, far more so than most autobiographers, and why they hardly even speculate about how they may have affected people who play an important role in their lives.[40]

Again, there is evidence here of "changing the rules" so that the lack of theory of mind thesis will still hold up. In prior work, the story was that one had to acquire a theory of mind first in order to have knowledge of one's own mind. Now it appears that one can have knowledge of one's own mind while still lacking an understanding of other minds. Additionally, it seems odd to judge someone's capacity for empathy by how much time he spends in his memoir—which is, after all, a literary genre devoted to the self—exploring other people's feelings rather than his own. Furthermore, Frith provides no evidence of research to support her comparisons between autistic memoirs and those of "most autobiographers."

THE "VOICES OF AUTISM"

At the beginning of each chapter of her book, Barnbaum provides a brief summary of a published autobiographical work by a person labeled with autism. Each summary focuses on the philosophical theme of the chapter.[41] Barnbaum presumably includes these summaries, which she calls "voices of autism," to show that her conclusions resonate with experiences reported by autistic people themselves. The problem is that Barnbaum leaves out details in her summaries that disturb the close fit between the "voices of autism" and Barbaum's belief that autistic people lack a theory of mind, empathy, and the ability to form close connections with others.

In her summary of Jim Sinclair's essay "Bridging the Gaps," Barnbaum describes him as not needing connection with others (which is an accurate representation of his words), conveys his description of how intense those connections he chooses to form are, but finishes with his quote about how those connections can be transient ("I don't stick"). By sandwiching her summary of how deeply Sinclair connects with specific friends between a reference to his feeling that he does not need this connection and his comfort with connections being transient, the overall picture is of someone who is less rather than more interested in human relationships.[42]

Here are Sinclair's actual words, however:

> But I don't stick. That confuses people sometimes. A friend once asked me for assurance that I really wanted to be together. I answered, "I can leave and be just fine, or I can stay and be *even better* (my emphasis)." Isn't it enough to be just fine on my own, and to be able to choose connections that will make my life even better? I have exactly as many relationships as I want. I relate only as myself, only in ways that are authentic to me. I value people only as themselves, not for their roles or status, and not because I need someone to fill empty spaces in my life. Are these the severe deficits in communicating and relating that I keep reading about?[43]

Furthermore, Sinclair speaks directly to the stereotype that autistic people lack empathy, but Barnbaum does not convey that aspect of his essay in her summary:

> Sometimes I'm not aware of social cues because of the same perceptual problems that affect my understanding of other aspects of the environment. My visual processing problems are no more the result of indifference than blindness is—are blind people considered insensitive if they fail to recognize people or to respond to others' facial expressions? Sometimes I notice the cues but I don't know what they mean. I have to develop a separate translation code for every person I meet—does it indicate an uncooperative attitude if someone doesn't understand information conveyed in a foreign language? Even if I can tell what the cues mean, I may not know what to do about them. The first time

I ever realized that someone needed to be touched was during an encounter with a grief-stricken, hysterically sobbing person who was in no condition to respond to my questions about what I should do to help. I could certainly tell that he was upset. I could even figure out that there was *something* I could do that would be better than doing nothing. But I didn't know what that something was. It's very insulting, and also very discouraging, to be told that if I don't understand someone, it's because I don't care.[44]

In her summary of Wendy Lawson's book *Life Behind Glass*, Barnbaum describes Lawson's friendships and marriage as "transient," although in the next sentence she acknowledges in passing that Lawson's marriage lasted for twenty years. She mentions Lawson's close friend Lesley, but does not include the detail that this was a friendship that had been ongoing for thirty years at the time Lawson wrote her book.[45] Furthermore, Barnbaum says of Lawson, "She cautions those who would make friends with someone who is autistic that 'the autistic person needs to manipulate their surroundings in order to maintain a sense of control of their environment'; this manipulation can extend to those with whom autistic people try to relate."[46]

By using the term "caution," Barnbaum suggests that Lawson is offering a warning. But this shows more clearly how Barnbaum interprets Lawson than what Lawson herself says. The passage about friendship with autistic people appears in Lawson's book under the heading "A Point to Ponder." The full passage is:

> It takes a special kind of commitment on behalf of "friends" to relate on a long-term basis to an autistic individual. The autistic person needs to manipulate their surroundings in order to maintain a sense of control over their environment. This will mean that those people closely relating to the autistic person will feel manipulated and "used." Reciprocity is quite an art and one that does not come naturally if you are autistic. However, it can be learnt. Just as a child is taught to say "please" and "thank you," so too can an autistic person learn how to express appreciation, thoughtfulness or concern.[47]

To say that friends of autistic people will *feel* manipulated is not the same as saying that people labeled with autism intentionally manipulate their friends. Furthermore, by editing the quote as she does, Barnbaum leaves off Lawson's important point that the challenge for people labeled with autism is to *express* their feelings of appreciation and concern—not that they do not have such feelings—and that the skills necessary to express one's reciprocal feelings can be learned.

Barnbaum also misrepresents the words of Donna Williams. According to Barnbaum:

> Williams stresses that persons with autism cannot simply be taught to experience certain thoughts or feelings, or be made to feel emotionally for others. A

person with autism can learn what he or she is supposed to feel in a particular situation, and then act in keeping with those feelings, "but that doesn't make it your own, and an idea is never a feeling, just a memory or a stored mental repertoire of how one appears."[48]

By omitting the context of the quote, Barnbaum gives the impression that Williams is saying that people labeled with autism will never feel certain emotions. On the contrary, Williams is disagreeing in this passage with the notion that a person labeled with autism has been "cured" if he learns to perform *as if* he feels the emotions that his performance appears to reflect. Her point is that "any other process of more real growth takes time."[49] Nowhere does she deny the possibility of emotional development in people labeled with autism. Indeed, her own story is an example of just that growth.

Furthermore, Williams provides ample evidence throughout *Somebody Somewhere* of her empathy—both for other autistic people and for her neurotypical friends and business associates—and her moral sensibility. The latter is reflected throughout the book in her righteous indignation at the treatment suffered by people who appear abnormal. She also discusses how she made the painful decision to expose herself by writing her first book, *Nobody Nowhere* because she felt an obligation to help others.[50] Barnbaum chose not to mention these facets of Williams's personality in her summary.

Finally, in the few details of Temple Grandin's life that Barnbaum summarizes, she passes up the opportunity to share with her readers Grandin's insights into how autism involves sensory overload and sensory processing challenges (which support the sensory and movement challenges interpretation over the lack of theory of mind interpretation),[51] and Grandin's ability to engage in moral reasoning and her capacity to empathize.[52]

BLAMING THE VICTIM

My concern in this chapter is to convey to the reader that the lack of theory of mind interpretation of autism is not only a questionable explanation of the behaviors labeled autistic, but is actually harmful. It is harmful in part because it suggests that professionals should ignore the sensory and movement challenges that people labeled with autism identify as their greatest obstacles, which means that those who could have provided the most helpful support will fail to do so. The lack of theory of mind interpretation of autism is also harmful because it supports the erroneous conclusion that people labeled with autism lack empathy and therefore the capacity to be moral agents. Denying moral agency and hence full personhood status to people labeled with autism on the basis of their supposed lack of empathy and moral understanding is an insidious form of blaming the victim.

Barnbaum provides a clear illustration of this in her summary of Gunilla Gerland's autobiography, *A Real Person*. This "voice of autism" introduces Barnbaum's chapter on "Autism and Moral Theories," and Barnbaum uses her discussion of Gerland to illustrate how people labeled with autism lack a moral sense:

> Gerland describes the failure to recognize the moral import of actions and events around her. A variety of stories capture this confusion. In one, she tells of her sister's lack of interest in playing the game "cars," and the bribes that she had to pay Kerstin to induce her to play. Gerland paid the bribes by stealing from her mother, saying "I didn't mind doing that at all." [53]

What Barnbaum neglects to mention in relaying this story is that Gerland was only four years old at the time.

Barnbaum continues:

> School posed equal challenges to Gerland's moral assessment of actions. She was routinely taken to the lavatories at her school and punched in the stomach by some of the boys. This went on for some time until another student disclosed this harassment to a teacher who made the boys stop. Gerland was upset that she was manipulated by the boys, and upset that the teacher put an end to the maltreatment: "It was now quite clear that I had been deceived in some way, so I felt stupid. Hadn't I gone and found those boys myself, in case on some days they had forgotten to hit me?" [54]

There are three problems with how Barnbaum interprets this part of Gerland's story. First, again, this happened when Gerland was very young, in early elementary school. Second, Gerland tells the story in the context of explaining how, due to her sensory and movement challenges, she found school to be a very confusing place. But one thing she grasped was that adults had told her that "you will like school," so she believed that she should, in fact, like everything that happened in school. She also grasped that school was about following the rules. The boys, who were older and bigger, told her "We're going to hit you once a day," and so she simply took it for granted that this was something that was supposed to happen at school. [55] So many other facets of school were unpleasant that there was no reason for her to question this additional unpleasant aspect. Third, Gerland did not want the teacher interfering because the teacher had, like Gerland's parents, already made it clear that she did not understand Gerland. This teacher, for example, was convinced that Gerland was cheating on spelling tests because she always spelled every word correctly and refused to believe Gerland's protestations to the contrary. [56] So Gerland had already learned that teachers did not believe her, that what she thought and felt did not matter, and that school meant putting up with lots of unpleasantness. She, with good reason, did not see the teacher as someone she could trust to protect her. And, in fact, after the initial fuss when the teacher found out what the boys were doing and those particular lavatories were locked up, they went on hitting Gerland behind the school anyway: there was no follow-up after the initial discovery to make sure that the bullying had ended.[57]

To use this example to impugn Gerland's moral sensibility is analogous to blaming a woman for "asking to be raped" if she, through choices that were not coerced (e.g., going to a party, drinking, interacting with a man or men she finds attractive and does not suspect of harboring malicious intentions), finds herself in a situation where men without scruples violate her. The people demonstrating their lack of moral sense in Gerland's narrative are the bullies and the teacher, not Gerland.

Barnbaum proceeds: "Gerland continues to be confronted with similar challenges in adult life. Unlike people who are not autistic, Gerland finds that she is '…unable to perceive whether people wish me well or ill.'"[58]

The problem in Barnbaum's interpretation is the phrase *unlike people who are not autistic*. It implies that neurotypical people never have trouble perceiving whether people wish them well or ill. Try telling that to Bernard Madoff's victims. If we follow Barnbaum's logic, they demonstrated that they are autistic by failing to realize they were being bilked. If we follow her logic to its conclusion, having allowed Madoff to cheat them by failing to intuit his intentions thereby disqualifies them from moral agency.

Barnbaum concludes that "in addition to complicating her relationships with other people, autism has affected Gerland's ability to make sense of the moral landscape."[59]

Reading Gerland's book, I draw different conclusions. Gerland explains how, in her childhood, her sensory and movement challenges made her behave in ways that were abnormal from her parents' point of view, and she describes how they responded with anger and by making fun of her. She perceived from their behavior towards her that they did not understand her and did not love her for who she was. She writes, "If I couldn't be loved, then I wanted to be left alone…I thought I had a right to be as I was, that I had a right to have my sense of integrity respected."[60] This sounds like a perfectly well-developed sense of the moral landscape to me.

Every person included as a "voice of autism" in Barnbaum's book experienced emotional or physical or sexual abuse, or all three. That Grandin benefitted by being surrounded by fewer people who were abusive (she did experience intense teasing in school) and from interacting with some people who were intuitively helpful to her is evident. Yet she still identifies herself as different from neurotypicals, because she processes information in ways that are less common and because she experiences sensory and anxiety overload more intensely and persistently than neurotypical people do. Sensory processing and movement challenges are a permanent feature of life for people labeled autistic. But before we consign people labeled autistic to the margins of moral personhood on the basis of their supposed lack of empathy and moral sensibility, we should first try seeing how they develop when their sensory processing and movement challenges are understood, their skills are appreciated, their friendship is valued, and they are protected from abuse.[61]

THE ETHICS OF AUTISM

Although developing this line of thought would require another chapter, if not a book, I want to conclude by offering the suggestion that thinking about the ethics of autism provides a means through which we can evaluate more generally what we mean by empathy. I mean this NOT in the sense of exploring the ways in which people labeled autistic supposedly lack empathy, but rather in the sense of exploring (1) double standards in respect to empathy that we hold for neurotypicals and people labeled autistic; (2) how neurotypicals have failed to practice empathy in respect to people labeled autistic; and (3) ways in which we can help all people be more empathetic.

Many people who clearly have poorly developed empathy skills nonetheless end up in positions of social power in our society. Indeed, we all too frequently vote them into power. In doing so, we acknowledge that they have full status as moral agents. We do not discriminate against them for their lack of empathy by denying their moral agency because we have already classified them as normal. This indicates that what really matters in our society is people's normality rather than their empathy skills *per se*, a stance we should question. For example, Barnbaum relays from Jeanette Kennett an anecdote about an autistic teenager named Jack who "was tremendously bothered by the notion that some homes lack perfectly tuned pianos, to the point that he suggested a constitutional amendment be adopted to remedy the situation. Jack was unable to suspend his own beliefs and preferences sufficiently so as to simulate what it would be like to be someone who was indifferent to the condition of the ill-tuned piano."[62]

Barnbaum presents Jack's unusual suggestion as evidence of lack of theory of mind and empathy skills in autistic people and as support for her claim that people labeled autistic are incapable of moral agency.[63] But consider the following example. There are people in the United States who are so very bothered by the notion of homosexual couples being married that they have proposed a constitutional amendment to ban same-sex marriage. Despite evidence that many, many people are not at all bothered by the idea of same-sex marriage, those who propose the amendment are clearly unable to suspend their own beliefs and preferences sufficiently so as to simulate what it would be like to be someone who is indifferent to the sexual preferences of his fellow citizens. If these are not grounds for denying the empathy and moral agency of people with a fixation on heterosexuality, then Jack's concern about out-of-tune pianos should not be used as evidence to deny his empathy and moral agency. Indeed, Jack's concern is harmless, while the concern of those opposing same-sex marriage causes needless suffering to others.

Autism is a challenge to the empathy skills of neurotypicals. Grandin, Sinclair, and others write that they feel like extraterrestrials as they navigate neurotypical society. But neurotypicals should be careful about how they choose to interpret that. I am not suggesting that neurotypicals should ignore what people who are labeled autistic say about themselves. But neurotypicals can choose to interpret autistic descriptions of alienation as part of "what it means to be autistic"—that is, as part of the condition of autism—or, on the other hand, neurotypicals can choose to entertain the very likely possibility that that sense of alienation is the result of how incredibly lacking in empathy neurotypicals have been in their interactions with people labeled autistic. If neurotypicals developed their own empathy skills better, put their understanding into practice by supporting autistic people in their sensory processing and motor challenges, reconsidered their obsession with conformity and gregariousness, and thereby presented themselves to people labeled with autism in a better light, people labeled with autism would feel comfortable and welcomed.

Empathy is not a quality that we either have by birthright or lack as an impairment. It is a skill that we learn. We know that empathy breaks down when others seem too different from us or we have come to believe that they are different from us. It has broken down in white people regarding nonwhite people, in upper-class people regarding working-class people, in "natives" regarding "foreigners," in men regarding women, in heterosexuals regarding LGBTI people, and in enabled people regarding disabled people. Barnbaum's book, unfortunately, reproduces and encourages such a lapse in empathy. The more neurotypicals believe that people labeled austistic are "among us but not of us," the less reason they have to learn to empathize. Yes, the ways in which people labeled autistic behave can seem strange to people who do not understand the effects of the sensory processing and movement challenges they experience. But the more neurotypicals listen to how people labeled autistic experience the world, and the more time they spend getting to know them and learning from them how to be supportive, the more skills in empathy all parties will attain.

People with autism in our society are survivors of a violence that is all the more insidious for being dressed up as conventionally accepted care. By violence I do not mean only the bullying, torture, and sexual abuse that the vast majority of people labeled with autism experience. I also mean the violence of constantly being told by parents and teachers—the people who are supposed to understand and nurture and protect you—that you are a bad person who does not behave properly. Of being told over and over to "act normal." Of enduring hours and hours of "therapies" that are supposed to help you achieve normality when what you are being asked to do, and why, does not make any sense, because it does not take into account the sensory processing and movement challenges you experience. And then hearing that you are a failure, or lazy, or lacking intelligence when you do not improve. I mean the violence of having no one in your life who empathizes with you, who understands you, who connects with you. As a society, we practice violence against people who are neurologically atypical, and then say that there is something wrong with them because they supposedly lack the capacity to adhere to "our" high moral standards.

REFERENCES

ARC of New Jersey. 2009. *The Future of Individuals with Developmental Disabilities and New Jersey's Developmental Centers* (May 15).

Autism Society of Michigan v. Fuller. 2005. United States District Court, W. D. Michigan, Southern Division.

Barnbaum, Deborah. 2008. *The Ethics of Autism.* Bloomington and Indianapolis: Indiana University Press.

Baron-Cohen, S. 1989. Do Autistic Children Have Obsessions and Compulsions? *British Journal of Clinical Psychology* 28:193–200.

Begeer, Sander; Malle, Bertram; Nieuwland, Mante and Keysar, Boaz. 2010. Using Theory of Mind to Represent and Take Part in Social Interactions: Comparing Individuals with High-Functioning Autism and Typically Developing Controls. *European Journal of Developmental Psychology* 7(1):104–22.

Biklen, Douglas. 2005. *Autism and the Myth of the Person Alone.* New York: New York University Press.

Blackburn, J.; Gottschewski, K.; George, Elsa, and Niki L. 2000. A Discussion about Theory of Mind: From an Autistic Perspective. *Proceedings of Autism Europe's 6th International Congress*, Glasgow, May 19–21.

Broderick, Alicia. 2011. Autism as Rhetoric: Exploring Watershed Moments in Applied Behavior Analysis Discourse. *Disability Studies Quarterly* 31(3).

Colle, Livia; Baron-Cohen, Simon and Hill, Jacqueline. 2007. Do Children with Autism Have a Theory of Mind? A Non-verbal Test of Autism vs. Specific Language Impairment. *Journal of Autism and Developmental Disorders* 37:716–23.

Courchesne, Eric et al. 2007. Mapping Early Brain Development in Autism. *Neuron* 56:1–15.

Donnellan, Anne; Hill, David, and Leary, Martha. 2010. Rethinking Autism: Implications of Sensory and Movement Differences. *Disability Studies Quarterly* 30(1).

Endow, Judy. 2006. *Making Lemonade: Hints for Autism's Helpers.* Cambridge Book Review Press.

Ford, Liam. 2005. Autistic Man Dies in Police Struggle. *Chicago Tribune*, November 22.

Frith, Uta. 2003. *Autism: Explaining the Enigma*, 2nd Edition. Malden, MA: Blackwell.

Frith, Uta and Happé, Francesca. 1999. Theory of Mind and Self-Consciousness: What Is It Like To Be Autistic? *Mind and Language*, 14(1):1–22.

Gerland, Gunilla. 1997. *A Real Person: Life on the Outside*, trans. Joan Tate. London: Souvenir Press.

Gernsbacher, M. A. 2006. Toward a Behavior of Reciprocity. *Journal of Developmental Processes* 1:139–52.

Gernsbacher, M. A. and Frymiare, J. 2005. Does the Autistic Brain Lack Core Modules? *Journal of Developmental and Learning Disorders* 9:3–16.

Grandin, Temple. 2006. *Thinking in Pictures: And Other Reports from My Life with Autism*, 2nd Edition. New York: Vintage Books.

Grinker, Roy Richard. 2007. *Unstrange Minds: Remapping the World of Autism*. New York: Basic Books.

Hakim, Danny. 2011. A Disabled Boy's Death, and a System in Disarray. *New York Times*, June 5.

Happé, F. 1991. The Autobiographical Writings of Three Asperger Syndrome Adults: Problems of Interpretation and Implications for Theory, in Frith, U., ed., *Autism and Asperger syndrome*. Cambridge, UK: Cambridge University Press. 207–42.

Kennett, Jeanette. 2002. Autism, Empathy, and Moral Agency. *The Philosophical Quarterly* 52:340–57.

Kliewer, C., Biklen, D., and Kasa-Hendrickson, C. 2006. Who May Be Literate? Disability and Resistance to the Cultural Denial of Competence. *American Educational Research Journal* 43:163–92.

Lawson, Wendy. 1998. *Life Behind Glass: A Personal Account of Autism Spectrum Disorder*. London and Philadelphia: Jessica Kingsley Publishers.

McGeer, Victoria. 2004. Autistic Self-Awareness. *Philosophy, Psychiatry & Psychology* 11(3):235–51.

Minshew, Nancy and Williams, Diane. 2007. The New Neurobiology of Autism: Cortex, Connectivity, and Neuronal Organization. *Archives of Neurology* 64(7):945–50.

National Disability Rights Network. 2009. *School Is Not Supposed to Hurt: Investigative Report on Abusive Restraint and Seclusion in Schools*.

National Disability Rights Network. 2010. *School Is Not Supposed to Hurt: Update on Progress in 2009 to Prevent and Reduce Restraint and Seclusion in Schools*.

Pentzell, Nick. 2012. I Think, Therefore I Am. I Am Verbal, Therefore I Live. *The Philosophy of Autism*. Lanham, MD: Rowman & Littlefield.

Perner, J., Frith, U., Leslie, A. M., and Leekam, S. R. 1989. Exploration of the Autistic Child's Theory of Mind: Knowledge, Belief and Communication. *Child Development* 60:688–700.

Rajendran, G. and Mitchell, P. 2007. Cognitive Theories of Autism. *Developmental Review* 27:224–60.

Regan, Tom. 1983. *The Case for Animal Rights*. Berkeley and Los Angeles: University of California Press.

Robertson, Scott Michael. 2010. Neurodiversity, Quality of Life, and Autistic Adults: Shifting Research and Professional Focuses Onto Real-Life Challenges. *Disability Studies Quarterly* 30(1).

Rusin, Carolyn. 2006. Death of Autistic Man Ruled Homicide. *Chicago Tribune*, February 8.

Shore, Stephen. 2003. *Beyond the Wall: Personal Experiences with Autism and Asperger Syndrome, 2nd Edition*. Overland Park, KS: Autism Asperger Publishing Company.

Sinclair, Jim. 1989. Bridging the Gaps: An Inside-Out View of Autism (Or, Do You Know What I Don't Know?).

TASH. 2009. *Inclusive Education and Implications for Policy: The State of the Art and the Promise*. Congressional Briefing on Inclusive Education.

Williams, Donna. 2008. *The Jumbled Jigsaw: An Insider's Approach to the Treatment of Autism's "Fruit Salads."* London: Jessica Kingsley Publishers.

———. 1994. *Somebody Somewhere*. New York: Times Books.

NOTES

1. Regan 1983, 152.
2. Barnbaum 2008, 89.
3. TASH 2009.
4. ARC of New Jersey 2009, 2.
5. Kliewer, *et al.* 2006; Biklen 2005; Robertson 2010.
6. Hakim 2011; National Disability Rights Network 2009; National Disability Rights Network 2010.

7. *Autism Society of Michigan v. Fuller*.
8. Ford 2005; Rusin 2006.
9. Hakim 2011.
10. Barnbaum 2008, 102–04.
11. Barnbaum 2008, 47, 57, 73.
12. Biklen 2005, 12; see also Broderick 2011; Donnellan et al. 2010; Grinker 2007.
13. Minshew and Williams 2007; Courchesne et al. 2007.
14. For further discussion and examples, see Shore 2003; Endow 2006; Williams 2008.
15. Donnellan *et al.* 2010.
16. Barnbaum 2008, 6.
17. Frith 2003, 80.
18. Gernsbacher and Frymiare 2005, 7; Biklen 2005, 38.
19. Perner et al. 1989.
20. Gernsbacher and Frymiare 2005, 5.
21. Gernsbacher and Frymiare 2005, 6.
22. Begeer *et al.* 2010, 105–06.
23. Begeer *et al.* 2010, 111–12.
24. Begeer *et al.* 2010, 114.
25. See Donnellan *et al.* 2010, 15.
26. Blackburn *et al.* 2000.
27. Pentzell 2012, chapter 4.
28. Rajendran and Mitchell 2007, 229.
29. Rajendran and Mitchell 2007, 230–31.
30. Frith and Happé 1999.
31. McGeer 2004, 240.
32. McGeer 2004, 240.
33. McGeer 2004, 241.
34. Baron-Cohen 1989.
35. Happé 1991.
36. McGeer 2004, 241.
37. McGeer 2004, 242–43.
38. Grandin 2006, 165–66.
39. Frith 2003, 211.
40. Frith 2003, 210.
41. Barnbaum 2008, 5.
42. Barnbaum 2008, 15.
43. Sinclair 1989.
44. Sinclair 1989.
45. Lawson 1998, 49.
46. Lawson 1998, 19; Barnbaum 2008, 68.
47. Lawson 1998, 19.
48. Williams 1994, 214; Barnbaum 2008, 143.
49. Williams 1994, 215.
50. Williams 1994, 174.
51. Grandin 2006, chapter 3 and throughout.
52. Grandin 2006, 97–99; 107–15; 156–57.
53. Barnbaum 2008, 106.
54. Barnbaum 2008, 106.
55. Gerland 1997, 92.
56. Gerland 1997, 93.
57. Gerland 1997, 92.
58. Barnbaum 2008, 106.
59. Barnbaum 2008, 106.
60. Gerland 1997, 23.
61. Studies have shown that when parents of young children labeled with autism learn skills that help them to interact more empathetically with their autistic offspring, the children im-

prove measurably in their social skills compared with control groups in which the parents did not receive training. In these studies, only the parents received intervention, not the children (Gernsbacher 2006, 147–49).

62. Barnbaum 2008, 119.

63. Barnbaum again plays fast and loose with her summarizing, in that she did not bother to include the fact that Jack later "outgrew the notion that this could be corrected by a constitutional amendment" (Kennett 2002, 351). She thereby reinforces the erroneous impression of autism as involving permanent deficits in empathy or moral reasoning.

Chapter Seven

Autism, Empathy, and Affective Framing

Michelle Maiese

Autism is a psychiatric condition that starts early in childhood and is characterized by abnormal social development, decreased capacity for communication, and impoverished imagination. Subjects typically fail to connect socially with others, find it difficult to communicate, have little interest in meeting another's eyes, demonstrate a decreased tendency to engage in social referencing behaviors or shared attention, and seem to have limited understanding of how their behavior affects others.[1] To make sense of these deficits, many theorists have looked to the theory-theory (TT) of social cognition, which asserts that ordinary human adults make use of causal-explanatory generalizations (a tacit folk psychological theory) to "read minds" and thereby make sense of and predict other people's behavior. By relying on a set of causal laws that interrelate inputs, internal states, and behavioral outputs, they are able to attribute mental states and make inferences about an agent's future behavior.[2] The capacity for employing this folk psychological theory depends on higher-order cognitive processes such as theorizing and inference making, and ordinarily surfaces at about four years of age.

Simon Baron-Cohen makes sense of empathy along these lines, as inherently involving a capacity to mentalize, identify another person's emotions and thoughts, and predict his or her behavior.[3] In his view, we theorize "an enormous amount, as a natural way of thinking about why people do what they do."[4] Empathizing involves both the ability to attribute mental states to others by applying a "theory of mind" (ToM), and also the capacity for appropriate affective response to another person's mental state. It is a process that "involves an imaginative leap in the dark, in the absence of much data" and renders a causal explanation that "is at best a 'maybe.'"[5] For example, the thought that "Maybe she didn't phone me because she was feeling hurt by my comment" illustrates the ordinary human ability to take these sorts of imaginative leaps, which Baron-Cohen claims is our "most powerful way of understanding and predicting the social world."[6] The capacity for empathizing is brain-based, and it is because autistics are lacking in a ToM that they are lacking in their capacity for empathy.

However, in my view, mentalizing is *not* the most powerful way of making sense of the social world, nor is it how empathy most commonly arises. Developing a fuller understanding of empathy requires that we focus more on the *essentially embodied, emotive, enactive* interaction processes involved in social cognition. To make sense of the way in which interpersonal understanding and empathy are essentially embodied, I maintain that our ability to interpret other people's actions, thoughts, feelings, and expressions largely depends on our capacity for bodily attunement and *affective framing*.

One way to understand an affective frame is as a sort of *emotionally colored lens*, whereby our bodily feelings and cares influence our patterns of cognitive focus and attention. Elsewhere I have argued that all of our judgment, deliberation, and decision making take place against the backdrop of our needs and concerns, whose associated desiderative bodily feelings influence and modulate our interpretations of our environment. At a very basic level, our framing is nonconceptual and nondeliberative and involves bodily engagement, bodily fluency, and bodily attunement. An affective frame operates, in effect, as an *egocentric caring-contoured map* that helps the subject to find definite points, lines, and contours of salience in the complex world around her. As a result, her interpretations are shaped to a large extent by her desires, goals, fears, and values, and grounded in her habitual patterns of bodily response. While the prefrontal lobe and other regions of the brain no doubt play a crucial role, the provision of affective and motivational color or tone to events is best understood as distributed over a complex network of brain *and* bodily processes. Affective arousal engages not only neural circuitry, but also metabolic systems and endocrine responses, and the impact of this arousal is spread throughout the body in muscles, increased blood flood, heart rate and blood pressure increases, and vascular constriction. Affectivity, together with corresponding physiology and bodily feelings, directly bias the competition for processing resources according to *what we care about* and in favor of information we *feel* is important.

In the context of interpersonal interaction, such framing affords us an implicit, spontaneous, embodied understanding of social behavior and renders other people's actions decipherable. It does so in part by providing us with an immediate sense of what others are thinking and feeling, by focusing our attention on various aspects of their movements, posture, facial expressions, gestures, and overall bodily comportment. In many cases, affective framing reveals subtle aspects of behavior that allow us to "get a feel" for others and form first impressions. In addition, affective framing and bodily attunement facilitate the coordination of activity that often occurs among interaction partners. By way of participatory sense making and the mutual modulation of *affective framing patterns*, subjects are able to take up an 'I-Thou' stance and develop an understanding of one another. Subjects engaged in conversation, for example, do not observe and then infer, but instead enter into a shared dance with their conversation partner(s). Empathy involves modulation of one's mental and emotional state by coming into bodily contact with other persons' mental states, so that one literally *feels with them*. Understanding other people's minds and behavior thus relies necessarily on the embodied interaction process itself, and among ordinary subjects, the cognitive and affective processes of empathy ordinarily are fused and intertwined. In autism, however, because these cognitive and affective processes operate in isolation, subjects' bodily feelings do not play their usual role in focusing attention or attuning them to other people's mental states. As a result of their impaired capacity for affective framing, autistic subjects do not exhibit the same sort of bodily modulation that ordinarily takes place during face-to-face interpersonal interactions, and therefore have a decreased capacity for empathy. At the end of the chapter, I will comment briefly on how my proposed account of empathy can help to explain why autistics are sensitive to moral considerations in certain respects, and yet lack moral competence in other respects.

BEYOND MIND READING AND BODY READING

The common presupposition among proponents of TT is that folk psychology represents a commonplace, accurate description of everyday interpersonal understanding, and that the ability to attribute internal propositional attitudes and deploy psychological concepts lies at the core of all social scenarios we encounter. This theory characterizes social cognition as an individual achievement that happens within a particular person's brain and body and treats social phenomena as external events that require interpretation.[7] On this view, we first perceive the other person's behaviors and expressions, and then use mind reading to understand him. However, as many theorists have noted, understanding other people's mental states is very different from applying a theory or solving a scientific problem. We typically do not have to ask ourselves, "What emotions or desires does this behavior express?" since this would require us to take up a certain distance from the other person. Shaun Gallagher, in particular, has repeatedly challenged the Cartesian idea that others' mental states are hidden away and inaccessible and rejects the notion that we ordinarily act as spectators of others' behavior. In his view,

TT fails to capture the primary way in which we relate to, interact with, and understand others.

Gallagher's proposed alternative, "interaction theory," emphasizes how our ability to understand other persons ultimately rests on a form of embodied practice that is emotional, sensory–motor, perceptual, and nonconceptual.[8] These are our basic ways of understanding others, and whatever theory-of-mind abilities we have depend on these embodied practices that we carry out during interpersonal interaction. From the very beginning, the perception of others' intentional actions engages our own motor and affective processes in a way that TT fails to acknowledge. In neonate imitation, the newborn demonstrates proprioceptive awareness of her own body, the recognition of a distinction between self and nonself, and also the recognition that the other is in fact the same sort of entity as herself. The newborn infant not only can pick out a human face from the crowd of objects in its surroundings, but also can imitate the gesture it sees on that face and use facial gesture to provoke response from others. This imitation of facial gestures is not mediated by theorizing or even strictly cognitive simulation, (as some versions of simulation theory suggest), but instead occurs in a direct, unmediated, and fully embodied manner. Infants appeal to their innate body schema, which allows them to map others' facial expressions and bodily movements onto their proprioceptive bodily experiences.[9] They also are attracted to their caregiver's voice, and have what might be called an "eye direction detector" and an "intentionality detector." Infants as young as six months perceive grasping as goal-directed; at nine months they follow the other person's eyes and start to perceive various body movements as goal-directed movements; and at ten to eleven months they are able to parse some kinds of continuous action according to intentional boundaries.[10] This ability to interpret bodily movement as goal-directed clearly does not require advanced cognitive abilities, since it surfaces at such a young age and appears to operate quickly and automatically. This evidence supports the idea that infants are capable of a nonmentalistic, perceptually based understanding of the intentions and dispositions of other persons, and that they look to others' bodies and expressive movements to make sense of their behavior.

For this reason, Gallagher has maintained that the ability to "read" others is primarily a form of *body reading* rather than mind reading. The basic bodily capacities that make humans naturally attuned to the expressions of others are largely pre-reflective, emotional, sensory–motor, perceptual, and not intellectually governed. Primary, embodied intersubjectivity serves as the basis for all face-to-face interactions, and even comes into play in instances of more detached explanation or prediction. While of course I fully agree with Gallagher's emphasis on the body, I think that social cognition is even more fully embodied and participatory than he acknowledges. In my view, by describing social cognition as "body reading," Gallagher is in danger of reaffirming the notion that interpersonal understanding is a detached, individual achievement, resulting entirely from cognitive processing going on inside one party's head. He would agree, I think, that there is good reason to think that social understanding typically emerges *through the process of second-person interaction itself*. Our appreciation of others as people is relational and involves a disposition to affect them, and to be affected by them, in various ways. It is during this process of mutual affection that joint meanings are generated and individuals' distinct perspectives are intersubjectively fused and modified.

Social understanding therefore should be understood as a product of the embodied social interactions of primary intersubjectivity, which are both *enactive* and *essentially emotive*. Interpersonal engagement is *enactive* in the sense that individuals "do not passively receive information from their environments, which they then translate into internal representations whose significant value is to be added later," but instead actively participate in the generation of meaning.[11] How individuals engage with, attend to, and make sense of their surroundings has much to do with their desires and concerns. Even in the early stages of interpersonal engagement, the infant's body serves as sense-giving orientation through which all experience is structured, and surroundings take on meaning and significance on the basis of the infant's basic needs and preferences. This is not only because the infant must depend on others to satisfy her basic needs and ensure her continued existence and well-being, but also because the infant spontaneously *cares* about other persons. Just as the enactive approach suggests that one perceives a car not as some object among others, but as something one can use, it also suggests that one sees others as beings with whom one can communicate, who can either help one achieve one's goals or thwart them, and who can be the targets of one's love or empathy. Thus, this early phase of social attunement necessarily involves "the emotions, the affections, and the desire to communicate."[12]

From the very beginning, people use expressions, gestures, and other bodily movements to invite the infant into some sort of "conversation" or communicative activity with them. This includes smiling, gesturing, sticking out their tongues, cooing, and grasping the infant's hand. Infants, in turn, typically rely on various forms of nonverbal communication, such as a bodily contact, posture, head nods, facial expression, gestures, eye contact, and pitch/volume of speech to interact with others. In early interactions between child and caregiver, such as play, joint attention, and gesture, the body plays a key role in allowing the infant to gain familiarity with her caregiver's intentions and attune her behavior accordingly. This is because the infant directly perceives others' desiderative feelings in their actions, gestures, and expressions, and also becomes directly aware of the mutual influence that exists between her and her caregiver. By engaging in direct "I–Thou" rela-

tions, caregiver and infant come to relate to each other as essentially embodied subjects whose interactions are influenced by each other's needs and
interests. A mother cuddling or breast-feeding her infant is a prime example.
Caregivers who act to satisfy the infants' needs (whether for food, warmth,
or social connection) quickly are perceived as another locus of agency, and
the infant also becomes aware of herself as an active subject who is capable
of prompting a response from the other person via her own bodily movements. It is striking that after only six weeks of interactive experience, infants display a classic still-face effect. In response to a social partner who
suddenly stops interacting, they first reduce their smiling and gazing, and
then attempt to re-engage the social partner.[13] This indicates that very young
children have some basic awareness of their own ability to modulate and
impact the behavior of others. In addition, the infant's experiences inform her
that others can elicit gestures, actions, and expressions from her. She impli-
citly senses that where adults point their fingers or direct their eyes, for
example, often shapes her own patterns of attention. As a social agent involved in a social interaction, the infant is "at once prodder and prodded,"
and so is her caregiver.[14] Thus, from the very beginning, social cognition is a
matter of bodily, perceptual, affective relatedness between people.[15] Even
something as simple as a father or mother matching his or her own emotions
to those of the child illustrates how intersubjectivity is a matter of *reciprocal
bodily attunement.*[16]

Some of the bodily processes that help to give rise to this sense of relatedness and cooperation include the key elements of primary intersubjectivity
identified by Gallagher: (a) a perceptual "intentionality detector;" (b) an "eye
direction detector;" and, (c) a "shared attention mechanism." This suggests
that there is a link between the perception of others and the goal-oriented
potentialities of one's own body, and that the direct perception of others as
persons involves bodily responsiveness. This includes patterns of motor-
readiness as well as an "affective sensibility to gestures and expressions."[17]
We interact with people by responding to feelings, gestures, and expressions
with our own feelings, gestures, and expressions. Various contemporary
theorists have called attention to this sort of bodily responsiveness or "motor
resonance." According to Daniel Hutto, imitation and motor mimicry can be
characterized as "instinctual responses to situations or other people, for
which our innate systems naturally are calibrated."[18] Because the information to which they are calibrated is bound up with a kind of intentional
directedness informed by our biological needs, perception of one's social
environment often is quick and reliable. To engage in acts of imitation and
mimicry, infants or adults need not rely on psychological principles or make
inferences about people's beliefs and desires, since in many cases subjects
simply read another person's basic desires and goals straight off her reactions
and expressions.[19]

While I agree with Hutto that such capacities are adaptive, and rooted in our needs and interests, I find the metaphor of "reading others," whether their minds or their bodies, far too Cartesian and intellectualist. Instead, during ordinary face-to-face interaction, a spontaneous and intuitive sort of bodily attunement occurs. This suggests that intersubjectivity is best understood as "a communion of flesh and not a relationship between separate persons."[20] In my view, the metaphor of "dancing with other people" more effectively captures the sense in which social cognition is essentially embodied, emotive, and interactive. *Social cognition, roughly, is a shared dance of sense-making whereby we come to understand other people.* If so, there is little doubt that prior to developing a capacity for theorizing or explicit inference-making, we are involved with others, and that "it is our joint cohabitation that secures our living consciousness for each other."[21] Typically others' conscious intentions and desires are directly manifest in their essentially embodied comportment, and it is the sensorimotor and perceptual processes of bodily attunement which serve as our primary basis for understanding others. In the next section, I will elaborate on the role of bodily attunement and discuss how the mutual modulation of interactors' affective framing patterns underlies the human capacity for empathy.

THE SHARED DANCE OF SOCIAL COGNITION

To make sense of the reciprocity and interactivity involved in interpersonal interaction, Gallagher appeals to the work of Husserl and maintains that social cognition involves processes that occur on the level of kinesthesis, or sensory experience of one's own movement.[22] When we see someone else act in a certain way, our own kinesthetic (sensory–motor) system is activated in a way that mirrors the perceived action of the other person. Gallagher then goes on to assert that mirror neurons are an important part of this account and that they can help to explain how this intermodal link between proprioception and perception of others is innate. Mirror neurons are activated when we perceive another animate body doing an intentional action, but are not activated if we see the very same action performed by a tool or machine. They also code for intentional action abstractly, without regard to who is performing the action or to the specific context. As a result of activation of the mirror neuronal system, there is a natural "pairing" that takes place from body to body, at the kinesthetic or proprioceptive level, in a way that shapes our perceptual experience.[23] For example, we recognize a specific emotion in others on the basis of the activation of brain areas responsible for the experience of that emotion in ourselves. Such activation thus contributes to the perceptual understanding of another person's instrumental or expressive actions.

While Gallagher's acknowledgment of a natural "pairing" at the bodily level is extremely important, I believe that pointing to mirror neurons for a complete explanation of how this occurs reaffirms the false idea that the brain is the source of our capacity for social cognition. First, in my view, it is as a result of *overall bodily attunement* that we understand others' emotions, and sometimes even experience real, even if secondhand, emotion when we perceive their expressions and gestures. Such bodily attunement is not simply a matter of mirror neuron activation, but also involves a vast array of bodily dynamics, including muscles, increased blood flow, heart rate and blood pressure increases, vascular constriction, and metabolic and endocrine responses. One can perceive others' desiderative bodily feelings on the basis of their expressions, gestures, and bodily movements, to which one becomes bodily attuned via a cognitive–emotional mode of understanding that I have termed "affective framing." As will be discussed further below, it seems clear that during interpersonal interaction, *our whole bodies, not just our brains, resonate with the other person.* This sort of bodily attunement, through which one enters into a reciprocal relationship with others, ensures that intersubjectivity is essentially a matter of *intercorporeality.* [24]

Second, as De Jaegher and Di Paulo rightly point out, an appeal to mirror neurons does not explain the dynamics of the interaction process itself, or how social cognition emerges and is modulated by specific patterns of engagement and interaction among the parties involved. [25] These theorists argue that social cognition involves ongoing engagement and *coordination*, which is the nonaccidental correlation between the behaviors of two or more coupled systems. This involves coherence or matching of behavior over and above what is expected given what those systems are capable of doing. Examples of coordination in the realm of human activity include synchronization, mirroring, anticipation, and imitation, all of which are displayed by infants from a very early age. One striking example is how when see a smiling face or some other facial gesture, we immediately and involuntarily attune to it with an enactive, mimetic response. [26] And perhaps even more striking is the phenomenon of infectious laughter, since it's more obviously fully embodied. We laugh with our diaphragms, stomachs, throats, and the central parts of our body, not merely with our lips. When other people laugh, we are inclined to laugh too; when other people are anxious, we become anxious; and when others are at ease, this puts us at ease. These are just a few very common examples of emotional contagion or what some theorists have described as "automatic emotional resonance." [27] In addition, interaction partners mirror each other's movements, anticipate them, temporally synchronize or desynchronize them, and alter them in accordance with the intricate to-and-fro glances, utterances, and gestures that occur between them. [28] Second-person interactions between infants and caregivers are characterized by reciprocation of affect and emotions, and infants naturally become distressed when others stop interacting with them.[29] This suggests, once again, that from the very beginning we modulate, and are being modulated and affected by, the expressions, gestures, and actions of the other person, and that this mutual modulation impacts how we make sense of others as well as our surroundings.

De Jaegher and DiPaulo maintain that the concept of coordination can help us to make sense of this "natural pairing" of bodily behavior, and recommend that we understand social cognition as an ongoing process in which the patterns of interaction can directly influence individuals' efforts to sustain, modify, or discontinue a social encounter. They seek to uncover how "the physical, interactional coordination of behavior, in particular movements, relate[s] to our capacity to share meanings and to understand each other." As the behavior of individual interactors becomes coordinated in the way De Jeagher and Di Paulo describe, the gestures, utterances, facial expressions, and intonations that arise over the course of the interaction themselves influence what kinds of behavior coordination are likely to occur. Being engaged in a second-person interaction reduces the number of ways in which the individual parties can behave and also gives them new functional roles. For example, the infant who reduces her smiling and gazing, and then attempts to reengage her social partner through smiles and vocalization, is in effect inviting her social partner to communicate with her and coordinate his behavior. Whether and how this social partner responds, or simply ignores her, will shape what the infant does next. Therefore, even this extremely simple social encounter influences the activity of the persons involved, so that the encounter as a whole is not reducible to individual behaviors. The individuals involved do remain autonomous interactors, but the relationship that arises between them has its own properties that constrain and modulate individual behavior. For example, consider the behavior dynamics of two adults engaged in an ordinary conversation. Now that they are "components" of a larger system, the individual interactors cannot do certain things (such as break off a conversation mid-sentence without explanation), and the interaction process as a whole influences the behavior of each party involved. On the other hand, the relational whole also has a qualitatively different repertoire of states and behaviors, and thus has greater potential than the previously uncorrelated "parts." De Jeagher and Di Paulo describe participatory sense-making as "the coordination of intentional activity in interaction, whereby individual sense-making processes are affected and new domains of social sense-making can be generated that were not available to each individual on her own."[30]

Indeed, there are a wide range of examples that illustrate how, through the coordination of intentional activity, the way that each individual understands a situation is mediated by the sense-making activities of the other person(s) involved in the encounter.[31] Just as a smiling face invites us to smile back, somebody singing a song in a sense invites us to join them in that activity. We involuntarily attune to them with a mimetic response, and our patterns of bodily attunement shift. Of course, in many cases, we do not actually mirror others' actions, because these motor impulses are suppressed at the spinal level. However, there is still a sense in which the other person's desires, intentions, and actions engage us at a bodily level. Hutto notes that we often find ourselves adopting bodily stances similar to those of others when we take an interest in their projects. [32] And perceptual–motor coupling is particularly evident in situations of intricate bodily coordination, such as dance or sport, in cases where there is a great deal of bodily attunement and mutual modulation. In such cases there is motor mimicry, matched or coordinated body positions, and complementary movements or gestures. Such mutual modulation also is evident in kissing, where someone's being a "good kisser," just like being a good dancer, is largely a matter of his or her being appropriately attuned to another's body by way of motor mimicry and coordinated bodily positions. However, it is clear that sport, dancing, and kissing are not modulated by theorizing or inference -making, since this would make substantial demands on our cognitive and intellectual resources and likely would make these activities become awkward and uncoordinated. Instead, these are instances in which an action is directly and spontaneously apprehended, and one immediately responds with a similar or complementary gesture that allows the other person to see that one has recognized the meaning of her action. [33] Because it captures the sort of bodily coordination, reciprocity, and interactivity crucially involved in bodily attunement, I believe that dancing is not just a striking example of social cognition, but also a particularly apt basic metaphor for the process whereby it occurs.

In many instances of coordination, the sense-making activity of one party orients the attention of the other. For example, when one interactor visually scans the room in search of a lost object, and the other grabs his attention and points to it, the sense-making activity of one person modulates the sense-making of the other. As a result, the two individuals are able to participate in an act of joint sense-making. Another example that De Jaegher and Di Paulo present is that of Janet, who stands in front of an open window and takes an appreciative breath of fresh air in such a way as to make sure that John notices it. In their view, this is a communicative act whereby Janet is trying to adjust "John's cognitive and affective take on the world." [34] Janet wants John to attend to a particular salient part of the world and notice certain things that are visible to both of them, "to engage imaginatively with certain possibilities which these things present," and "to frame the visible world in a certain way." [35] During such orientation, John does not relate to Janet as a detached observer seeking to read her mind or body. Instead, his bodily dynamics and sense-making activities are directly affected by hers, so that there is no need for explicit deciphering.

As I indicated earlier, I do not think that such coordination and modulation can be explained simply via appeal to mirror neurons or brain activity, though of course I do not deny that brain activity plays a central role. In my view, we need to take seriously Ratcliffe's suggestion that the dynamics of "mutual influence"[36] described above are rooted in "a distinctive kind of bodily responsiveness comprised, at least in part, of patterns of motor-readiness and an affective sensibility to gestures and expressions."[37] Such bodily responsiveness, I believe, can be understood as a matter of deep bodily attunement and the entrainment of interactors' affective framing patterns. Particularly in instances of direct, face-to-face social encounters, subjects undergo a pronounced "affective reorientation" that changes how they view and interpret their surroundings. This is because once two interactors become part of a coupled system, their bodily dynamics and affective framing patterns become entrained to some extent, so that each person's expressions, behaviors, and desires modulate those of the other person. In addition, the dynamics of the interpersonal interaction as a whole causally affects and constrains the outlook and behavior of each party involved in the interaction. Insofar as their affective framing patterns (their patterns of focus and attention) are correlated and coordinated, two interactors are made interdependent and their desires and point of view are altered. What is crucial to point out is that this entrainment of affective framing patterns is a matter of interactors' lived bodily dynamics, which is exemplified by the many examples of so-called motor resonance, bodily reverberation, affective transformation, bodily attunement, and bodily coordination highlighted earlier. During second-person interaction, the cares and concerns of each party shift, the bodily dynamics of individual interactors are modulated, and each one's "caring-contoured map" is modified as a result.

One might say that Janet is trying to get John to adjust his affective framing patterns, so that coordination proceeds by way of bodily attunement. John understands Janet's intentions insofar as his own perspective and patterns of affective framing are influenced and shifted by Janet during the encounter. During second-person interaction, other people's desires and cares impact how we make sense of things and shift our patterns of attention. To see this, note that John understands Janet's desires, thoughts, and emotions in large part because of the impact that her expressive behavior and action has on his perspective and patterns of attention, and because of the joint sense-making that unfolds. His affective framing processes are shifted over the course of the interaction in accordance with Janet's desires. This change in affective framing patterns involves changes in his bodily dynamics (including his posture, heart race, blood flow, and gaze), which together constitute a shift in attention that attunes him to Janet and helps him to understand her perspective.

In moments of empathy, a shift in affective framing patterns goes a long way toward allowing us to see the world through another person's perspective. Empathy relies heavily on the dynamics of emotional contagion, bodily resonance, and mutual modulation. To take just one example, after being knocked backward into an awkward knee bend, a young football player grimaces as his body is contorted in pain. Watching on the sidelines, his mother grimaces, her heart rate quickens, and her legs ache. Something similar happens, of course, when people are in emotional pain. Upon coming into contact with another person's embodied emotional state, I take an "I-Thou" stance whereby my body resonates with hers. Her sadness is infectious, and suddenly her facial expressions and posture are mimicked to some extent by my own body. Because of this modulation of my bodily state, as a result of coming into contact with her essentially embodied emotions, I literally *feel with her*. Likewise, if I hope to cheer her up, I smile at her and give her a hug, hoping that some of my strength and good cheer will *rub off on her*. (Even this way of speaking is testament to the embodied nature of social interaction, especially where intense emotions are concerned.) I do not observe and then infer, but instead enter a shared dance with my interaction partner, whereby each of our affective framings and patterns of bodily attunement are influenced and modified. As a result of the bodily modulation that I undergo, my patterns of attention and focus shift and I begin to make sense of my surroundings in new ways. Thus, the reason why social interactions often are so transparent and direct, and also are potentially *transformative*, is that they engage us at a basic bodily level. This is evidenced by "motor resonance," galvanic skin responses, hormone fluctuations, and changes in heart rate and blood pressure.

MAKING SENSE OF AUTISM

If the account of bodily attunement and affective framing that I have presented above is correct, then autism should not be understood as "mindblindness," or an impairment in the ability to theorize about what is going on in others' minds, infer their mental states, and predict their behavior. Instead, the central social cognition deficits involved in autism should be understood as a direct result of impaired affective framing capacities and deficient patterns of bodily attunement. Therefore, I believe that Simon Baron-Cohen's well-known claim that children with autism are conscious of the physical world, and yet relatively unaware of the mental world, should be rethought. There is, in fact, a great deal of evidence which indicates that in addition to their impaired ability to understand other people's mental states, autistic subjects exhibit wide-ranging sensory abnormalities that make their bodily engagement with the physical world dramatically different from that of ordinary subjects. As Victoria McGeer notes, some of the abnormalities associated with autism clearly have little to do with "mind-reading" capacities.[38] These include sensory–motor problems, unusual physical sensitivities and insensitivities, slowed orienting of attention, oddities of posture and gait, tics, twitches, and abnormalities in perceptual processing. A study by Susan Leekam et al. showed that over 90 percent of children with autism have sensory abnormalities, with symptoms in multiple sensory domains.[39] First-person autobiographical accounts likewise reveal that subjects have unusual sensory experiences, including insensitivity to pain and atypical responses to auditory, visual, tactile, and olfactory stimuli. Some of the abnormalities most commonly found among autistic subjects include being distressed or unusually fascinated by certain sounds; exhibiting an unusual degree of interest in bright lights, shiny things, and the feel of certain surfaces; aimlessly manipulating objects to seek sensory stimulation; peculiar gesturing or hand-flapping; and exhibiting a negative reaction to gentle touch.[40] In addition, Stuart Shanker notes that autistic children display atypical facial expressions of positive emotion, marked by asymmetry, reduced movements in the eye and mouth regions, shorter durations, and lower intensity.[41] Lastly, autistic infants between eight months and one year of age do not use the noises found to be common among normal babies to express their needs and feelings, and Ricks and Wang found that nonverbal forms of communication were not used easily or naturally by older children.[42]

In light of such evidence, Gallagher claims that the source of autism is a range of neurological disruptions that impact sensory–motor processes.[43] He cites brain activity as the ultimate source of autism and points to research indicating that the normal timing of apoptosis (the natural pruning of the excess neuronal cells with which we were born) is disrupted in the autistic brain. Some of the brain-based sensory–motor problems Gallagher cites include movement disturbances, problems with sitting, walking and crawling, and abnormal motor patterns. In my view, while Gallagher is correct to emphasize the sensory–motor problems associated with autism, his account mistakenly affirms the assumption that brain dysfunction alone is the source of autism. Why not suppose that sensory–motor problems *themselves*, while perhaps associated with the disruption of the normal timing of apoptosis (or some other dysfunction) in the brain, play a direct role in interfering with social understanding by way of decreasing subjects' capacity for bodily attunement?

As discussed previously, there is evidence that a subject's understanding of another person's actions and intentions depends importantly on a mirrored reverberation in the subject's own motor system. Gallagher rightly notes that "problems with our own motor or body-schematic system could significantly interfere with our capacities for understanding others."[44] Thus, disruption of one's own sensory–motor processes could contribute directly to deficits in social cognition. Along these lines, Stuart Shanker maintains that the source of autism is a set of "sensory challenges" that impede children's abilities to engage in co-regulated affective interactions with caregivers.[45] Due to an over- or under-reactivity to stimuli, the infant's opportunity to engage in important learning experiences is undermined, making it difficult for autistic children to undergo healthy emotional and social development. Deficits in facial expressions, for example, may exacerbate problems with social interaction and the development of intersubjectivity insofar as they impact a caregiver's responsiveness to the child. On the other hand, a child who is overreactive to visual stimuli may resort to tuning out the world (for example, by averting his gaze) as a way to cope with the sense of being overwhelmed by stimuli. According to Shanker, the more this child avoids interaction with others, the more difficult it is for him or her to build up the range of thoughts, feelings, and emotions that would allow her to engage socially.[46] McGeer likewise maintains that autistic sensory disturbances lead autistic children to shut out other people, making it difficult for them to develop the social, communicative, and imaginative skills needed to make good regulative use of other people. The innate capacity for imitation, for example, "would hardly be evoked in a sustained and potentially regulatory manner if autistic children find their contact with others, on the whole, far too stimulating to be tolerated."[47]

Both of these theorists highlight how sensory disturbances cause autistics to shut out others and thereby make it difficult for autistic children to develop the sorts of skills that are needed for productive social engagement and interpersonal understanding. Such accounts imply that withdrawing from the social world is a way of coping with overwhelming stimuli and thus a defense mechanism for autistic children. No doubt this is true to some extent. However, I believe that sensory disturbances play an even more direct role in the sense that they render autistic subjects incapable of entering into relationships of *mutual bodily attunement*. Although sensory experiences may be especially intense, associated stimuli are not experienced as *mattering* and bodily feelings are devoid of their usual desiderative element. Because a child whose affective framing capacities are impaired is unable to make sense of the meaning of such stimuli, he or she may very well feel overwhelmed or distressed and withdraw from the situation in order to escape being bombarded by intense, seemingly meaningless stimuli. But perhaps even more importantly, because their own bodily experience is attenuated and distorted, such children likely will find it difficult to coordinate their own expressions, gestures, and movements with those of others. If the bridge between self and other is sustained by perceiving and reproducing the expressed bodily feelings of others (smile for smile, frown for frown) and participating in mutual modulation, certainly this will be disrupted if one's own bodily feelings lack salience and felt meaning. As a result, others' gestures and expressions will not arouse the subject's own embodied, deside-rative feelings, and she will not clue in to other people's emotional comport-ment or intentions. In short, because autistics *lack a clear sense of the mean-ing and significance of their own bodily feelings*, they will find it difficult to engage in social referencing behaviors or shared attention. Thus, the sensory disturbances commonly associated with autism, which are symptomatic of a disruption in embodied emotional consciousness, lead directly to an inability to become attuned to other people.

For this reason, the distinction that Baron-Cohen makes between under-standing the physical world and understanding the mental world is mistaken to the extent that it fails to acknowledge the sense in which understanding other minds is largely a matter of *becoming attuned to others' living, lived bodies*. As Baron-Cohen himself highlights, pointing gestures, gaze monitor-ing, showing gestures, and other aspects of joint attention often are absent in children with autism. They are deficient in their ability to monitor or direct another person's focus of attention, use gesture to engage in social communi-cation, and coordinate their own behavior and attention with that of others.[48] Indeed, it appears that from an early age, the essentially embodied practices of primary intersubjectivity among autistic children are *broken or out of sync*. It is not surprising, then, that many high-functioning autistic individu-als, who would be capable of passing false-belief tests, nevertheless exhibit certain abnormalities of social behavior that impact reciprocal relating and communication. Consequently, it seems unlikely that autism results funda-mentally from a disruption in meta-cognitive or higher-level mechanisms of mentalizing or theorizing. Social cognition rests largely on the capacity for *body attunement* rather than theorizing, and it is disrupted or etiolated pat-terns of essentially embodied experience and bodily attunement that make it difficult for autistic subjects to connect with and understand others.

Ratcliffe rightly maintains that "an absence of the to-and-fro of expres-sion and gesture that ordinarily operates as a harmonious backdrop for mutu-al understanding" results in a breakdown of interpersonal understanding.[49] We normally interact with others by responding to feelings with feelings, which are conveyed via a patterned system of bodily gestures and coordinat-ed movements. While one might characterize this as "body language," the linguistic metaphor is potentially misleading. I have suggested that an even more apt analogy, which is appropriately less cerebral and intellectual, is *dancing*. Ordinary subjects perceive actions, gestures, and expressions through activation of their own motor systems and bodily feelings, and there-by "know how to dance" with others. The perception of another's body comportment spontaneously arouses various bodily feelings in the perceiver, and also various responsive movements, such as turning to face a speaker and looking him or her in the eye. In the case of autism, on the other hand, lack of expression on the part of the autistic subject is met by lack of expression by the other party, resulting in disrupted patterns of affective response. Because this capacity for everyday bodily attunement and responsiveness—this "knowing how to dance" with others—is disrupted in those with autism, their capacity to connect and affectively interact with others is diminished. First-person social interactions come to be ruled by third-person "It–It" dynamics, resulting in more or less "disembodied" social relationships. Due to their lack of bodily attunement with other minded subjects, autistic subjects find it difficult to understand the significance and nuanced meaning of various social acts and encounters.

Moreover, because autistic subjects cannot perceive the intentions or emotions of others in their bodily comportment or participate fully in reciprocal bodily modulation, high-functioning autistics may employ theorizing strategies or mentalizing as a way to compensate. However, this is because they lack the ordinary way of understanding others, and so must try to make algorithmic and explicit what for most of us is second nature.[50] In autism, a first-person perspective based on pre-reflective, essentially nonconceptual bodily attunement (affective framing) often is replaced with a third-person perspective involving the application of algorithms, general principles, and abstract rules.[51] Along these lines, Frederique de Vignemont and Uta Frith depict social cognition among autistic subjects as relying primarily on "abstract allocentrism."[52] They maintain that ordinary subjects adopt an egocentric stance during direct, face-to-face interactions with others, and thereby understand the other person in relationship to themselves. A subject who takes an egocentric stance is immersed in the social interaction and directly connected with the other person. Taking an allocentric stance, on the other hand, is more detached from interactions with others and allows one to understand that others exist outside of their relationship to oneself. No doubt it is important that subjects be capable of assuming both of these stances. The problem is that autistic subjects take up the allocentric stance even when they are involved in direct social interaction. They rely heavily on rules and predict other people's behavior on the basis of regularities between inputs and outputs. Therefore, while autistics are able to understand social structures and interpersonal relationships in a detached way, their sense of how the social world should work often is very logical, formal, and far removed from the reality of most everyday social encounters. In my view, this is because their own bodies do not resonate with the postures, facial expressions, tones of voice, and gestures of other people. Because they are capable only of an abstract allocentric stance that is disconnected from embodied, face-to-face interactions, they tend to rely on normative rules rather than the desiderative bodily feelings of affective framing when empathizing with others. One might say that people with autism operate in the way one might expect all humans to operate if TT were true, by appealing to a set of generalizations and approaching social cognition from a detached, third-person perspective. As Stuart Shanker points out, autism thus exemplifies the Cartesian view of "normal" social cognition and empathy often articulated by proponents of TT.[53] However, it is important to keep in mind that this sort of rule following is not the way the ordinary subjects understand other people, but instead a way that high-functioning autistics attempt to compensate for their social cognition deficits.

This reliance on "abstract allocentrism" and the application of rules helps to make sense of why autistic subjects appear to be sensitive to moral considerations in certain respects, and yet lack moral competence in other respects. To be clear, my claim is not that autistic people are devoid of emotions or that they do not care about other people. As Vignemont and Frith note, the available evidence does not indicate that children with autism are impaired with respect to emotion recognition, but instead that they suffer from emotion processing abnormalities and find it more difficult to regulate and reflect on their emotions.[54] This may mean that although they have an autonomic affective response, they are unable to decipher fully the meaning or significance of what they are feeling. As a result, their emotions do not fully come into play during information processing. One way to make sense of this is to point out that empathy ordinarily involves both an affective and cognitive component, and that these components are *fused together* by way of affective framing. In autism, however, these cognitive and affective elements come apart, so that the desiderative bodily feelings of affective framing no longer effectively focus attention or guide the subject in making sense of others' behavior. Thus, the problem is not that they are insensitive to the distress of others or that they simply do not care, but rather that their caring is more detached from cognitive processing than it is for ordinary subjects. I have argued that this apparent detachment can be explained as a deficiency in bodily attunement and an impaired capacity for affective framing.

However, although autistics do exhibit a weakened sense of emotional connectedness, they still are able to participate in moral life to some extent and are capable of some mode of empathy. This is because through the development of moral rules and principles of conduct, they can fashion long-term stable values and concerns for themselves and care about the interests of others. Jean Kennett has maintained that underlying this capacity for rule-governed conduct is "generalized moral concern," which enables autistic subjects to recognize that other people's interests *matter* and are reason giving, and thus renders them capable of deep moral concern.[55] She points out that while many of us are empathically engaged spontaneously and become immediately attuned to the concerns of others, autistics rely more on rules of conduct and general principles in order to navigate the social landscape. This might be described as a "cold" methodology that engages the intellect to a great extent in order to bring about the sort of affective, bodily attunement that for ordinary subjects occurs spontaneously and pre-reflectively via affective framing. Because their mode of empathy is more rule driven, their participation in social and moral life differs somewhat from that of ordinary subjects. Indeed, Temple Grandin reports that she has learned how to approach social relationships and social situations by applying rules and using her intellect, and reports having great difficulty with new social situations if she does not have a similar situation from the past to use as a guide. Because she is unable to grasp human emotions intuitively and pre-reflectively by way of bodily attunement, she instead relies on pure logic and has devised a rule system to guide her social interactions and behavior. Using the metaphor of dancing once again, one might say that among autistic subjects, performance of the "dance steps of social cognition" becomes explicit and rule driven rather than flowing, pre-reflective, and spontaneous. Because the affective, bodily mappings of affective framing that normally guide face-to-face interpersonal interactions have broken down, empathizing takes on a different, less fully embodied form. However, this does not entail that empathy and social understanding disappear altogether.

REFERENCES

Baron-Cohen, S. 1999. Can Studies of Autism Teach Us About Consciousness of the Physical and the Mental? *Philosophical Explorations* 3:175–88.

Baron-Cohen, S. 2002. The Extreme Male Brain Theory of Autism. *Trends in Cognitive Science* 6(6):248–54.

De Jaegher, H. 2009. Social Understanding Through Direct Perception? Yes, By Interaction. *Consciousness and Cognition* 18:535–42.

De Jaegher, H. and Di Paolo, E. 2007. Participatory Sense-Making: An Enactive Approach to Social Cognition.*Phenomenology and Cognitive Science* 6:485–507.

Gallagher, S. 2001. The Practice of Mind: Theory, Simulation, or Primary Interaction? *Journal of Consciousness Studies* 8(5-7):83–108.

Gallagher, S. 2004. Understanding Interpersonal Problems in Austism: Interaction Theory as an Alternative to Theory of Mind. *Philosophy, Psychiatry, and Psychology* 11(3):199–217.

Gallagher, S. 2005. Phenomenological Contributions to a Theory of Social Cognition. *Husserl Studies* 21:95–110.

Gallagher, S. 2008. Inference or Interaction: Social Cognition Without Precursors. *Philosophical Explorations* 11(3):163–74.

Goldman, A. 1995. Empathy, Mind, and Morals, in *Mental Simulation,* eds. M. Davies and T. Stone, 185–208. Oxford: Blackwell Publishers.

Hatfield, E., Cacioppo, J., and Rapson, R. *Emotional Contagion.* 1994. Cambridge, UK: Cambridge University Press.

Hutto, D. 2004. The Limits of Spectatorial Folk Psychology. *Mind and Language* 19(5):548–73.

Kennett, J. 2002. Autism, Empathy, and Moral Agency. *The Philosophical Quarterly* 52 (208):340–57.

Leekam, S. *et al.* 2007. Describing the Sensory Abnormalities of Children and Adults with Autism. *Journal of Autism Development Disorder* 37: 894–910.

McGeer, V. 2001. Psycho-practice, Psycho-theory, and the Contrastive Case of Autism: How Practices of Mind Become Second-Nature. *Journal of Consciousness Studies* 8(5-7):109–132.

Noë, A. 2009. *Out of Our Heads: Why You Are Not Your Brain, and Other Lessons from the Biology of Consciousness.* New York: Hill and Wang.

Ratcliffe, M. 2007. *Rethinking Commonsense Psychology: A Critique of Folk Psychology, Theory of Mind, and Simulation*. Hampshire, UK: Palgrave Macmillan.

Shanker, S. 2004. Autism and the Dynamic Developmental Model of Emotions. *Philosophy, Psychiatry, and Psychology* 11(3):219–33.

Sparaci, L. 2008. Embodying Gestures: The Social Orienting Model and the Study of Early Gestures in Autism. *Phenomenology and Cognitive Science* 7:203–23.

Stanghellini, G. 2004. *Disembodied Spirits and Deanimated Bodies: The Pyschopathology of Common Sense*. New York: Oxford University Press.

Stanghellini, G. and Ballerini, M. 2004. Autism: Disembodied Existence. *Philosophy, Psychiatry, and Psychology* 11(3):259–68.

Striano, T. and Reid, V. 2006. Social Cognition in the First Year. *Trends in Cognitive Science* 10(10): 471–76.

Vignemont, de, F. and Frith, U. 2007. Autism, Morality and Empathy, in *Moral Psychology* 3: *The Neuroscience of Morality,* ed. W. Sinnott-Armstrong, 273–80. Cambridge, MA: MIT Press.

NOTES

1. Baron-Cohen 1999, 177.
2. Goldman 1995, 186.
3. Baron-Cohen 1999; 2002.
4. Baron-Cohen 1999, 177.
5. Baron-Cohen 2002, 248.
6. Baron-Cohen 2002, 248.
7. De Jaegher 2009, 537.
8. Gallagher 2001, 85.
9. Of course this could be construed as a type of simulation, but what is crucial to note is that such simulation is essentially embodied. We create "living pictures" of other people with our own bodies, by means of our proprioceptive responses to them. For example, this is illustrated by the way in which people stand and modulate their facial expressions when they are talking to each other at social gatherings. Thus, the theory I present here might be understood as a non-cognitivist version of simulation theory.
10. Gallagher 2008, 166.
11. De Jaegher and Di Paulo 2007, 488.
12. Stanghellini 2004, 68.
13. Striano and Reid 2006, 471.
14. DeJaegher 2009, 540.
15. Ratcliffe 2007, 129.
16. Stanghellini 2004, 91.
17. Ratcliffe 2007, 149.
18. Hutto 2004, 551.
19. Hutto 2004, 554.
20. Stanghellini and Ballerini 2004, 263.
21. Noë 2009, 33.
22. Gallagher 2005, 97.
23. Gallagher 2005, 101.
24. Stanghellini 2004, 68.
25. De Jaegher and Di Paulo 2007.
26. Gallagher 2008.
27. Hatfield, Cacioppo, and Rapson 1994, 2.
28. De Jaeagher 2009, 539.
29. Striano and Redi 2006, 471.
30. De Jeagher and Di Paulo 2007, 497.
31. De Jaegher and Di Paulo 2007.
32. Hutto 2004, 551.

33. Ratcliffe 2007, 141.
34. De Jaegher and Di Paulo 2007, 499.
35. De Jaegher and Di Paulo 2007, 499.
36. Ratcliffe 2007, 149.
37. Ratcliffe 2007, 158.
38. McGeer 2001.
39. Susan Leekam et al. 2007.
40. Leekam et al. 2007, 897.
41. Stuart Shanker 2004.
42. Ricks and Wang 1975.
43. Gallagher 2004.
44. Gallagher 2004, 210–11.
45. Shanker 2004.
46. Shanker 2004, 229.
47. McGeer 2001, 129.
48. Sparaci 2008, 215–16.
49. Ratcliffe 2007, 169.
50. Shanker 2004, 212.
51. Stanghellini and Ballerini 2004, 266.
52. Vignemont and Frith 2007.
53. Shanker 2004.
54. Vignemont and Frith 2007.
55. Kennett 2002.

Chapter Eight

Advocacy, Autism and Autonomy

David DeVidi

While I'd normally prefer to avoid doing so, I feel that it is important to begin this chapter with a bit of autobiography. My approach to issues surrounding autism is conditioned by my experience as an *advocate* for people with autism, and people with developmental disorders more generally. The groups I am involved in advocate for the right of those with developmental disabilities to live self-directed, fulfilling lives in the community. In practice, this involves trying to take concrete steps that will create mechanisms and a context that will allow people to live richer, community-based lives. These mechanisms include appropriate social and health services, new housing options, more flexible funding arrangements that put control of support funding in the hands of individuals, and supported decision making to make best use of those resources, while the desired context is pursued by increasing public awareness, helping build "support circles" around individuals, and so on.

The point is not merely that people be happy and safe, though obviously that would be nice too, but that they have a chance to live lives that are *satisfying* and *productive* in the community. The values that motivate this work, we announce, are *full citizenship, reciprocal relationships, self-determination* and *community*.[1]

Questions confront any philosopher using such rhetoric, particularly in advocacy for people with autism. The *DSM-IV*, for instance, lists impairments of social interactions, including "lack of social or emotional reciprocity" and "failure to develop peer relationships appropriate to developmental level" as key diagnostic criteria for autism.[2] This looks rather like it might make it a matter of definition that the goal of enabling meaningful reciprocal relationships for those with autism is quixotic. Moreover, it has been argued that psychopathy is "moral death," on the grounds that *empathy* is a necessary condition for moral agency.[3] Since the diagnostic criteria for autism are often read as entailing a lack of empathy, it is natural to ask, as Jeanette Kennett has, "why is the autistic person, morally speaking, not worse off than the psychopath?"[4] Kennett suggests an interesting response, and in any case her presupposition is that knowing people with autism makes obvious that they are moral agents, so that something has gone wrong in the reasoning that leads up to the question. But if the question of whether people with autism are "worse off" than morally dead is on the table, the appropriateness of the rhetoric is certainly in question since it is, to say the least, not obviously appropriate to argue for "full citizenship" for those who are not moral agents.

The question, then, is one of good faith. When this sort of advocacy rhetoric is employed, can we really *mean it*? Of course, even if not, it wouldn't immediately follow that we have to *stop* using it. If the point is not merely to understand the world but to change it, and such rhetorical devices are part of an effective campaign that creates change beneficial to individuals with autism, then there is a case to be made for carrying on. Alternatively, it might be that the use of terms such as "citizenship," "relationship" and "self-determination" are best understood as something similar to the coded language used, for instance, in diplomacy ("free and frank discussion") or in journalism (e.g., describing a member of parliament suspected of drunkenness as "tired and emotional") when a too-blunt statement risks adverse effects. But before resorting to a justification of either of these sorts for the style of rhetoric in question, one would want to be sure that no *direct* justification of such terminology is forthcoming.

For the present, my specific focus will be on the question of autonomy. Much of the rhetoric produced by advocates rather directly involves the assumption that people with autism are capable of, and ought to be enabled to lead, autonomous lives. Consider that we advocate for self-determination, or make claims like "leading a good life means *leading* that life." But other rhetoric also involves such a claim by implication, as when we argue for a right to "full citizenship," which in a democratic society involves a role in social decision making that, at least arguably, is only appropriately played by autonomous individuals.[5]

In certain respects what I have to say will overlap with what might be said by someone considering this rhetoric with respect to other developmental disabilities. Nevertheless, as I shall try to show, there are many respects in which the question of autonomy is a particularly vexed one for individuals with autism.

Autonomy in the abstract is, of course, the subject of a thriving literature in its own right, but the immediate topic is sufficiently rich that I intend in what follows to mostly steer clear of detailed consideration of debates within this literature. The lessons to be drawn here will for the most part require us only to consider the common core shared by most notions of autonomy. As a convenient summary of that common content, we could do much worse than to borrow this characterization, due to John Christman: "Put most simply, to be autonomous is to be one's own person, to be directed by considerations, desires, conditions, and characteristics that are not simply imposed upon one, but are part of what can somehow be considered one's authentic self."[6]

It is unfortunate, if understandable given the goals of their specific projects, that so many of the discussions of autism in the philosophical literature focus on those with Asperger's syndrome and others at the "high functioning" end of the autism spectrum. This risks an ironic compounding of a problem of "invisibility" that some in the autism community feel they have long confronted. Many people with autism do not speak.[7] This, coupled with their highly idiosyncratic and usually complex needs, often makes people with autism easy and convenient to ignore. Disabilities where individuals are more socially adaptable and less likely to be explosive are "more telegenic"; a duty to maximize the effectiveness of limited resources suggests concentrating on developing programs and services that will serve groups where needs are more similar between individuals; and people who do not speak for themselves are obviously disadvantaged when it comes to self-advocacy. Now that autism can no longer claim to be a hidden problem nor to lack for attention compared to other "more telegenic" disabilities, the danger is that those autistic persons who are highly articulate, easier to study, and for some purposes easier to work with will be taken as typical and representative of the whole spectrum. There is a general worry here, since it could distort the picture of what autism involves, possibly resulting in the use of scarce resources to provide accommodations that disproportionately suit only those on part of the spectrum; and anyway, it pushes those on the rest of the spectrum, once again, into background invisibility.

For the present inquiry it is important to have in mind people elsewhere on the spectrum. I will mostly have in mind people with "classic autism,"[8] which usually involves profound difficulties with language and with self-control that exacerbate the complications in their lives, and that make the claim to autonomy more difficult to sustain.

There is a reason for this focus. As we shall see, linguistic differences are central to the question of whether people with autism are (or have the capacity for being) autonomous. I shall argue that the linguistic deficits characteristic of autism lead to *overestimation* of the contrast between people with autism and other, uncontroversially autonomous agents along certain dimensions relevant to the question of autonomy. As I shall try to show, once these differences are seen in the correct light, being a person with autism, even in a severe form, is compatible with being an autonomous agent.

THE CHALLENGE

There are many ways in which autism calls into question whether a genuine capacity for autonomy is in the cards. I will focus on three. I suggest, though I will not try to argue in a chapter of this length, that the sort of response I will make to these three considerations would apply, *mutatis mutandis*, to others.

1. Inflexibility: People with autism characteristically have difficulty adapting to changes in routine. This rules out the sort of on-the-fly decision making that is available to, and expected of, autonomous citizens in the community. Some opportunities come around only rarely and taking advantage of them requires a certain dexterity and willingness to change tracks. One readily imagines ways that options passed over due to discomfort with change might be more consonant with an individual's "true nature," and so this inflexibility prevents that individual from measuring up to Christman's characterization of an autonomous agent.

2. Poor impulse control: Difficulty with impulse control is a common trait among those with autism. Personal autonomy is often thought to involve the capacity to make choices among one's own desires, and moreover to make them stick; one way to flesh out the talk of desires that govern a person's behavior being "authentically one's own" is that the desires are the ones the person has *chosen* for herself. Such desires about desires are often referred to as *higher-order desires*, and variations on the idea that the presence and effectiveness of higher-order desires is a precondition of autonomy are frequently voiced in the philosophical literature. [9]

3. Communication differences: The communication difficulties characteristic of autism can raise questions about autonomy in several ways. First, the characteristic communication deficits having to do with interpreting the pragmatic component of the communicative content of speech limits the capacity for autonomy in a couple of ways. Some life paths (professional poker player, labor negotiator) are probably ruled out by such an inability to read people. More generally, though, the inability to grasp significant components of what is being said means that often, in the normal run of conversation, a person with autism will not be in a position to appreciate the range of options actually on offer.

But when we consider people with classic autism, especially those who do not speak, other questions arise. For concreteness, consider someone who communicates by supported typing—for instance, as sometimes happens, the person can type answers to questions, provided they have another person's arm to press against as they direct their hands towards the keyboard. [10] Often this works with people only after the typist and the assistant have had a lot of time to work together, so can only happen in the presence of particular others. This level of dependence on particular others to modulate one's inter-actions with the world runs counter to the usual picture of autonomy as of a piece with independence. [11]

These three characteristics have implications for how decisions, especial-ly decisions about important matters, are made by people with autism, espe-cially in circumstances of "supported decision making." It will be useful to have in front of us a couple of fairly specific, and (insofar as anything is typical of people with autism) not atypical examples of what I mean. [12]

One complicating factor can (at some risk of oversimplification) be phrased thus: "No" often doesn't mean no. While this is subject to a great deal of individual variation, when a person with autism is asked whether or not a particular activity (going for a walk, stopping in at the bank, etc.) would be a good idea, especially when the suggestion is outside of routine, the first response can be an "automatic no." Repeated discussion can be required before the routine-breaking activity can happen. For instance, if we ask someone "Would you like to go for a walk with Bob?" where Bob is a new acquaintance, "no" might well be interpreted by family members as simple discomfort with change. And the family members might well be confident that the "no" is merely a matter of the question coming out of the blue. A few different things might ground this confidence, such as past instances where asking a few times during the course of a day led to a changed answer, or longstanding expressions of a desire for more excursions and a wider variety of friends to share excursions with.

For more complicated questions, the interpretive role of those close to the person is correspondingly more complicated. For a question such as "Who would you be willing to share your home with?" the result can be a fluctuat-ing answer as the question is asked repeatedly. Indeed, it is regarded as bad practice to accept the first response to such important questions. After repeat-edly asking the same questions over time, the answers usually settle into being consistently the same, at which point it is natural to think that the answer reflects the person's true wishes. But it takes someone who knows the person well to know when the fluctuation has settled into a decision.

Finally, the dependence on others has further consequences. People with autism often have limited experience of the world around them. It is some-times difficult for them to understand the likely results of various options. Sometimes they will not even be aware of the options typical of common situations. Such information is, of course, essential to reasonable decision making. So a key part of the support in supported decision making is provid-ing this essential information, and working to help the person understand it.

This list raises questions of two broad types. First, there is a certain sort of epistemological complication in supported decisions. Even supposing there is a definite core of beliefs and desires that reflect an autistic person's "true self," the mechanisms described above call into question our ability to reliably access it—we are depending on those who "know the person best" to act as interpreters, after all, in cases of the sort described. If the decision maker is dependent on others to bring the decision into effect, the possibility of acting on that true self is doubtful.

This is further complicated by the fact that the ability to detect subtle cues, to "read" a particular individual, that make someone an appropriate communication assistant depends on establishing trust and good will. As a practical matter, this makes it more difficult to disentangle the contribution of the individual from that of the assistant. By no means do I want to impute ill-will or intent to deceive to the assistant. But consider again the simple example of saying "no" to a walk. The tendency to regard decisions that turn out well to have been one's own idea all along seems to be near universal, so the fact that someone asked after the fact might say "yes, I did really want to go for the walk, but my first reaction is very often no in a new situation" might merely reflect this tendency. In such cases it will be hard for the assistant to disentangle what she knows to be *in the person's interests* from what she takes to be *what the person wants to do*.

But we also must ask whether the "deeper desires" are there in the first place. One must confront the question of whether the influence of assistants in supported decision making mean that they ought to be called not merely assistants, but the *decision makers*. In a complex decision, like where and with whom one will live, it would not be unusual for people assisting with the decision to provide evidence about what sort of options are available in the region; help the person think through the implications of the various choices; and decide when a person's statements on the matter are sufficiently consistent and well-informed to count as settled. There are distinct sorts of worry here. How the information is presented can tip the decision, of course (Does the assistant point out that group homes are often noisy and chaotic? Or is the emphasis on sharing the house with people who might share interests and provide opportunities for interesting activities?) But there's also a worry about continuing to ask the question until the desired answer is delivered.

THE DEFENSE

Nevertheless, I think it is possible to defend the claim to autonomy, or more precisely of the capacity for autonomy, of people with autism. More precisely still, I think the defensible claim is that autistic people are capable of autonomy if anyone is. The case for this is in two parts. First, it is easy to overestimate the significance of the considerations raised above by overestimating the difference it shows between people with autism and others, usually because we do not appropriately assess the implications of communication differences. The second step is to argue that the remaining significant differences involve the *externalization* of certain parts of the decision making process that are not typically externalized, but this externalization does not undermine the claim to autonomy for the decision maker. The key to this second argument is to make clear that externalization of key parts of decision making is common, but for most decisions made by most people it is invisible because social structures are in place that make the supports ubiquitous and automatic.

First, let us consider the question of impulse control. Difficulty with compulsive eating, self-stimulation, pacing, shouting, and more, can make people with autism challenging for those who support them day-to-day and disconcerting company for people who don't know them.[13] But of course, problems with impulse control are not exclusive to those with disabilities. It is a familiar feature of human existence that, for most of us much of the time, the process of keeping on track to meet longer-term goals requires avoiding falling into temptation. That is, we must avoid being diverted into pursuing more immediate, highly appealing satisfactions that would prevent or greatly reduce the likelihood of achieving longer term goals that, given the opportunity to evaluate them side by side, we would judge more important to us. Indeed, addictive behavior is plausibly viewed as consistent failure on just this score.

How do most of us cope? Willpower strikes me as a fundamentally implausible answer.[14] But even those less sceptical of the idea of willpower in general will admit it is not always sufficient to the task. Instead, we take preemptive action to avoid being confronted with temptations or opportunities to make mistakes. Pilots in training are told "The superior pilot uses superior judgment to avoid situations requiring superior skill."[15] We take similar precautions to avoid crashes in our own lives. To resort again to autobiography, I left my home town to attend a distant university in part as a way to get out of the circumstances that led me to binge drinking every weekend during the last half of high school. I had other goals and thought, plausibly, that alcoholism was likely to thwart them.

Consider another simple example: my spouse, who has more willpower than most, can't resist eating chocolate chips if they're in the cupboard, so we don't keep them in the house. This example may seem trivial, but it usefully illustrates some important points. It's *me* who does the grocery shopping in our house. It is therefore not in my spouse's direct control whether there are chocolate chips in the house.[16] Instead, she *asks* me not to buy them, and unless I'm being a jerk, I oblige. What's important about this is just how mundane and common it is that the strategies we use for impulse control involve *the assistance and cooperation of others*. Notice, too, that had my spouse been blessed with a more considerate partner she may never have had to ask me to avoid buying chocolate chips. This hypothetical considerate partner might have used what he knew of her considered preferences for a healthy diet, and readily available evidence about how difficult it is for her to leave chocolate chips alone, to make an easy inference and decide to help her by leaving the chips at the store. People do this sort of thing all the time, sometimes to save the other person the trouble of asking when it could be embarrassing, and sometimes because the person might never ask and so would end up worse off without someone else taking the initiative to implement the avoidance of temptation on the person's behalf.

The ease with which we could multiply examples of this sort makes it plausible that there is at most a difference of degree between the role others must play in helping those with autism with their impulse control and their role in impulse control for others. The dietary examples will be close to home for many people who live with people with autism, as people with autism often have food sensitivities, are aware that certain foods are a problem for them, but have limited ability to avoid eating those foods when they're around. It is thus up to the people who support them day-to-day to ensure that the danger foods are not readily accessible.

What we should say about the implications of needing this sort of support from others for one's autonomy will be sensitive to the details of particular cases. An occasional unhealthy dessert that doesn't significantly derail a basically healthy diet is probably best regarded as not impugning a person's claim to autonomy at all, even if regretted shortly after it's eaten. If a person is genuinely powerless in the face of a particular sort of temptation, but is able to engage in avoidance behavior, perhaps by enlisting the assistance of others, it seems to me that we ought not to question the person's autonomy—he is able to act on his true desires—but cases like this make clear that actual autonomy can depend on the circumstances in which one finds oneself. Finally, suppose that there were no practical options for my spouse to avoid chocolate chips, with or without the assistance of others (e.g., suppose I bought them every week, but the obvious expedient of upgrading her spouse was for some reason ruled out). In that case, we may conclude that she is not autonomous about chocolate chips. But this is dependent on unfortunate circumstances, and so does not imply a lack of *capacity* for autonomy in this respect (had she the appropriate supports). And we'd hardly decide on the basis of her chocolate chip addiction that she is not an autonomous person, since her ability to act in accordance with her more fundamental desires in other areas of her life is clear. Autonomy is not an all-or-nothing thing. The same lesson must apply to people with autism, so that even those impulses that are not within their control, with or without external supports, would only limit the scope of their autonomy.

The two-step strategy applies to the limited ability of people with autism to make decisions "on the fly," whether caused by limited ability to understand all aspects of conversations or by problems adapting to sudden change. These difficulties are of apiece with the sorts of circumstantial limitations confronting every decision maker. One's physical capacities and intellectual talents obviously condition what options are available for pursuing. There is a plausible parallel between an individual with autism who does not even consider pursuing otherwise attractive options because of discomfort with change and, say, a short and uncoordinated person never considering pursuing a career in basketball or a shy person not considering a job in public relations.

The inability to take part in the sorts of conversations where options are revealed to those able to discern them, whether negotiating in a board room or a bar, presents a different sort of limitation. Here the options that never become available need not be ones the person would be uninterested in or incapable of successfully pursuing. Rather, the characteristic deficits in grasping implicatures and other pragmatic aspects of communication can prevent recognition that appealing options are available. But these limits, too, have their analogue in the lives of most nonautistic people. They are rather more like limitations due to lack of financial resources, or (more directly to the point) lack of social connections and the mannerisms that often signal them. Notoriously, people often attend particular universities for programs in law or business, not for the quality of the education they will get, but for the connections they can make. The connections open up options that never come to the attention of the possibly smarter and better-educated graduates of other programs. But extra options don't always go to the more powerful. The gang at work might carefully avoid having the boss hear them planning a trip to the pub at the end of the work week. The very good reason might be that joking with the boss is a dangerous business, since the boss doesn't understand the teasing humor likely to ensue, and is a dangerous business since causing offense has consequences of a different order from offending the person in the next cubicle.

That some options are available only to those who attend the right school, and other such limits on people's options, certainly smack of social injustice and as something worth striving to eliminate. But for present purposes, it is more important to note what would be required to overcome these restrictions. There are thriving consultancy businesses that teach people from the wrong schools how better to pass in the corporate world: how to pick the right wine, which fork to use, how firmly to shake someone's hand. In the other direction, millionaires educated at Yale who want to become politicians need to learn to look like "someone you could have a beer with." External

supports are needed to decode implicit messages for all of us, at least sometimes. There is, of course, an important difference in the degree to which this
is so for people with autism. But those to whom a particular class of options
never becomes available do not lack autonomy *tout court*. Rather, this is a
kind of limitation that all decision makers confront in some measure. They
are the sorts of limits that any plausible account of autonomy is going to have
to make room for if *anyone*, autistic or not, is going to count as autonomous.

Finally, let us turn to the issues raised by the supported decision-making
process itself (considering both prongs of the defense at once, since it is
impossible to put off discussion of externalization when discussing this topic). As noted, people with severe autism often lead rather sheltered lives that
provide them with relatively little information. In some enlightened regions,
people can hire "facilitators," one of whose key duties is providing information about options, about the implications of particular choices leading up to
important decisions. The same facilitator often then plays a role, sometimes
described as "brokering personal supports" or "navigating the system," of
finding services, making contacts in the community, and so on. In all these
respects, facilitators are playing a role that many people, for most decisions,
play for themselves. In the absence of such expert assistance, this "external"
role can fall to others, perhaps family members or friends. But if autonomy
requires the ability to make reasonable and so informed decisions then to
bring them into effect, someone has to play this role. As already noted, this
sort of dependence for information is fraught with potential for manipulation,
though the manipulation need be neither deliberate nor with bad intent.

Once again, though, it is important to recognize that, while supported
decision making involves a higher degree of externalization of this sort, it is
not an unknown phenomenon for others. While it is increasingly common for
high school students to find information about various universities from the
Internet, until recently information about postsecondary options was the
province of parents and guidance counselors, and these continue to be important sources of advice about how to weigh up the consequences of various
educational choices. These choices are similarly fraught with opportunity for
unintended manipulation, which is why university recruiting offices have
traditionally been so interested in building relationships with guidance counselors. Other examples are plentiful: decisions about what sort of cancer
treatment to undertake, where to invest one's money, etc. The proliferation of
such factors in the lives of children and teens may lead us to think they have
less autonomy than adults typically do. But it hardly leads us to suppose they
have none, still less that they are *capable* of none.

The fundamental worry posed by supported decision making, though, has
to do with whether the resulting decisions reflect the person's "true self." I
see two related strands to this worry. First, it's one thing to externalize
something like information gathering, but especially for those who have

intellectual disabilities in addition to their autism, as is common, or for decisions where one might expect that empathy plays an important role in good decision making for most of us, one might suspect that it's the *thinking* that is being externalized, not just the information gathering. [17]

Secondly, one might well doubt that there is a well-determined set of preferences in advance of the extended process likely to be required to make an important decision. Limited experience of the world and few opportunities to make important decisions make it likely that for many pairs of possible outcomes (for someone who has always lived with his family: noisy but friendly housemates or quiet but lonely living?) the person will simply have no opinion as to which is preferable, not having experience of either and never having had to consider them in the abstract.

The first worry is, I think, a real one. It is important not to lose the distinction between *helping someone to think something through* and *doing someone's thinking for him*. [18] The risk of falling from one into the other is very real, as people involved in supporting someone's decision making are often family members who are concerned to keep the person from harm or those having a legal obligation to keep the person safe. Especially with someone as vulnerable as a person with serious autism, the urge to preempt mistakes on paternalistic grounds is often overwhelming. [19] If the person is making his own decision, then it has to be possible that the decision of the person be different from the one the supporters would have made on his behalf. In practice, what is less in question is that this is possible than that this contrary decision will be put into effect. If contrary decisions are sure to be ruled out on paternalistic grounds, then there is no autonomous decision making going on. But the reason is that the person's choices are not being implemented, a rather familiar sort of thwarting of autonomy, rather than anything that shows a lack of capacity for autonomy.

As for the second point, it is once again important not to overestimate the difference between the situation for people with autism and others. When it comes to important decisions, people do not typically have their preferences sorted out sufficiently that it is a mere matter of "doing the sums" to see which available option is the one to pick. If someone offers me free tickets to the hockey game on Friday, but the game is a three-hour drive away, what should I do? Among the salient factors is that my wife will probably decide to come along because she knows that I love hockey, but she loves it considerably less than I do (so I would be imposing my tastes on her); I will have to get away from work early to get to the game, which will cause some inconvenience for others; if I don't take the tickets, the person offering them may well be insulted; my night vision is not what it once was, so there is some increase in the risk of driving that far at night; and so on. The suggestion that I've got anything like a suitable calculus for weighing inconvenience to colleagues against projected satisfaction from watching grown men push a rubber disk across a sheet of ice seems to me highly unlikely. A decision like this, I think it is plausible to say, could turn in either direction depending on who I talk to along the way. If I talk to the department chair, a hockey fan, and he says "How often have you inconvenienced yourself to help a colleague out?" the effect will be quite different than if I talk to someone who reminds me of my misgivings about the public subsidies that enrich the owners of professional sports franchises. My preexisting preferences and attitudes do not determine a unique solution, even in a relatively straightforward and not-too-consequential decision like this one.

It is, I think, unfair to demand of people with autism a greater degree of presorting of preferences than we expect of the rest of us. Insofar as the idea of a decision being in accordance with one's "true self" requires that the decision be determined by some fixed, predetermined set of preferences or characteristics, it is one that will rarely be satisfied by anyone, autistic or not. Since the suggestion that my decision about whether to go to the hockey game is not autonomous on these grounds is outlandish, there is clearly something wrong with that sort of picture of "true selves" and their role in autonomous decision making. But it's clear that whichever way my decision goes, it is going to be based on things that are important to me. However trivial my love of hockey, it is a characteristic of long standing, and one I have no inclination to give up; similarly, I pride myself on being conscientious about doing my share of work when there are joint projects afoot, and concerns about city governments being bamboozled by developers are a central feature of my mental economy. What is required of an autonomous choice is that it arise from one's "true self," not that it be the only decision which could have so arisen in the circumstances.

With this weaker understanding of the requirement, the worry is undermined. Plausibly, at the start of the supported decision-making process people with autism have some well worked-out higher-order preferences, as they must if they are to meet even this weaker condition, though they might be as general as higher-order desires for order, quiet, and to do useful work. The supported decision making process is a slower one than is standard decision making for others, and will often involve not merely deciding on courses of action for the present context, but working out new long-term preferences that can be added to the stock that are part of the person's "true self." But that the process leads to a decision that arises out of (though it is not determined by) this "true self" is a satisfiable condition. [20]

CONCLUSION

The lesson I take from this is that advocating for self-determination for people with autism need be no mere rhetorical ploy, but can be done with a clear conscience. The *potential* for autonomy is in place. The existence of autonomy is dependent, for many people with autism, on our putting suitable external supports in place too. But so, too, does the autonomy of the nonautistic depend on the existence of external supports. The main difference between the cases is that the supports needed by people with autism are not the usual ones, and so are not already in place, ubiquitous, and so invisible to us. But that autistic people are statistically unusual is not a surprise, and the sorts of supports needed are not fundamentally different in kind from the usual ones. It is only just, then, to push for the creation of the right sorts of supports to make this autonomy more than potential, and so to provide people with autism with the respect and consideration that comes along with being an autonomous agent.

REFERENCES

Kennett, J. 2002. Autism, Empathy, and Moral Agency. *Philosophical Quarterly* 52:341–57.
Murphy, J. 1972. Moral Death: A Kantian Essay on Psychopathy. *Ethics* 82:284–98.

NOTES

1. This nice summary list is taken from the list of values behind the Modeling Community Change and Innovation project in Ontario, Canada (http://www.modelingcommunitychange.com). Similarly, the Individualized Funding Coalition for Ontario lists as its core values Citizenship, Inclusion, Self Determination, Community, and Supports for a Whole Life (http://www.individualizedfunding.ca/about.html), and the Family Alliance Ontario describes its goal to be a society where people with developmental disabilities have "valued relationships, choice and control in their lives, and … inclusion through meaningful contribution and participation in their communities" (http://www.family-alliance.com/about.html). But this sort of advocacy and rhetoric is hardly specific to Ontario.

2. The *DSM-IV* diagnostic criteria for "Autistic Disorder" are reproduced in many places, for instance at http://www.cdc.gov/ncbddd/autism/hcp-dsm.html.

3. Murphy 1972.

4. Kennett 2002, 349.

5. The issues here are tangled. That it is at least arguable is shown by the fact that people do argue for this claim. See, for instance: Habermas, Jűrgen. 1994. *Between Facts and Norms*. Cambridge, UK: Cambridge University Press.

6. http://plato.stanford.edu/entries/autonomy-moral/.

7. "Do not speak with our voices" as some of them who communicate via other modalities such as supported typing would say. See *Bridges-Over-Barriers: In Our Own Words* (Bloomfield, Andrew, ed. 2010. Ontario: Bridges-Over-Barriers.); a Guelph, Ontario, based group of people with autism "find their voices through supported typing." I will stick with the more idiomatic use of "speak" where it involves use of one's voice, and use "communicate" for the more general concept that includes alternative modes, even when those alternative modes are linguistic.

8. This is an informal term used to refer to those manifesting the cluster of symptoms used to identify autism since its first description in the 1940s. One sometimes also sees the name "Kanner's Syndrome" used in much the same way. These are much the same as the criteria listed in the *DSM-IV* for Autistic Disorder, though there is a rather startling lack of reference in the *DSM* criteria to (both voluntary and involuntary) movement impairments, though these have been part of descriptions of cases of autism all the way back to the 1940s. The prevalence

of Autistic Disorder is assumed to be much the same as that long suspected for classic autism—about four to five per 10,000. In total, the much wider definition of Autism Spectrum Disorder (ASD) may apply to at least 1 percent of the population, with half of these people having Asperger's syndrome. (See http://www.cdc.gov/ncbddd/autism/hcp-dsm.html for the *DSM-IV* definitions.) Since the *DSM-IV* was published in 1994, autism has become more commonly understood in neurodevelopmental terms characterized by unusual response to sensory stimuli and movement disorders. It will be a matter of wide interest to see how autism and ASD are characterized in the *DSM-V*.

9.   The view is probably best known as it is advanced by Harry Frankfurt (Frankfurt, Harry. 1987. "Freedom of the Will and the Concept of a Person." *The Importance of What We Care About*. Cambridge: Cambridge University Press.), but is endorsed in some form by many others.

10.   One of my autistic friends can touch-type very successfully when copying things he has already written, or when copying the work of others, but he needs someone to help him by providing resistance for him to press against when typing his own thoughts.

11.   Ideally for some purposes, of course, people competent to provide communication support would live with the person with autism, perhaps providing other needed supports as well, which lessens the practical impact of this dependence. However, if dependence of this sort undermines autonomy, lessening its degree does not prevent the undermining.

12.   These examples are gathered from conversations with people with autism and people, including family members, directly involved in supporting people with autism.

13.   Those who do know them attest to how hard people with autism struggle to control these behaviors. It is important to recognize how insulting people with autism and those closest to them find it when people who do not know them take such behavior as willful, or as evidence of a lack of intelligence.

14.   And I'm not alone in this. See, for instance: Ainslie, George. 2001. *Breakdown of Will*. Cambridge, UK: Cambridge University Press.

15.   I owe this example to my colleague, Tim Kenyon, who heard it from his older brother shortly after the brother began his pilot training.

16.   Except in the sense that once bought they are not in the house for long.

17.   To merely note some relevant philosophical issue I shall not attempt to engage, there may well be philosophers (perhaps advocates of the "extended mind" school) who would not see externalization of the thinking" as in itself problematic, and others might question whether there's a principled line between "thinking" and "information gathering."

18.   Though this is not a sharp distinction with agreed boundaries—consider that some, but only some, people suggest that use of a calculator puts elementary school students on the wrong side of the line when doing "word problems" for their math classes—it is one to which people engaged in the sort of advocacy in question here attach great importance, and that they worry will be lost. This is reflected in the ever-changing terminology for what is wanted from supported decision making: "individualized planning" became "person-centered planning," which in turn has become "person-directed planning." In each case the change was, in the opinion of some, necessitated by the earlier term's coming to be applied to planning where decisions are made *on behalf of* an individual, and with their interests at heart, but not *by* the individual.

19.   This, in essence, is my answer to an important question: Why would an advocate for the vulnerable focus on autonomy, with its liberal and individualistic presumptions? Unlike many vulnerable people, who are vulnerable because of a lack of supports and nobody looking out for their interests, for many people with autism the problem is an *excess* of care which strangles their ability to guide their own lives. I think it is probably obvious that my own view is that "guiding one's life" only takes place when one is suitably embedded in an appropriately supportive social environment, whether one is disabled or not.

20.   There are two groups of people I want to thank. For sharing information about autism, what it's like to live with autism, and what it's like to support someone who is living with autism, I want to thank Andrew, Elizabeth and Gerry Bloomfield. For comments on an earlier draft of this paper I want to again thank Elizabeth Bloomfield, and also my colleagues Tim Kenyon, Shannon Dea, Matt Doucet, and Patricia Marino.

Index

Contributors

Jami L. Anderson is an Associate Professor in the Philosophy Department at the University of Michigan-Flint. Her research interests began with Hegel, puzzling about justifying the state punishment of crimes committed by the so-called rabble. She then took detours into gender and race theory and, then, disability studies. She does hope, one day, to write once again on Hegel. *Maybe*.

Simon Cushing is an Associate Professor in the Philosophy Department of the University of Michigan-Flint. His interests are in social and political theory and the metaphysical issues surrounding ethics. He was working on a book called "Is Sex Essential?" when autism derailed that project.

David DeVidi is a Professor of Philosophy at the University of Waterloo in Waterloo, Canada. Most of his research is in analytical metaphysics, philosophical logic and philosophy of mathematics. He is currently Chair of the Wellington-Dufferin Committee for Independent Facilitation and Planning, and was named an Honorary Lifetime Member of the Board of Directors of Guelph Services for the Autistic for his years of service to that organization.

Michael D. Doan is a PhD student in Philosophy at Dalhousie University. He specializes in the philosophy of emotions and moral psychology and has interests in neurodiversity and ethics. He has worked as a research assistant at the Autism Research Centre, located at IWK Health Centre in Halifax, Nova Scotia, where he conducted research in the fields of cognitive science and developmental psychopathology. He has also worked as a counsellor at the Autism Summer Camp in Halifax, Nova Scotia.

Andrew Fenton is a Postdoctoral Research Fellow at Novel Tech Ethics, Dalhousie University. His research interests include the nature and extent of cognitive diversity in humans, as well as other animals, and how this ought to impact societal approaches to difference in cognitive capacities. This interest has led Fenton to work on the philosophical foundations of the Neurodiversity movement. He is particularly interested in how 'neurotypical' understandings of Autism, even within the relevant professional literature, distort the (intellectual or agential) capacities of those diagnosed on the Spectrum as well as how embodied theories of cognition might provide a way out of these distortions. Fenton's other research interests include changing views of embodiment that arise, or are perceived to arise, from current work in neuroprostheses; problems associated with neurocentric views of mind (e.g., challenges from situated cognition); and issues of animal welfare within the context of animal laboratory science.

Michelle Maiese is an Assistant Professor of Philosophy at Emmanuel College in Boston, Massachusetts. Her research focuses on philosophy of mind and psychology, philosophy of action, and the emotions.

Nick Pentzell is a college student and "diffability" advocate for people on the autism spectrum. Nick Pentzell is one of the "FC speakers" featured in Sally R. Young's book about facilitated communication, *Regular People, Regular Lives: Autism, Communication & Quality of Life* (2011), and he contributed to *Sharing Our Wisdom: A Collection of Presentations by People on the Autism Spectrum* (2003/2008). In 2002 he collaborated with Gwen Waltz on the award-winning video *Outside/Inside,* which has been shown at disability film festivals worldwide. Nick has presented at conferences hosted by organizations such as the Society for Disability Studies, Autism National Committee, and Youth Advocate Program and has published "Fools of God" in *The Other Side* 40:2 (March 2004), "Dissed Ability: Grappling with Stereotypes and the Internalized Oppression of Babyliss" in *Disability Studies Quarterly* 30:1 (2010), and "Beyond FC: Unlocking Codes of Social Cues to Open Wider the Door of Interpersonal Communication" in *The Communicator* 19:1 (Spring 2010). The 2006 SDS conference version of "I think, therefore I am. I am verbal, therefore I live" appeared briefly online in *The Autism Perspective* magazine (2008).

Ruth Sample is a philosophy professor at the University of New Hampshire specializing in Early Modern Philosophy, Ethics, Social and Political Philosophy, and Feminism. She graduated with a BA from Oberlin College in 1986 and a PhD. from the University of Pittsburgh in 1995. She has published articles on the philosophy of John Locke, libertarianism, feminism, contractarianism, and exploitation. She is the author of *Exploitation: What It Is and*

Why It's Wrong (Rowman and Littlefield, 2003) and the co-editor (along with Professors Charles Mills and James Sterba) of *Philosophy: The Big Questions* (Blackwell, 2004). She lives on a tree farm in Lee, New Hampshire with her husband Dean Rubine, her daughter Hannah, and her son, Sam.

Anna Stubblefield is an Associate Professor of Philosophy at Rutgers University-Newark. She received her doctoral degree from Rutgers University-New Brunswick in 2000, with a specialization in social and political philosophy, especially Africana philosophy. She is the author of *Ethics along the Color Line* (Cornell University Press, 2005). In recent years, she has written about contemporary understandings of intellectual ability and disability as social constructs that developed in Europe and the United States in conjunction with constructs of race, class, and gender. Her current work addresses ethical issues relating to cognitive disabilities, autism, and mediated forms of communication. She is an ethics consultant to agencies that serve people with autism and cognitive disability labels. She also provides communication support for four friends labeled with autism, is an ally of the autism self-advocacy movement, and a member of the Autism National Committee, which is run by and supports civil rights for people labeled autistic.